MW00988706

Investing in Resources

Investing in Resources

HOW TO PROFIT FROM THE OUTSIZED POTENTIAL AND AVOID THE RISKS

Adrian Day

WILEY

John Wiley & Sons, Inc.

Copyright © 2010 by Adrian Day. All rights reserved.

Published by John Wiley & Sons, Inc., Hoboken, New Jersey.
Published simultaneously in Canada.

No part of this publication may be reproduced, stored in a retrieval system, or transmitted in any form or by any means, electronic, mechanical, photocopying, recording, scanning, or otherwise, except as permitted under Section 107 or 108 of the 1976 United States Copyright Act, without either the prior written permission of the Publisher, or authorization through payment of the appropriate per-copy fee to the Copyright Clearance Center, Inc., 222 Rosewood Drive, Danvers, MA 01923, (978) 750-8400, fax (978) 646-8600, or on the web at www.copyright.com. Requests to the Publisher for permission should be addressed to the Permissions Department, John Wiley & Sons, Inc., 111 River Street, Hoboken, NJ 07030, (201) 748-6011, fax (201) 748-6008, or online at http://www.wiley.com/go/permissions.

Limit of Liability/Disclaimer of Warranty: While the publisher and author have used their best efforts in preparing this book, they make no representations or warranties with respect to the accuracy or completeness of the contents of this book and specifically disclaim any implied warranties of merchantability or fitness for a particular purpose. No warranty may be created or extended by sales representatives or written sales materials. The advice and strategies contained herein may not be suitable for your situation. You should consult with a professional where appropriate. Neither the publisher nor author shall be liable for any loss of profit or any other commercial damages, including but not limited to special, incidental, consequential, or other damages.

For general information on our other products and services or for technical support, please contact our Customer Care Department within the United States at (800) 762-2974, outside the United States at (317) 572-3993 or fax (317) 572-4002.

Wiley also publishes its books in a variety of electronic formats. Some content that appears in print may not be available in electronic books. For more information about Wiley products, visit our web site at www.wiley.com.

ISBN-13 978-0-470-61326-9; 978-0-470-89029-5 (ebk); 978-0-470-89030-1 (ebk); 978-0-470-89031-8 (ebk)

Printed in the United States of America.

10 9 8 7 6 5 4 3 2

To
Juliana,
and Emily
for the inspiration

Contents

Acknowledgments

Any achievement is the result of efforts of many people, whether they realize it or not. First, I should like to acknowledge the role played by my late parents, who sacrificed so much for my education and taught me the virtues and ethics that are part of my being.

I should particularly like to thank Karen Anderes and Candy Harmel, who not only helped so much with the book, but did so, evenings and weekends, unstintingly and with enthusiasm and energy. Without their assistance, the book would never have been finished anywhere close to deadline. A special thanks is due to Karen for preparation of the detailed index. Thanks also to Cyndi Schlegel, who helped in many ways whenever called upon. And thanks are also due to Robin Christhilf, and Denise Geasland at Global Resource Investments, who kept things running smoothly.

Thanks also to my agent, Al Zuckerman at Writers House, and my editor at John Wiley & Sons, Debra Englander, who first got me interested in writing this book. To her and other editors, Adrianna Johnson, Kelly O'Connor, and Chris Gage, thanks for their diligent efforts, as well as (no doubt like editors throughout the centuries) for their patience!

Many people responded unflinchingly to calls for assistance, including Bob Bishop, Paul van Eeden, Brent Cook, David Hargreaves, Ross Beaty, Robert Quartermain, Rick Rule, Michael Jones, and many others. I apologize to anyone I have omitted, but your assistance has been no less gratefully received. All errors, of course, are mine and mine alone.

There are also many who contributed to my education in this field, some knowingly and others not, but all appreciated. They include Pierre Lassonde, Peter Cavelti, Seymour Schulick, Marc Faber, Jim Rogers, Brian Kennedy, Andre Gaumond, Brian Dalton,

Anthony Deden, the late James Blanchard, the late Bob Kephart, Van Simmons, Frank Holmes, John Doody, Michael Checkan, Mark Skousen, William Bonner, Ian McAvity, Douglas Casey, Kerry Smith, John Lydall, Tanya Jakusconek, and many, many others in various circumstances over the years, standing on windy hilltops in the desert or over a bottle of wine and plate of food. It was an education, every time. Again, I offer my apologies to the many whose names are not included, but should have been. Many have given so generously of their time and knowledge over the years. For their friendship, advice, and help over the years, I am truly grateful.

All these people have made this business what it is, interesting, profitable, and also a lot of fun.

Last but not least, my appreciation to my dearest daughter, Emily, who forewent visits and made do with abbreviated holidays without complaint; and to my beloved Juliana who has been patiently waiting these many months, but who encouraged me, inspired me, and spurred me on. This book would not have been possible without such help.

Introduction

"To be rich is glorious." When Paramount Leader of the People's Republic of China Deng Xiaoping uttered those famous words in 1978, he let the genie out of the bottle. Since then, China's gross domestic product (GDP) has gone up tenfold, making it the second largest economy in the world, overtaking Japan. China is poised to regain its historical role as the leading economy in the world.

Yes, for most of world history, as far back as comparative statistics have any meaning, China was the world's dominant economy, with 25 to 30 percent of global GDP. In 1820, after Britain's Industrial Revolution was well under way, China's GDP represented one-third of world GDP, more than Britain, more than all of Europe, vastly more, of course, than the newly independent United States.

Over the next century and a half, as the Industrial Revolution spread throughout Europe and across the Atlantic, China turned inward, rejecting modernization. By 1950, after the Maoists had taken over, after the civil war and famine, the economy of that vast land was less than 5 percent of the world's GDP. After over a quarter of a century of harsh communism had dragged it down further, the true revolution began, and China has begun to catch up at a rate that is unprecedented in human history.

More People, More Demand

With 20 percent of the world's population, this economic growth would be staggering enough. But there is something more. As undeveloped, rural economies industrialize, there is a similar trajectory. At first, the growth starts slowly, then begins to accelerate, and finally reaches a take-off point, when the economy begins to advance rapidly. After 10 or 15 years (longer in previous periods), they reach a developed status, when growth levels off. Typically, economies reach that take-off point when average per-person GDP is between $3,000 and $5,000. That is right where China is today, and it is now at the cusp of that blast off.

Further, and crucially, when economies reach take off, the per-capita income starts to appreciate rapidly. At this point, people begin to want, and can afford, all the accoutrements of modern living that we take for granted. Motorbikes take the place of peddle bicycles; automobiles take the place of motorbikes. Ranges replace open fires. TVs, cell phones, and washing machines all become commonplace. Beef takes the place of soy. Men acquire more than one suit of clothes, and women more than one handbag.

And all these things require resources to manufacture. China's economic growth has been the prime factor driving the bull market in resources over the past decade. And with per-capita GDP about to move further upward, the potential demand for resources is about to explode.

It is not only China, of course. The world's population has doubled since the early 1960s. All those people need food, clothing, and housing. All of that requires resources. Behind China stands India, then Brazil, then other Asian emerging economies. In the more-developed United States, every baby born today will consume over 1,000 pounds of copper, 6 million cubic feet of gas, over half a million pounds of coal, and so on. The children of today's emerging economies are not far behind. As London mining consultant David Hargreaves states simply, "The long-term demand curve is well established."

But the amount of resources in the ground has not doubled since then, nor has the amount discovered. Indeed, across the broad resource spectrum, despite technological advances, it is becoming more difficult, more costly, and more time-consuming to find and develop new resources, particularly those that can be exploited at today's prices.

The combination of dramatically higher demand and constrained supply is an explosive combination, one that may well lead to resource wars and civil strife in the decades ahead. Important as that may be, however, it is not our concern in this book. For investors, this combination offers a once-in-a-generation opportunity for tremendous long-term profits. Rarely comes an opportunity so enormous yet so one-sided, so simple and so obvious that investors have time to get in, an opportunity investors can stay with for years, and on which fortunes are made.

The fundamental story is much the same for all resources, whether platinum or copper, coal or uranium, wheat or lithium. The nuances vary for different resources, and over time, things will shift. There will be times to favor oil, times to favor gas. In this book, while reiterating the basic story, I elucidate on the fundamentals, expand the nuances, and tell you the best ways to invest and avoid the pitfalls. I do not discuss every resource out there but focus on those I believe offer the best risk-reward characteristics and that offer you the easiest ways to participate.

Stick with the Big Picture

John Templeton bought U.S. stocks in the depths of World War II. He held on as the United States emerged from the War to become the world's dominant economic power. Then, in the early 1960s, he bought Japanese stocks as that economy emerged from the devastation of military defeat. The ideas were obvious and simple. Eventually, as we know, the dreams came to an end. In the United States, Vietnam and "Great Society" entitlement programs drained the United States of its energy and laid the groundwork for its slow decline. In Japan, growing debt and overpaying around the world burst the bubble. Yes, assets in both cases moved from being extremely undervalued to become, eventually, manias. Subsequently, the U.S. stock market was flat from 1968 to 1980. Japan's stock market collapsed by 70 percent over the ensuing 20 years. But before the bubbles burst, fortunes were made.

And so it will be with resources. Eventually, there will be manic buying, pushing up prices exponentially, beyond any rational interpretation of value. Some might say that I have swallowed my own poison. All I can say is that the more research I undertook, focusing on the long-term fundamentals, the more convinced I became of the validity of the long-term story, as well as, frankly, scared of the potential for price levels and the horrific social implications.

Despite the moves up in prices over the past decade, we are far from a bubble in resources. The fundamental story remains true. Resources have always moved in long cycles up and down, for reasons I explain, and this time will be no different. You and I have the opportunity to buy while prices are still reasonable. Yes, they are higher than they were a decade ago. But as Winston Churchill said in another context, this is only the end of the beginning. Long before this cycle is over in a rush of irrational exuberance, when you and I will be moving out of the sector, we will have made fortunes.

ADRIAN DAY
Annapolis, Maryland
April 2010

PART

I

COMMODITIES:
WHY THEY'RE GOING UP

CHAPTER 1

Commodity Cycles

On January 10, 1980, Dr. Albert Johnson, a dentist in Oklahoma City, withdrew $10,000 from his savings account and marched determinedly down to a local coin shop. Despite the scenes he had watched on television, he was surprised to see a line snaking around the corner, but he waited patiently for 40 minutes to buy some gold coins. Little did he know that he would have to wait a lot longer to turn a profit . . . 28 years to be precise. At the beginning of 2008, he finally had a profit.

Long Cycles for Commodities

To everything there is a season, as the Good Book tells us. For commodities, the cycles tend to be longer and more extreme than for many other products or services. There are sound economic reasons for this, far beyond the excessive speculative nature of resource investors or the natural tendency of investors—humans, really, in all their pursuits—to assume trends will continue.

First, we should recognize that the very long-term trend for most resource prices is downward. This is not true, however, for gold and silver, which have monetary attributes and tend to hold their value. But for commodities generally, prices today, for example, are still below, in real terms, prices in the mid-nineteenth century.

Why is that? As economies develop, they move away from basic industry toward more high technology and services. Moreover, there is much more efficiency in the use of resources; despite the United States' reputation as a "gas-guzzler" nation, the input of energy into each unit of production is far less today than it was 20 and 30 years ago. Technology plays a role, creating more efficient substitutes with less resource usage; fiber optics replacing copper wire is a clear example. Technology also plays a role in improving exploration and production of resources; think of the massive "pre-salt" oil fields off Brazil's coast. Twenty years ago, they would not have been discovered nor would anyone be thinking seriously of producing from them in any realistic time frame. The ultra-deep-sea technology did not exist.

None of this invalidates the theme and conclusions of this book, namely that we are only in the middle of a long-term "super cycle" for commodities, one that will see significantly higher prices. Within this very long-term downtrend in prices are periods, sometimes quite long, of dramatically increasing prices. I am not referring to price spikes caused by supply disruptions resulting from wars or natural disasters, but rather to the multiyear periods of upward price move-ment caused usually by a new source of demand, be it in the early nineteenth century from Britain, in the late nineteenth century from Germany, in the 1910s from the United States, and after World War II from the rebuilding of Europe followed by Japan, Korea, and Taiwan. Once the economies of these newly developing countries mature, demand reaches a new plateau and the inexorable decline in prices resumes. (See Figure 1.1.)

Higher prices can also come about because of easy credit, spark-ing a false economic boom. (I will have much more to say about this later.) Similarly, low prices tend to come about from broad declines in economic activity. However, from time to time, lower prices can re-sult from specific developments, such as a major new discovery (e.g., the California gold rush) or new technologies that enable erstwhile uneconomic ores to be mined profitably. Such price adjustments tend to be temporary, however.

The Cycle of Production

But within this long-term trend—beyond the horizon for most investors—are the inevitable booms and busts of the cycle. There are many reasons why these ups and downs tend to be longer and more extreme for commodities than for most other goods and services. For the underlying reason, though, we have to turn to economic theory. The Austrian theory of the structure of production provides a logical explanation. Dr. Mark Skousen has written the clearest exposition

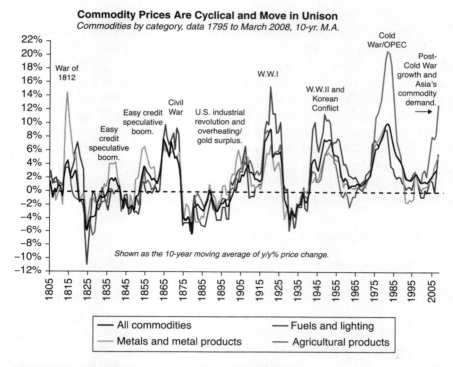

Commodity Prices Are Cyclical and Move in Unison
Commodities by category, data 1795 to March 2008, 10-yr. M.A.

— All commodities   — Fuels and lighting
— Metals and metal products   — Agricultural products

Figure 1.1   Commodity Prices Are Very Volatile

Source: Stifel Nicolaus & Co.; Data: Historical Statistics of the United States.

from what he calls "the businessman's common sense" approach in which he emphasizes the importance of time.[1] All goods move through various stages of production, from raw materials to semifinished goods to wholesale and ultimately to retail for sale to the final consumer. Ploughs are needed to harvest the wheat that eventually becomes bread. Hides become leather, which is fashioned into shoes. The earlier in the production cycle a product is, the longer the price cycles and the more volatile it will be. It is for the same reason that capital goods tend to be more volatile than consumer goods.

This same principle helps explain why exploration companies tend to be far more volatile than producers; they are further away from the end consumer.

---

[1]See Mark Skousen's masterly *The Structure of Production* (New York University Press), a book the late Peter Drucker called "a monumental achievement."

All production has a time and money component; the further from the end consumption, the longer the time. When consumption patterns change, retailers can respond quickly. If prices decline, stores cut back on ordering at the first possible opportunity and then wholesalers order less. The signals from the market typically take longer to reach the beginning of the production process. But even when the signals are received, huge amounts of capital have already been invested in response to earlier higher demand, and production increased. Mine production cannot be cut off as readily as many further down the supply chain can cut supply (or end users can cut demand). The mines are still producing copper and zinc, but the consumer is not buying homes or automobiles.

Booms Go Further and Last Longer

In a boom, conversely, prices rise more. Because the resource business is so capital intensive, relative to, say, a retail store, easy credit has a far more meaningful impact on the ability and propensity to invest more (and ultimately produce more). Since most resources require significant amounts of energy, far more than many down the supply chain, energy prices tend to be more volatile than even other resources. And note also that whereas a store owner, for example, can open a new store relatively quickly to accommodate increased demand, for the resource producer it takes far longer from the time demand starts to increase, until new production can be brought on. In the meantime, increased demand outstrips supply, forcing up prices.

In an extended period of increased demand, producers first increase production from existing mines, perhaps by stepping up to full capacity, by undertaking expansions, and by reopening closed mines. These are the first steps, but even these take time to implement. Beyond that, new mines are considered; perhaps the property that was marginally profitable at a certain price becomes profitable at the new price. But before committing millions or perhaps hundreds of millions of dollars to develop the project and bring it into production, the company will want to be reasonably sure that the new higher prices are sustainable. Even once the decision is finally made, the company will have to raise the capital, obtain all the permits, and construct the mines. At best, this is a 12- to 18-month process. Again, one can see why mining companies do not respond immediately at the first upward blip in prices. Then, of course, the company starts speeding development of properties in the pipeline, and finally undertakes new exploration.

There are differences even among the various commodities, with farm output able to respond quickest to new price signals (albeit always dependent upon nature) and oil output, the slowest. In addition, for oil and extractive industries generally, there are heightened political, environmental, and social obstacles to overcome, which also take time. Few people object to a new farm starting operations; many complain of a new mine.

We can see how the cycle works, however, for resources (as for any good). Increased demand leads to higher prices, which curb demand and lead to decreased production, which leads to lower prices, which leads to increased demand and so on. (See Figure 1.2.) Or as resource broker and investor Rick Rule puts it: The cure for high prices is high prices, and for low prices, low prices. The length of the cycles and their volatility depend to the greatest extent on how early they are in the production cycle and therefore how quickly they can respond to changing price signals.

So cycles tend to be long. According to researcher Martin Murenbeeld at Dundee Wealth Economics, the shortest cycle for gold, up or down, since 1800 was 10 years (in the 1970s), while for copper, the shortest cycle was 14 years, a long bear market ending in

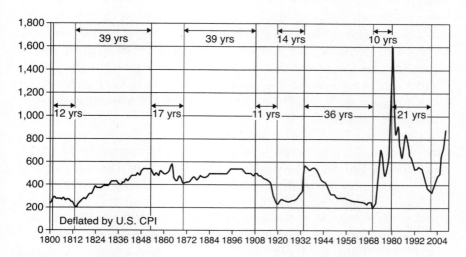

Figure 1.2   Gold Moves in Long Cycles

Source: Global Financial; Data: U.S. Bureau of Labor Statistics.

1932. Even within these long cycles, however, corrections are normal and can be violent. For example, near the onset of its 1970s bull market, gold fell almost 50 percent in the 18 months from the beginning of 1974. Copper, like most resources, was in a bear market from the end of the inflationary 1970s until 2001, yet during that period it more than doubled from 1987 to 1989, and again in the 18 months from the beginning of 1994, with several lesser but still appreciable rallies along the way. So countertrend rallies are normal, and in resources can be quite extended and very powerful, more so than in goods and services closer to the end of the supply chain.

Slowly Out of the Long Winter

For most resources, there was a very long period of low prices from the end of the 1980s inflationary boom to the onset of the new millennium. That 20-year winter caused underinvestment and mine closures and led fewer people to enter the profession. The people who were on top of their game in the last boom, whether company executives or humble field geologists, had in many cases made a lot of money. These people were often approaching retirement, and many retired early or moved to other industries. As the downturn dragged on, after 10 and 20 years, top students moved into MBA programs, not geology or mining engineering courses. By the time the next upturn started, the people who ran the industry in the 1970s were retired, and few new graduates had entered the business. Indeed, Robert Quartermain, who just recently stepped down as president of Silver Standard, told me that he believes the biggest challenge the industry seeks today is finding enough skilled personnel, particularly those with the skills sets "to operate in a competitive and regulated global environment."

There was a deficit of capital as well as of experienced people. When demand is low and prices are low, capital wants to go elsewhere and there is no interest or need for new capacity. (Environmental issues compound the problem.) The last smelter in the United States was built in 1969. Only one new lead mine was opened in the past 25 years. So mines were often old and inefficient. When prices started to move, executives did not at first believe the sustainability of higher prices; they had been fooled by a few short-lived rallies during the bear years, another reason the response was slower and delayed.

Eventually of course, they do "believe," and expand mines, proceed with new mines, speed up development, and increase exploration. Unlike the proverbial widget maker, however, a mining company is far more physically restrained in its response to higher demand; there are very defined, natural limits to just how much output can be increased over a certain period for time, even with the best will and other conditions being right.

Higher prices also spur the move toward improved technology for exploration or mining and there have been numerous examples of this in recent decades: In the 1970s, heap-leaching for gold and copper, which enabled many low-grade disseminated deposits to be mined economically; SX-EW techniques, which enabled copper to be extracted from smaller, erstwhile uneconomic ores; later, improved magnetic and satellite imagery, which facilitated more efficient exploration; and horizontal drilling, which allowed for the exploration of oil deposits hitherto hidden. The list goes on. And a sustained period of higher prices leads more students to choose relevant fields, boosting the knowledgeable manpower. In addition, banks want to invest more capital in the booming sector.

It Takes Time to Cut Back Production

Similarly, when prices start to decline, new products can be delayed, but the mining company tends to be slower, for example, to lay off exploration personnel in the field, whose success may be measured in years, than the shoe store owner who lays off a salesman or two promptly. But exploration geologists are deemed expendable compared with head office staff, exacerbating the supply response on the other side of the valley; if the exploration has not been undertaken, then companies don't have the projects to develop.

Even reducing production is not such an easy task. Many mature mines, particularly underground ones, realistically may never come back into production once they are closed. Capital for mine expansions may have already been raised, the trucks ordered, and the new mining camp built. A company does not easily or readily abandon the decision to proceed. The geologist laid off by the big company that is scaling back exploration may start his own small exploration company or perhaps become a consultant, so the exploration work continues for some time, even as prices decline.

So we see why the response from resource producers, whether to higher or lower prices, tends to be delayed.

These shifts in production can be very long term, the classic example being Argentina. In the 1920s, Argentina boasted the world's fourth-largest GDP and was called "the bead-basket of the world." It has since declined to such a point that no one thinks of the country as an economic powerhouse, and this year's planting of wheat being recorded as the smallest acreage in a century. There can also be extreme volatility within the sector. We saw how energy tends to be more volatile with longer cycles than, say, farm produce because response time to higher or lower demand is longer. But even apart from these fundamental forces, specific developments can lead to great volatility within the sector. This might be a major new mine coming on stream or perhaps production difficulties at a big producer.

Great Volatility within Cycles

Let's look at the first decade of the millennium. Of 14 major commodities, gas was the top performer in 2000 (up 320 percent), again in 2002 (up 86 percent), and in 2005 (up 83 percent), but in two of the years that followed these, it came in dead last, down 74 percent in 2001 and down 44 percent in 2006. This is a classic example of the mean reversion principle. Frank Holmes, CEO of United Services, which specializes in resource mutual funds, emphasizes this as a central principle. He points out that, over the decade not one commodity consistently outperformed. The swings are not always so dramatic or so immediate, of course; you can't always buy the worst performer and expect it to be the best the following year. Palladium was the worst performer in 2002 and again in 2003, and close to the bottom the next year. But more often than not, a huge upswing—above the rest of the group—in one year will mean underperformance in the not-too-distant future.[2]

We have discussed how the supply response tends to be delayed and slow, both from higher and from lower prices. Occasionally, it can be relatively quick, however, though still slower than the shoe store or car dealer. This is when the economy drops rapidly. This was

---

[2]See www.usglobaladvisors.com. This Web site has a wealth of educational material for investors, including a dynamic table of resource returns over the past decade (www.usfunds.com/research/2009-commodities-periodic-table-of-returns/).

most clearly seen following the credit crisis of 2008, a very dramatic and unusual period, when access to capital dried up overnight. It was this lack of access to capital amid an economic meltdown, rather than low commodity prices themselves, that caused the sharp cutback in supply.

To gauge how dramatic was the response, look at the news headlines from just a three-week period beginning on the last day of March 2009, production cut announcements "the likes of which I don't ever recall seeing before, so quickly," as analyst Ian McAvity put it.

March 31

- Glencore announces it has suspended operations at its Iscaycruz lead/zinc mine in Peru.

April 1

- Japan's copper smelters plan to cut output for the remainder of the year.
- A Russian consortium postpones launching a new aluminum smelter for two years.
- Montenegro suspends operations at its loss-making aluminum smelter.
- Bosnia's only alumina plant says it is cutting output for 2009 by two-thirds.

April 2

- Most of Japan's refined lead and zinc producers plan to cut output in the year ahead.
- Alcoa announces it is cutting aluminum output at its New York smelter to just 20 percent of normal output.

April 7

- Tajikstan cuts aluminum output by 17 percent.
- Rio Tinto is cutting bauxite production at an Australian mine by 23 percent.
- Rio Tinto is slowing the expansion of a Queensland alumina refinery.

April 8

- Greece's Larco is cutting nickel output by almost 50 percent.

April 9

- Vedanta is shutting part of an Indian smelter.
- Xstrate says it is halting operations at its Sinclair nickel mine in Australia in August if prices do not rebound.
- The Novokuznetsk smelter in Russia is cutting output by a third.

April 10

- Zambia's Luanshya copper mine is delaying a planned resumption of operation.

April 14

- Indonesia's Timah Tbk it cutting tin output by 8 percent this year.

April 16

- Vale announces it will delay the start-up of a new nickel mine in Brazil by at least one year.
- Vale also announced a two-month closure of its Sudbury nickel mines and plants in Canada.

April 17

- FNX Mining says it is considering suspending all production in Sudbury following Vale's announcement yesterday.

April 21

- Russia's RUSAL aid aluminum production falls over 7 percent in the first quarter, halfway toward its full year goal.

April 22

- Indonesian tin output may not reach 90,000 tonnes this year, the energy ministry says, well below initial plans to cut production to 105,000 tonnes.

April 22

- Indonesian state-owned miner Aneka Tambang says first quarter ferro-nickel output fell 24 percent.
- BHP says output from its huge Escondida copper mine in Chile will fall 30 percent this year.
- BHP also says that output from all its operations are under review.
- Freeport Copper says its spending plans continue to be reviewed and may be further cut.

April 23

- Southern Copper says it is cutting its capital and exploration budget for 2009 by 25 percent.
- Mexico's mining chamber says new investment in the sector dropped 25 percent this year.

April 24

- BHP says the economic viability of its Bayside aluminum smelter in South Africa is at risk following a sharp decline in demand.

And it didn't stop there. The supply response from companies was much more dramatic than in previous cycles, partly because the drop in prices and demand was very sharp. To some extent, also, these decisions were forced on companies because of lack of credit, but it is certainly true to say that the supply response to lower demand at the end of 2008 and early 2009 was far deeper and quicker than in previous cycles. It is also true to say that, notwithstanding this, in absolute numbers, production cuts still tend to be more modest and take longer than, say, the output of automobiles or for our shoe store owner.

Cycles tend to be long, and if what we have seen so far in the new millennium is to be all there is, that would make these the shortest cycles on record for most resources. In short, I strongly believe we have many years of higher prices ahead, and both the dramatic emergence of China as an economic superpower and increased supply constraints suggest this cycle will last longer than most.

CHAPTER 2

Demand for Raw Materials

In 1866, John White stepped off the boat from Southampton, England, a relatively new iron-hulled monster, having spent several months on his journey, with stops in Cairo and Bombay. He was overwhelmed by the hustle and bustle of Shanghai, but as he lay in his hotel bed, unable to sleep because of a mixture of tiredness, excitement, and the stifling heat of mid-July, the enormity of the country, its population, and its potential dawned on him.

"Why," thought the London clock manufacturer, "if I could sell just one clock to each family, I would be rich beyond my wildest dreams."

Dreams of Huge Market

And so it has gone, with each businessman or entrepreneur who steps afoot the *Bund* as each generation passes—just one pair of socks, just one knife and fork, one refrigerator, one automobile, one iPod. One enterprising cloth maker, perhaps apocryphally, wanted to persuade the Chinese that long shirt tails were necessary. "Just one inch more fabric, and I'll be as rich as Croesus."

The hopes and dreams of each generation are the same. But now China is at that critical take-off point in economic development. Three decades after Chinese leader Deng Xiaoping proclaimed "to be rich is glorious" and initiated the process of opening up internally and externally, and of globalization where China's goods flowed freely to North America and Europe, those dreams are about to become a reality.

It is not the socks or knives and forks, and certainly not that extra inch of fabric on shirt tails, that is fueling China's growth, but rather infrastructure and the accouterments of modern life. With cell phones, computers, motorbikes, and automobiles, the Chinese consumer is catching up with Western standards and wants the things that we take for granted.

Everything from railroads and bridges to pots, pans, refrigerators, and automobiles uses metal and energy, in great quantities. Phones, televisions, and other high-tech gadgets require yet more resources, often expensive rare elements in small amounts for highly specialized uses.

Growth in China behind Resource Boom

The driver of this resource bull market—and the reason it is going to continue for many more years—has been the tremendous growth in demand from China, India, and other emerging economies. Developing economies tend to follow similar paths, with long periods of steady growth before a take-off period that can last for years before leveling off. In recent years, we have seen this with Japan in the period after World War II, and later Singapore, Taiwan, and Korea.

You don't have to be an international economics wonk to see this happening. It is reflected in the exports with which people in the West are familiar, itself a reflection of manufacturing capabilities. Older readers will remember when "Made in Japan" was treated with the same kind of derision reserved today for "Made in China." Yet no one laughs today at products made in Japan: Sony, Canon, and a host of other companies are world leaders in quality and innovation as well as sales and price. They are beating U.S. manufacturers hands down.

The same story played out on a lesser scale with Korean goods, from cheap plastic toys to electronics and automobiles known for low-cost quality.

When the average U.S. consumer thinks of goods made in China, he thinks of cheap Christmas ornaments and toys made of lead with parts that fall off. But the reality is changing. Increasingly, in a variety of areas, China is making inroads into the higher end and it will not be long before "Made in China" is no longer a source of derision.

China Is Catching Up, Rapidly

My own experiences back up this changing reality. Not so long ago, I purchased three wine refrigerators, two by U.S. manufacturers, one made in China by a Chinese company (Haier). You may have guessed the end of the story. Within two years, both of the U.S. products had broken—destroying thousands of dollars worth of wine, I might add—and "are not worth repairing," while the Chinese product continues to hum along.

When I recently needed a new laptop, the product with the features I wanted was a Lenovo, a Chinese product. I admit to being a little hesitant at purchasing a computer from what was then to me a relatively unknown Chinese company. I need not have been. My customized laptop arrived in my office, shipped directly from Shanghai, within four days of my placing the order online, with a very efficient and helpful order taker (for whom English was not his first language), in a completely hassle-free experience. It works perfectly and, albeit for a somewhat higher price than competitors, is the lightest and most powerful and flexible laptop available.

Yes, a higher price. No longer are consumers going to Chinese products only for price; they are going for quality as well.

This is a reflection of manufacturers' capabilities, itself an indication of China's stage in the development cycle. The manufacture of all these products for export requires tremendous amounts of raw materials. The increase in manufacture and exports has lead to a boom in the economy that is fueling increased domestic demand. China's economy is now approaching that critical take-off point, and because of the sheer size of China's population, the impact will be so much more dramatic for the global economy than it was for Korea or even Japan.

Following China are other Asian countries such as Thailand and Malaysia (if it can put aside its ethnic and religious conflicts), as well as two other high-population countries: India, already a major force in many areas, but well behind China on the overall development path; and Brazil, a major resource exporter whose long-term potential is finally about to be realized.

But most of the countries that experienced this rapid economic take off in recent decades, as well as those to come, pale when compared with China, the 900-pound gorilla about to devour the world's available resources, not for the manufacture of cheap exports but for its own internal development.

We should not forget—if we ever knew—that China, now the world's third-largest economy and gaining, as recently as the early nineteenth century accounted for one-third of the total world GDP, almost 50 percent more than western Europe at that time. Then came the Industrial Revolution, led by Europe and distrusted by China, leaving the Middle Kingdom way behind in the economic size league. Isolation, civil wars, and 50 years of Maoism did not help. Now, China can be seen as catching up, simply regaining its historical place in the economic world.

The results will be staggering. Indeed, the world will have to change fundamentally in many ways because there simply are not enough resources readily exploitable to meet China's likely demand without staggering price increases and frequent shortages. Most likely, the decades ahead will see all of this: shortages, changes in consumption patterns, changes in technology, political changes, and price increases. The astute investor with a long-term view stands to reap the benefits of this key opportunity, and the biggest danger will be in short-changing himself, either believing he has "missed the opportunity" or selling too soon. This is a once-in-a-generation, nay, once-in-a-century opportunity wherein fortunes will be built.

Changing of the Guard

The growth potential of emerging countries is staggering. In the broad range of developed economies, from Greece and Spain to the United States and Switzerland, the average gross domestic product (GDP) per person is around $40,000. In emerging countries, from Mexico and Hungary to Pakistan and Egypt, the average is around $4,000. No country is as close to take off and as large as China (with Brazil a close second); yet the per-capita GDP in China is just over $3,500. The potential as it moves toward developed status over the next 20 or 30 years is truly without precedent, given the country's size. (See Figure 2.1.)

Let's put this in perspective. The U.S. economy continues to dwarf that of China, at approximately $14 trillion GDP against $5 trillion. (This measures China's economy using official currency exchange rates. On a purchasing power parity basis [PPP], the CIA puts China's economy at well over $8 trillion, making it the second largest rather than the third, after Japan, at official exchange rates.) But China is rapidly catching up. In the 30 years since thrice-purged

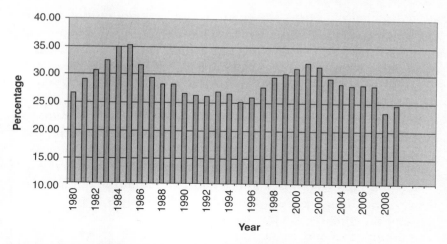

Figure 2.1   U.S. Share of World Economy Declines

Source: International Monetary Fund, *World Economic Outlook Handbook*, April 2010; *CIA World Factbook*, May 2010; World Bank World Economic Development Indicators, July 2009; and prior annual reports.

Deng Xiaoping and—surprise—Mao's henchman Zhou Enlai initiated the reform program, China's GDP has doubled every seven and a half years, surpassing Germany's economy in 2008 and poised to overtake Japan. Consider this: In 1971, not so long ago, India and China combined accounted for less than 1 percent of world GDP.

In a well-publicized 2003 study, at a time when the U.S. economy was still growing rapidly, Goldman Sachs forecast that China's economy would edge ahead of the United States by 2041. In subsequent reports, Goldman Sachs brought forward that projection, and in its latest forecast, from 2007, suggested that China's GDP would be comfortably ahead of the United States by 2030. Further, it predicted that India would be the world's third-largest economy, ahead of Japan, while Russia and Brazil would be sixth and seventh, ahead of European powerhouses Germany, Britain, and France. That would be a changed world indeed.

In all, Goldman predicted that the four BRIC countries (Brazil, Russia, India, and China) would surpass the six largest Western economies by 2041. Their researchers later revised that target to 2039 and then again to 2032. There's nothing like a trend in motion. Interestingly, when Goldman's chief economist in London, Jim O'Neill, came up with the BRIC acronym in 2001, he had never even visited three of the four countries. It was perhaps at the time just a snappy tag to enliven a research report, and some economists dismissed the term. "Really just marketing," sniffed respected London analyst Charles Dumas in a January 2010 *Financial Times* article. "It's nonsense." But the rapidity with which the phrase caught on, strictly nonsense or not, suggests there was a need to refer to rapidly developing large emerging economies in a way that did not seem condescending, as "emerging" does. After all, by many measures, these countries are already ahead of their more developed colleagues.

All along, the U.S. share of world GDP is shrinking. Indeed, it reached its peak as far back as the mid-1980s, and though it has not been a straight-line path downward, the direction is clear. The U.S. share of the global economy has declined from in excess of 35 percent to under 25 percent, a stunning relative decline in such a short period. Only part of that, and recently, can be attributable to the collapse in the U.S. economy after the credit crisis; the rest an inexorable changing of the guard as China, the rest of Asia, and other emerging countries grow dramatically. Note that comparing the size of the nations' economies is not straightforward. One can use official exchange rates or adjust for purchasing power. One can use official numbers or include estimates of the black (or underground) economy. The numbers, in absolute as well as relative terms, will vary considerably. Using generous estimates of the size of the global economy would put the U.S. share at just a tad over 20 percent, but in the accompanying table (Figure 2.1), I've used the more conservative of the official estimates. What is important for our purposes is the trend rather than absolute numbers. The latest estimates from the International Monetary Fund, April 2010, predict that by 2015, despite sharp growth in the U.S. economy, its share of the world economy will have farther declines to just over 22 percent, with China's economy nearly doubling.

The last century belonged to America, just as the nineteenth century belonged to Britain; this century belongs to others, to China.

There Will Be Setbacks

Of course, the economic development won't be a straight line, just as it was not for other major countries in the past. The United States had a significant setback with the 1870s depression, as well as various bank runs, panics, and social upheavals in the years before World War I, which itself was followed by another depression. For investors, these economic setbacks mean investment declines, while even over the period when the United States became the world's dominant military and economic power many individual schemes investing in America went bankrupt. Yet throughout all this, demand for resources and their prices kept increasing.

China's economy, too, will experience setbacks. One cause for concern is the large number of unmarried young males (the result of the country's one-child policy, which favored boys), a combustible mix. The increasing protectionist tenor in the U.S. Congress is also disturbing; it could lead to trade retaliation and set off an economic retrenchment. Do they know anything about the Great Depression? To date, though, the setbacks have been relatively mild when seen against the long-term growth outlook. This is also true for other emerging nations. China's growth rate, from a torrid 14 percent in 2007, fell to between 6 and 8 percent in 2009. That's growth the Western world can only dream of at a time when the United States, Western Europe, and Japan were all in recessions. Brazil's growth fell sharply at the end of 2008, amid the credit crisis, and then promptly recovered, with growth of 4 to 5 percent in 2009.

Of note, the Chinese economy started slowing as early as mid-2007, ahead of the onset of the credit crisis in the United States, when monetary authorities concerned at the too-fast pace of growth and increased speculative activity deliberately engineered a decline. It is significant that this was well before the slowdown in the United States and Europe, well ahead of the collapse in China's exports to these countries. Their fiscal position is reasonably strong, with high savings and low debt levels (partly because credit cards, home equity loans, and other forms of consumer credit are not widely developed).

Increased Wealth and Urbanization

The economic development of China—and of other countries—is important because consumption per capita increases as a country's wealth increases, eventually increasing exponentially. This partly reflects higher incomes but also growing urbanization, which brings with it different demand necessities, as well as a growing middle class, with different consumption wants, including the "stuff" of modern life and the continual replacement with the ever newer.

Resource broker and entrepreneur Rick Rule notes that when rich people get more money, they tend to spend more on services. But when poor people get money, they spend it on things, and that requires additional resources.

The farmer in a rural area has less time and money and need for trinkets—for multiple pairs of dress shoes, for the latest iPod, for larger and thinner TV screens as part of home entertainment systems. The farmer's wife likely has one practical handbag, and certainly not faux crocodile designer bags in a multitude of colors. Urbanization and a growing middle class changes demand patterns.

Though the Chinese economy is at the take-off point, where the economy and demand for basic raw materials will likely increase dramatically in the years ahead, consumer demand is still at a very early stage relative to economic growth. Compare with the consumption patterns of the typical factory worker in the grim Northern England industrial cities in the mid-nineteenth century; he had one suit of clothes, his church suit, for example. But that changed, and so will China's, likely more rapidly, giving the demand for raw materials a second boost in the years ahead.

It is important to understand that this is a long-term phenomenon (and important for the investor not to see this as a normal economic cycle and sell too soon). Already, half the world's population lives in urban areas for the first time in human history; the total living in cities today is a larger number than was the entire world population in 1965.

China and India, the world's most populous countries, are more rural than the world at large, but both are urbanizing rapidly. The population of the greater Beijing area will increase from under 13 million to just over 16 million in the next decade. Overall in China, some 500 million people are expected to move to the cities over the next 30 years. In India, a total of some 540 million people will live in urban areas by 2025.

These are huge numbers, unprecedented in human history, with fundamental implications for social upheaval as well as demand for resources. We are less concerned here with the social implications than with the implications for resources.

Consider where China is today. In many areas it is lagging, as one would expect from a still largely rural economy. Sixty percent of the Chinese population is dependent on public transportation; nearly a quarter owns an electric bike; 17 percent uses a peddle bicycle;

about 5 percent a motorbike; and just 8 percent own a car. Yet fully one-third of car owners purchased in the last 12 months, many of them for the first time, while in a recent survey, 17 percent plan (not "would like") to buy a car in the next three years.

Changes Evident

Visitors to Beijing cannot help but notice these changes. Twenty years ago, looking out of my hotel room down on one of the broad thoroughfares into the city center, I was struck by the wall of bicyclists, literally tens of thousands of people filling the streets. The rare black Mercedes usually had a flag on the bonnet, and you could be it contained a high party official or foreign diplomat. Ten years ago, there was a sprinkling of electric or motor bikes as well as a few more modest cars, owned by the factory managers. Today, one still sees bicycles, but an automobile no longer stands out the way used to. Within not so many years, most of those bikes will be replaced by motor bikes or automobiles, with the commensurate increase in consumption of the raw materials that go into those products.

Compare this with the United States, which leads the world in car ownership. With about 200 million cars, virtually every family owns one car, most two. That is ahead of China and India by a wide margin, both in absolute numbers and even more so in terms of cars per person. China has about 30 million cars currently, but less than two cars for every 100 people. But though the number of cars in the United States is projected (in a 2006 study by Goldman Sachs) to increase steadily for the next three decades, already there are more cars bought in Asia than in the United States. The number of cars in China is expected to surpass that in the United States within 12 years, while India is expected to surpass the United States within the next quarter century. By 2040, the total number of cars in China will be double that in the United States while India will have 50 percent more vehicles than the United States, this despite cars-per-person being barely half in China, and significantly less than half in India. So within just a few years, the number of cars being purchased will be far greater in China and India than in the United States. (See Figures 2.2 and 2.3.)

China is reaching the point where everyone wants, and can afford, a car, mining consultant David Hargreaves told me. Eventually, when China catches up to the United States, it will have, he says,

Much to Catch Up On
Car Ownership per 1,000 Population of Driving Age,
2007

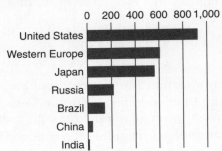

Figure 2.2   China and India Lag West in Auto Ownership...

Source: Platinum Group Metals; Data taken from Morgan Stanley.

460 times as many automobiles as it has now. "Close on a billion vehicles," he comments. "That is an awful lot of lead... and zinc... and
steel... and rubber tyres... and ..."

Yes, indeed. Over the next 30 years, therefore, the demand for
raw materials that go into automobiles will increase substantially, regardless of how depressed the U.S. auto market becomes and despite
increased manufacturing efficiencies.

China is catching up rapidly in many areas. In some, it already
surpasses the United States, areas as diverse as gambling revenues,
from Macau, already higher than in the United States; and mobile

Crossover Point
Car Sales,* m

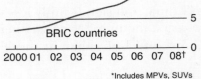

*Includes MPVs, SUVs
and LCVs   †forecast

Figure 2.3   But More Cars Sold in China Than United States

Source: Platinum Group Metals; Data taken from Morgan Stanley.

phones, with four times as many subscribers than the United States. That's not new purchases, but in absolute terms, China is already a larger market than the United States. On a per-capita basis, though, the country still lags but as it catches up, the demand for products and services of all types will increase exponentially, and with it the demand for raw materials essential to the manufacture of these products.

Urbanization itself goes through phases. When people first move to cities, they are largely, as in China today, unskilled or semiskilled. Because of the large numbers they are low-cost and productive workers.

Over time, this changes and we are seeing this change in China, to a more highly paid and more skilled workforce involved in capital-intensive industries. It is at that point when the demand for resources can expand rapidly. This can be seen clearly in the examples of both Korea and Taiwan.

Per-capita income between $2,000 and $5,000 (in current values) is the level when economies typically take off, growing rapidly until per-capita income reaches around $20,000, when economic growth and demand for resources levels off. China's per-capita income is currently right in the middle of that take-off range, just over $3,500 in 2010. (See Figure 2.4.)

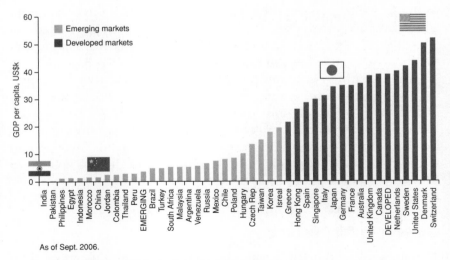

As of Sept. 2006.

- Poor countries grow faster than rich ones
- EM GDP per capita is US$5,000 vs. $40,000 in developed markets

Figure 2.4   China and India Behind, but Catching Up

Source: US Global Investors; Data from IMF, Merrill Lynch.

Just how dramatically demand for resources expands at this point is determined by many factors; in economies that are more urbanized, export oriented, and reliant on investment, the demand for resources tends to expand more dramatically. In those three criteria, China scores highly. Its high level of investment relative to its output suggests a high demand for resources. What all this means for resource prices is that it's far from over and "we ain't seen nothing yet."

Each Person Uses More

As GDP per capita increases, consumption of raw materials increases, and the patterns are remarkably similar across countries and across decades. Indeed, as countries develop, there is a remarkably similar pattern of resource consumption. We see this across a broad range of resources. It requires energy to make anything, and oil to run a modern economy. Though Japan and Korea developed decades apart, the pattern for each was similar. In Japan, per-capita consumption of oil went from around 2 barrels per year at the beginning of the 1960s to 15 billion barrels at the end of the decade and has remained more-or-less at that level since. When Japan was at the take-off point, Korea's consumption of oil was less than one barrel per year. It slowly moved up to just under 5 barrels before the country hit that take-off point in the late 1980s, and again, within a decade, Korea was consuming a little over 15 barrels per person, at which level it still is. The same is true of overall energy use per capita; China and India, with large populations, use well below the industrial economies. (See Figure 2.5.)

Today, China consumes just over 2 barrels per person, though that represents a steady increase since the early 1970s, at the onset of the modernization reforms of Deng Xiaoping. Already, China has moved from a country that produced sufficient energy for its needs to an important importer of energy and coal. Imagine the impact on global oil demand, oil resources, and the price of oil as China's 1.3 billion people start to move toward the developed country benchmark of 15 barrels per person.

Growth in All Resources

The situation is much the same for all commodities. For example, Korea and Taiwan each consume about 800 kgs of steel per capita per year. This number is ahead of the United States and Japan; typically, per-capita steel production accelerates rapidly during economic development and industrialization but then moderates as the economy

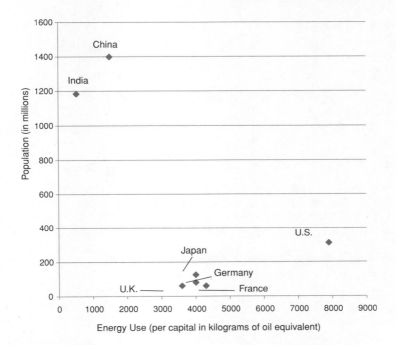

Figure 2.5   China and India Lag in Energy Consumption
Note: BCA estimate for Chinese oil consumption if China developments repeat Japan and Korea's experience.
Source: CIA World Factbook, December 2008.

matures. The volumes used by Korea and Taiwan, however, are not untypical for newly developed and industrialized countries. Comparative numbers for China and India are just 150 kgs and 30 kgs.

China and India may not reach the levels that Korea and Taiwan reached after a decade of industrialization—though China's goals are ambitious—but at even half those levels, the resulting impact on prices for iron and various steel alloys would be phenomenal. Or put another way: If it took them a quarter of a century to reach the levels the other countries reached in just a decade, that would equate to 5 percent growth annually for the next 25 years.

Look at copper, one of the most basic of resources (often referred to as "the metal with a PhD in economics" because its price tends to predict future economic activity). Whether it's Western Europe, the United States, or Japan, as per-capita GDP increases, so too does consumption of copper to a remarkably similar extent. (See Figure 2.6.)

We see this in electricity consumption. (See Figure 2.7.) No country uses as much electricity as the United States, over 12 kWhr per

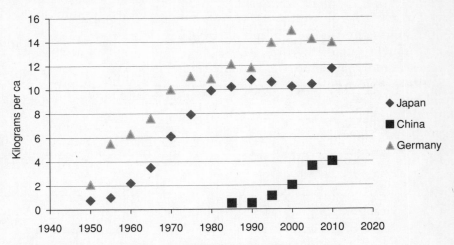

Figure 2.6   China's Copper Demand Catching Up
Data taken from, GSJBW Research.

Per-Capita Power Generation of Selected Countries

- China's per-capita power consumption is only 16% that of the United States

- India's is only 4% of per-capita U.S. consumption

- As per-capita income rises, power consumption likely to grow

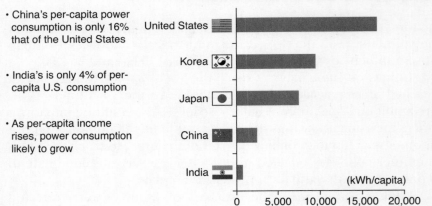

Figure 2.7   Electricity Usage Will Increase as Cities Grow
Source: US Global Investors.

capita. Other countries, as diverse as Western Europe, Japan, Korea, and Taiwan, are in the 5.5 to 6 kWhr range. China and India each consume less than 1 kWhr. As more and more people move into the cities, as more and more want and use televisions, washing machines, and other conveniences, the consumption of electricity will move up rapidly.

Per Person Use Multiplied by a Lot of People

China's per-capita GDP has moved up to where Western Europe's was in the early 1950s, and per-capita copper consumption is very similar, at just under 4 kgs per person. That would have to more than double before matching consumption in Western Europe and triple to match that in Japan. *And don't forget: We are talking about per-capita numbers.* China's population dwarfs that of Europe or the United States or Japan, so the potential for absolute growth in demand as the GDP grows is truly mind-blowing. The impact on prices is clear: catastrophic for other consumers, highly rewarding for those who invest in mining companies today.

Resource after resource, we can go through similar exercises, and the results are always the same: Countries experience similar growth patterns through economic development; they rise slowly as countries start to industrialize until a critical take-off point. China is close to that take off, India is well behind, but both are set to experience growth per capita of two times to three or four times over the next couple of decades before reaching other industrialized countries.

For most countries, the time from take off to developed plateau is a little more than 10 years; in earlier cases (e.g., Germany and Britain) it was longer, but most post-World War II examples are around a decade. In a 2007 report, Ross Garnaut and Ligang Song of the Australia National University concluded the *increase* in China's demand for metals over the next two decades "may be comparable to the total demand from the industrial world today." But even if China and India grow only half as much over twice as long, the result on demand for resources will be quite staggering and support a long-term supercycle increase in commodity prices.

China Now Dominant in Resource Demand

Most of the *growth* in demand for resources in the last eight years has come from China and other emerging economies. But that's not

Iron Ore Seaborne Trade

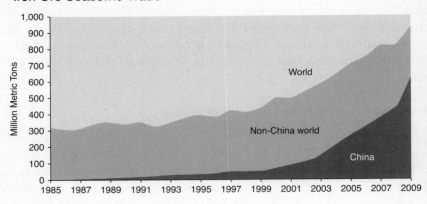

Figure 2.8   Chinese Imports Drive World Demand
Source: Vale SA.

just where the growth is. These countries are now significant if not dominant in *absolute* terms, with *growth* from emerging economies increasingly outweighing any *declines* in demand from the United States and Western Europe. (See Figure 2.8.)

China ranks first or second in global consumption in a whole range of resources; it ranks first in copper, steel, and aluminum consumption, and second in oil. It consumes between 22 and 33 percent of each of the world's main metals.

The BRIC countries consume between 10 and 60 percent of each significant commodity, from 15 to 20 percent for coffee and cocoa to 60 percent of total world demand for pork and cotton. For most of the important resources (copper, aluminum, zinc, and so forth), these four countries account for 30 to 50 percent of the world's consumption.

In the most important oil market, emerging economies as a whole now consume, for the first time, as much oil as all developed economies. In 1970, with more countries listed in the emerging category, nonetheless developed economies consumed 70 percent of the world's oil. The gap between developed and developing country oil consumption has been steadily closing over the past 40 years, to today's roughly equal level. In not so many years, developing countries will consume more than developed ones. The PIRA Energy Group projects that China's annual oil demand will grow at 5 percent in the next decade, well over twice any other region other than the Mid-East with a 3.6 percent projected annual growth.

Part of the decline in consumption of many resources is a long-term, gradual slide in mature economies as there are greater efficiencies in usage and concern for the environment. More recently, there has been economic sluggishness in major developed countries, including the United States, Western Europe, and Japan, but even without that, we might expect per-capita consumption of most resources to plateau and even decline modestly.

In short, what happens to these countries' economies is increasingly more significant for commodities than what happens to the U.S. or European economies.

Of the big four, Russia remains sluggish and heavily dependent on oil, though India and, particularly, Brazil are rapidly advancing toward the take-off phase behind China.

Brazil: Dramatic Reversal in Economy

Brazil, in my view, is the most likely to be a major force in the near term, after China. Indeed it already is. It has often been said of Brazil that "the country has a great future . . . and always will have." Indeed, visitors to Brazil in the 1960s, 1970s, and 1980s were struck by the spectacular and diverse scenery, the endless beaches, the beautiful girls in their small bikinis, the great sense of life of the people, and by the faded elegance. Then came the deeper thought of the unfulfilled potential.

The economy was in a shambles. Think of Brazil in the second half of the twentieth century and one thinks of runaway inflation and worthless currency. Indeed, in the time I've been visiting the country, the currency changed twice, with the old one becoming virtually worthless. Since I travel a lot, it is my practice to keep money from one trip unconverted so I have some cash for my next visit. On one trip to Rio, my first task was to write a few postcards and mail them. On arriving at the hotel, I pulled out my envelopes full of 10, 20, and 100 cruzados notes (remaining from a previous trip). "How much for a stamp to the United Kingdom?" I asked, plunking down a 10 note . . . then a 20 . . . then a 100. The clerk laughed. What two years before had bought me a great meal and bottle of wine now didn't purchase a postage stamp!

Runaway inflation and a worthless currency: That was Brazil's economy. But starting in the mid-1990s that all changed, and changed with a vengeance. As with Paul Volker at the Federal Reserve after Jimmy Carter's disastrous presidency (though the seeds of that inflation were planted many years before), interest rates were moved up dramatically, to over 50 percent, and government profligacy reigned in.

The harsh medicine worked and the patient recovered. Rates declined steadily, with bank deposit rates falling from 24 percent in early 2003 to under 12 percent today and still falling. Inflation was brought under control, from several thousands percent in the 1980s and early 1990s to a current 4.5 percent. And because of the underlying structural improvements in the economy, despite lower interest rates, the currency has appreciated, from over 3 to the dollar in the early part of this decade, to its current 1.8 to the dollar, making it one of the strongest currencies in the world in recent years.

Improved government policies worked, aided no doubt by the global resource boom (Brazil is a major resource producer and exporter).

Middle Class Emerges and Is Now Dominant.   This reversal in the economy has led to dramatic social changes as well. From a country with perhaps the widest inequality in the world, with only very rich and very poor and a few struggling in between, a vibrant middle class has emerged. Today, just over half the entire population is counted as "middle class," which in Brazilian terms means a job in the formal economy, ownership of a car, and access to credit, with an income between $600 and $2,500 a month. Significantly, the distribution of the middle class is broad throughout the country, though, naturally, centered in towns and cities.

This has led to significant changes in everyday life, and though by no means is life easy for middle-class Brazilians—after all, borrowing rates are over 12 percent and few have strong savings, while for businesses, a strong currency makes exports less competitive— nonetheless it is improving. No more do workers rush to spend cash before prices go up. No longer do businessmen have to factor in inflation expectations in daily price changes to goods. And, significantly, now there is growing access to credit, a prerequisite for capital formation and investment.

As recently as the turn of the millennium, there was essentially no residential mortgage market. At the onset of this century, mortgages in the entire country could be counted in the hundreds. Consider this: Who would want to lend money with inflation in the hundreds or thousands of percent, with a depreciating currency at best, a currency conversion at worst? And who could borrow with rates of 30, 40, and 50 percent?

Previously, one had to pay cash for a house or apartment, or one had to rent, severely limiting who could buy. Now a flourishing mortgage market is developing; though most residential mortgages are for only 10 years, and all are floating rate, nonetheless for upper-income and even lower-income people, mortgages are increasingly available. Chicago's famed property investor Sam Zell sold both his U.S. residential and commercial real estate companies before the credit bust and invested much of the proceeds into Brazilian real estate. Many scoffed at the time, but his timing was impeccable. Now Brazil is his international property company's favorite location, and Zell is the major investor in one rapidly growing local developer and mortgage provider called Gafisa (though he sold some of his shares in early 2010). One way to benefit from the resource supercycle boom is to invest in solid companies in resource exporting countries. Though less pure than a direct investment in the resources themselves, it is one part of the multipronged approach I advocate. I shall have much more to say on this later.

Brazil has a wealth of natural resources and is a major exporter of oil, iron ore, and soybeans, among other products, but the growth in the economy means a growing demand for raw materials and the finished products that use them. With a population just shy of 200 million, Brazil is the fifth most populous country in the world, with a growing middle class (as we've seen) and growing urbanization; it is at that take-off point, with a per-capita GDP of just over $4,000. It is a highly consumer-oriented society, extremely fashion and brand conscious, taking cues from the wildly popular TV soaps. But in addition to spending hundreds of dollars on tiny threads of fabric, they also want washing machines, dishwashers, cell phones, automobiles, and other products that use significant amounts of metals and other resources.

In addition, as the economy grows, capital spending increases, as does spending on massive projects to repair an aging infrastructure. And the wealth of resources in a stable country attracts investment from around the world, from the largest mining companies, such as AngloGold (which aims to almost double its Brazilian gold output), to the smallest explorers, all bringing in foreign capital and spending on, among other things, local infrastructure and mine sites. It takes metal to find metal.

India: From a Bureaucratic Socialist Morass to a Vibrant Economy

India, with the world's second-largest population, of 1.17 billion, is further behind in the development cycle. It too struggled for much of the second half of the twentieth century with policies not conducive to economic growth. Whereas Brazil had a profligate and inefficient central government, corrupt local government, an absence of the rule of law in much of the country, and in the 1960s and 1970s Cuban-trained guerrillas, India, for the half century after independence from Britain in 1947, in addition to its vicious religious civil war, was led by an ideological socialist dynasty that bankrupted the vast country. It also had a stifling bureaucracy.

That all changed with an economic reform program starting at the onset of the 1990s; since then, economic growth has been fairly consistently between 5 and 7 percent—solid, though well below the torrid pace of China or the East Asian tigers. In a few areas, particularly technology and software (not to mention cricket), India is a world leader, but overall the economy lags the rest of the region and other developing economies. Its first shopping mall—much as I dislike using such as a sign of progress—was not opened until late 1999. (The mall, in central Mumbai, actually opened a day earlier than planned. As the city's famous and glamorous sipped champagne at a pre-opening celebration, some 40,000 would-be shoppers pushed outside onto the mall's huge glass wall, actually bending it dangerously inward. In order to avoid a pre-opening tragedy, the mall doors were opened and the shopping began!)

India's export growth has been led by services and information technology (IT), which use far fewer raw materials than China's capital-intensive projects. Per-capita usage of virtually all other resources is half or less that of its huge neighbor to the east. India uses about one-third as much energy per person as does China, just one-eighth as much copper. This will change as India plans to boost its manufacturing sector in order to create more jobs, particularly for the unskilled, as well as improve its famously dreadful infrastructure.

The country's 3.4 million kilometers of roads, one of the biggest networks in the world, exemplifies this as much as anything. Roads are in a dreadful state, and in rural areas many roads just peter out, a huge hindrance to economic activity and development. The government, at the end of last year, announced a $20 billion plan to overhaul the country's road system, building new highways, including 12,000 kilometers of new roads this year alone, and repairing existing roads. Some analysts find it difficult to believe the ambitious goals, but the scale makes it clear that the problem is recognized.

India has some important fundamental advantages: common law and a strong judiciary; property rights; a highly educated and English-speaking population; established accounting standards; and developed capital markets. Holding it back is the infamous bureaucracy, one of the legacies (along with much that was good) of the British Empire, though taken to extremes; partly because of the mass of red tape required to do anything, there is a large informal economy. Though such economies can be vibrant, they typically lack access to credit and therefore capital formation is absent and they do not grow. The unwieldy democracy may also be a hindrance to rapid development compared with China's command economy (whatever its advantages). India also remains highly rural, compared with China and other emerging economies, with an agricultural sector accounting for 25 percent of the country's GDP and responsible for the livelihoods of many more.

It may be a few years more before India's economy reaches that critical take-off level, but it is approaching it inexorably, and the country's vast numbers suggest the importance that this will have to the world's economy and demand for resources. Long before the Chinese economy reaches maturity and levels off, India's growth will be accelerating, and it will assume the baton of demand growth. The resource boom has a long way to go and will become more dramatic long before it ends.

In all, the developed economies of the G-7 have 11 percent of the world's population and 55 percent of the GDP. The largest seven emerging economies have over half the world's population and just 16 percent of GDP. As those numbers begin to converge, as the GDP of the emerging economies begins to approach its share of world GDP based on population, the increase in demand for resources will be truly staggering.

Emerging Economies No Longer Depend on the United States

It should also be noted that economic growth in the emerging countries does not depend on economic strength in the developed world. It used to be well said that if the United States catches a cold, the rest of the world gets pneumonia. No more. We saw this very clearly in the 2008–2009 credit crisis: When Lehman went broke and AIG and others were bailed out, economies around the world slumped. But six months later, while the United States was still in a recession (as were Britain, Germany, Japan, and other developed countries), Brazil was growing at 4.5 percent, China at 8 percent, and many other emerging economies had resumed positive growth.

Emerging countries are no longer as dependent on the United States and Europe as once they were. All the statistics for foreign direct investment, and for exports, show this clearly; whereas as late as the 1990s, the United States accounted for a significant majority of inward investment and a majority of exports from these countries, that is no longer the case. Though still important, U.S. investment to emerging Asia is now less than that of Japan and China into the region. Asian exports to the United States have been steadily declining as a percentage of total exports since the late 1990s, from over 20 percent to under 10 percent today, while exports from smaller Asian countries to Japan and China have quintupled to over 25 percent of the total and are much more significant than exports to the United States.

Even for China, the importance of exports to the United States is often grossly overestimated, both in popular imagination as well as from a cursory look at the statistics. It is important to realize that, to a large extent, China is an "added value" assembler of goods whose parts are often made elsewhere. In looking at exports, therefore, one must also look at goods imported solely for the purpose of later re-export. If the economy of major importers, such as the United States and Europe, decline and with it the demand for China's products, then so too does the need for China to import so much. *Net* exports (net of the imports of goods later re-exported) accounts for only 10 percent of the Chinese economy, of which only 25 percent is exported to the United States. Thus, if the U.S. hunger for Chinese exports declines, it would not devastate the Chinese economy as much as expected. Increasingly, much of China's exports are consumed by the rest of Asia and the Middle East, and the *growth* is certainly not in the United States or Europe. China's exports to emerging countries have grown at 20 percent a year for the past five years; more recently, in 2007, its exports to the other BRIC countries rose over 60 percent. Meanwhile, even before the global credit collapse at the end of 2008, exports to the United States were increasing by less than 5 percent.

As time goes on, the United States is becoming less important to developing countries, certainly less than it was, and increasingly less than other countries. With the U.S-centric view so dominant in this country, consumers and politicians alike seem to believe that if the United States stops buying the trinkets made in emerging countries, their economies will collapse. In fact, exports to the United States account for just 5 percent of India's GDP, 3 percent of Brazil's, and only 1 percent of Russia's.

More and more, capital and goods are imported for the development of their domestic economies, rather than for re-export. So a weak United States and Europe does not in any way mean an end to the growth in global demand for resources. That supercycle boom will continue with or without the United States, and with it much higher prices for commodities. *The Economist* concluded in September 2006 that "the era of cheap raw materials is over."

CHAPTER 3

Supply

Normally, when the demand for a product increases, one would expect the supply to increase as businessmen respond in a rational manner. But that has not happened with commodities, and there are practical, economic, and political reasons why this has not been the case.

Supply Is Constrained in Many Ways

Most fundamentally, of course, the availability of commodities (other than agricultural commodities) is limited by what is there; unlike televisions or iPods or socks or widgets, one can't manufacture copper or zinc or nickel out of plain old soil. The supply of resources is finite. This is not a doomsday outlook; human ingenuity and higher prices will increase usable supply. But ultimately, supply is finite, and particularly limited with current technologies, current political realities, and at current prices.

Nor can one ramp up production of commodities as quickly as one can for most products, be it televisions or socks. As we have seen, resources tend to have very long cycles, for both economic and practical reasons. Even if the ore deposit exists, it takes time to fully understand the deposit, time to work out the best way of mining it, time to obtain government permits, time to raise the capital necessary, and time to construct the mine. Even when there are no obstacles or unexpected problems—which is rare—this is still a matter of years. Referring to Murphy's Law, it is said that, "In the mining business, Murphy works overtime."

In addition to these unavoidable reasons for the time lag, there are increasing political, social, and environmental hurdles that at best further delay projects coming on stream, at worst mean they never do. Two of the largest gold discoveries this decade have been delayed by government restrictions: Las Cristinas in Venezuela, dormant through a protracted permitting process, and Rosia Montana in Romania, the target of environmental protests and hurdles.

These are among the most extreme examples of delays caused by nontechnical or economic factors. Everywhere, it is becoming more difficult, costly, and time-consuming to develop resource projects, particularly mining. Everyone wants to benefit from the fruits of mining, but few want a project nearby. The "nimby" effect ("not in my backyard") is alive and well. In the United States, even in apparently mining-friendly states, the permitting process is getting stretched, with an average wait of seven years for a permit. That is now one of the longest wait times in the world. In fact, according to a new study by mining advisory group Behre Dolbear, the United States now ties last with Papua New Guinea for the longest permitting approval process among the top 25 mining countries in the world.

And when mines do finally come into production, governments tend to grab what they can. Government take is getting bigger; in many third-world countries, governments take as much as 50 percent of the project often with no investment.

It is not only third-world countries that get greedy. Australia's May 2010 proposal to introduce a resource "super profits tax" is a revival of an old idea that has demonstrably failed. In the 1960s, when miners were riding high, several countries introduced the tax, including Guyana, Jamaica, and Venezuela. Others, including Chile, Australia, and Zambia, rejected it. The contrast between development of the resource industry in the two groups is surely clear, even to the most blind left-wing academic. After Australia announced its new tax, several countries stated firmly that they would not introduce such a tax, including notably Canada. The response from miners active in Australia has been vociferous, with several already announcing delays in project approvals. Such a tax, if introduced, would defer expansions, reduce exploration, and cut acquisitions.

When I asked renowned mining consultant and long-time friend David Hargreaves what he thought were the biggest risks facing mining today, he answered without hesitation, "Political." He said that the long-term demand curve, particularly from India and China, "is well established" but supply is the question. Governments look on mining as a cash cow. "They forget there are good times and bad," he added. In mining, with its long cycles, deep depressions, and high capital cost, the good times have to cover the bad ones.

Supply Response Is Normally Slow

Even when prices decline, it is not a simple matter of cutting off production, though the supply response to lower prices can be quicker than on the way up. Certainly, as we have seen, price declines after the onset of the credit crisis in 2008 saw rapid response from mining companies, partly perhaps because of fears the economic downturn would be protracted. This was a far more rapid and severe curtailment of production than we typically see in a usual downturn.

When prices decline, mining companies can stop production at uneconomic or marginal deposits, slow or suspend development of mine expansions, and postpone development of new mines. But this is not so easy. Given the often large capital requirements for mines, the company may need to continue generating cash flow to service capital debt, even if it is only churning dollars. To stop production at a mature mine, particularly one near to the end of its natural life, may well mean the mine never comes back into production. This is especially true of deeper underground mines. So companies are faced with the decision to suffer what may be only temporary losses rather than abandon a mine. It can be expensive and time-consuming to restart a mine, even if it was put on careful care and maintenance. Permits may have expired, workers dispersed, and equipment leased or moved elsewhere. And there may be outside pressures. The lending banks may require the mine continue so cash flow can service the debt, even if the mine is not operating at a profit. There are numerous hurdles to suspending mining and more hurdles to restart. So cutting production is not as straightforward as turning off a spigot.

Often, the most significant cutbacks come from expansions and new mines, projects that would not have contributed additional production for some months or even years into the future. The further away from production, the more likely projects are to be cut. As the credit crisis took hold, exploration budgets worldwide were slashed, down a sharp 40 percent in 2009 from the record $12.6 billion spent on nonferrous exploration in 2008, according to the respected Metals Economic Group of Nova Scotia. Significantly, the Group notes, grassroots exploration was cut the most, by almost 50 percent, while mine site budgets declined least, less than 30 percent. There is also a response from other players, however, which frequently does not help the supply situation: stockpiles are sold off, end users stop building up inventories, and investors sell. Humans tend to think in straight-line terms; when a price declines, we tend to think it will continue to decline so our propensity is to delay purchases, the opposite of when prices are moving up.

This is perhaps especially true in the resource sector, which has particularly long cycles. For two long decades after 1980, all commodities were in slumps, albeit with occasional short-term price rallies. During that period, it often seemed that the industry would never recover, and there was very little investment in the sector. But as Rick Rule put it in a recent conversation, these industries require continuous reinvestment because "they are, by definition, self-depleting." Now that companies are prepared to reinvest in the sector, "they are playing catch up."

Whatever mining companies can do to cut back supply when prices decline is less difficult than what they can do on the way up. In those circumstances, maneuverability to affect near-term supply is more difficult, given many of the problems we have discussed here. They can accelerate production at existing mines, expand mines, restart closed mines, and accelerate development of new mines. But all this takes time (and money), so these decisions tend to be made after prices have already advanced and mining companies are convinced the price moves can be sustained, particularly for expensive, large-scale projects.

On the way up, however, we do see the opposite of what we see on the way down: Inventories start to build up; end users buy more in advance, accumulating stockpiles; and investors and "speculators" come in and buy.

Deposits Are Difficult to Find

One response to higher prices is to look for new deposits, so exploration spending increases while more marginal proven deposits are developed. So typically, over time, higher prices tend to lead to increased production and vice versa. Increasingly, however, the supply response in a broad range of resources is not keeping up with the surge in demand.

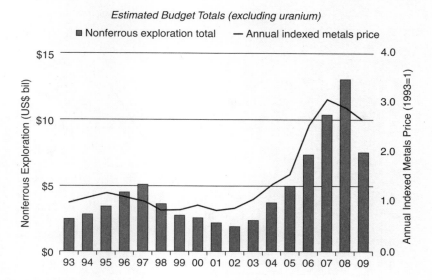

Figure 3.1   Exploration Spending Up . . .
Source: © Metals Economics Group, 2010. *World Exploration Trends Report.*

Consider the example of gold. Since the bull market began in 2001, the price of gold has nearly quintupled (as of May 2010). One might expect increased supply as a response. In fact, until 2009, global mine production experienced an accumulative drop of 14 percent. Production did increase in 2009, however, though it remains below the output at the beginning of the decade. Given the price appreciation, that is quite astonishing. The world's largest mines, in South Africa are mature and are more and more difficult and expensive to mine as they go ever deeper. Several of the oldest and largest mines there have experienced temporary closures in recent years because of rock blasts, flooding, or other accidents. South Africa, which used to account for some 70 percent of the world's output, now contributes just 15 percent.

Equally, as prices have increased, mining companies have quintupled their exploration budgets; nearly half of this is spent looking for gold. (See Figure 3.1.) One might expect with an increased exploration effort, and a higher price making more deposits economic, that discoveries would have increased. But on the contrary. The number of major discoveries has declined, and precipitously. More important, the number of major discoveries has declined even

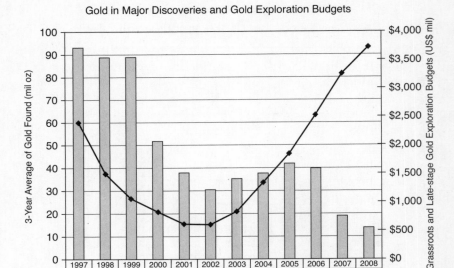

Figure 3.2   But Few New Discoveries

Source: © Metals Economics Group, 2009. *Strategies for Gold Reserves Replacement: The Costs of Finding and Acquiring Gold.*

more so, while increasingly discoveries are being found by juniors. This is well below the replacement level necessary just to maintain steady production. (For reference, approximately 74 million ounces was produced in 2009.) (See Figure 3.2.)

Even if the ounces are discovered, not all will be mined, as we have noted. Besides political roadblocks, many deposits may be in remote areas, making it very expensive to build mines. Hope Bay, a gold deposit in the remote central Canadian Arctic, will no doubt be mined one day. But it will be expensive to develop; all staff has to be flown in, while roads, a town, an airstrip, and power all have to be built and the cost factored into the cost of mining.

Total global spending on exploration for all nonferrous metals (metals other than those containing iron) has also increased in response to higher prices across the board. From just under $2 billion in 2002, it rose steadily to $13 billion in 2008, the year before the decline in prices and credit crisis had an impact on spending plans. Where are the results? Though there have been some discoveries in different metals, generally the results have not been spectacular. The difficulty and cost of finding new reserves to replace what is produced is significantly more than in earlier decades.

Increased Looking Does Not Mean More Finds

This replacement problem applies equally to other resources, including oil and gas. The peak years for new oil discoveries were the early 1960s, when both the North Sea and Prudhoe Bay were discovered. Since the mid-1960s, it has been a steady decline in the amount of new oil discovered. In 1966, almost 60 billion barrels were discovered. Since then, only one year has been above 40 billion barrels, and no year since 1980 has exceeded 20 billion. In the last few years, there have been discoveries totaling well under 10 billion barrels each day, considerably below the annual consumption.

Much the same is true of conventional natural gas. As the price moved up in the first part of the decade, the "rig count"—the number of drill rigs exploring for gas—rose appreciably, more than doubling in the six years to 2006.[1] The amount of conventional gas discovered was not commensurate with the increased activity, and much of what was found had fast-declining rates. The price of gas declined, not because of an increase in production so much as a series of mild winters diminishing demand and allowing stockpiles to build up. More recently, there has been a surge in production from nonconventional gas sources, such as shales, which we will discuss in a later chapter. This supports the view that technology and human ingenuity will increase production, but that traditional supplies are increasingly more difficult to find.

Let's look at copper from a different angle. Of the world's top 10 copper producers, half have been producing for more than half a century, three of the top six for more than 70 years. More significant for the long term is that newer mines tend to be small: Four of the seven mines with the largest recoverable reserves have been operating for more than 80 years, including Chile's Andina, which started operations in 1865.

As we saw with mature gold mines, old copper mines are more technically difficult, lower grade, and more expensive to mine, and they are more susceptible to problems leading to temporary supply disruptions. The average grade of copper mines around the world has declined from almost 1.5 percent in the early 1990s to just 1.2 percent last year, a dramatic decline in such a short period, and not attributable to any specific incident but rather to older mines becoming

---

[1]Baker Hughes rig count survey.

lower grade and lower-grade mines being brought into production.[2] Several old copper mines have experienced disruption in recent years, including multiple incidents at Chile's Chuquicamata, whose centennial will be this year (2010).

They're Not Making Any More of It

The critical factor to always bear in mind is that nonagricultural resources are a depleting asset; once mined, they are gone. A factory can keep churning out widgets, but not so with a mine. So it is necessary for companies to discover a lot just to take the place of what has been produced (so-called "reserve replacement"), let alone grow. For major companies, this is no easy task and is the most important reason that there has been so much merger activity in recent years. It is cheaper, and certainly easier and more certain, to buy reserves from other companies than to make discoveries. (We discuss this further in the chapter on the mining industry today.) Newmont Mining was for a while the world's largest non–South African gold producer, but replacing over 7 million ounces of production each year is no easy matter. In fact, Newmont's production has steadily declined in recent years, and the company has recently announced it intends to produce at a lower, steady-state rate for the next several years, eschewing growth targets.

It is important to realize that the world is not running out of resources any time soon. Though clearly the amount of copper or zinc or gold in the earth's crust is finite, at least for the meaningful future, I am not proclaiming that the end is nigh. We've seen that movie before, with Paul Erdman in the 1980s and now with brother Al Gore. Efficiencies and alternate sources will help on the demand side; the United States uses less oil for unit of output today than it did 20 years ago, and that's not because of new government mandates. Equally, wind and solar, though highly marginal in the overall picture today, may become more significant in years ahead, and displace some current demand.

On the supply side, new exploration, development, and mining technologies will continue to boost supply in unexpected ways. The introduction of heap-leach gold mining in the 1980s brought about a jump in production since it enabled many economically marginal

---

[2]U.S. Bureau of Mines, U.S. Geologic Survey.

and smaller mines to be mined profitably. The next major development could be mining from the sea bed. If this sounds fanciful, consider that it is quite standard in the oil and gas industry; it is just new to the minerals industry. Two of the pioneers are the aptly named Nautilus Minerals, which is exploring in the waters off Papua New Guinea, and Neptune Minerals, exploring around New Zealand. Underwater mining is seen as speculative, but as Dr. Kate Wilson, with the Commonwealth Scientific and Industrial Research Organisation in Australia commented, "perceptions of risks are heightened when the risks are unknown." But she believes the seafloor around Australia is increasingly seen as a new frontier for minerals. Now AngloGold, one of the world's leading gold miners, has teamed up with De Beers, which already mines gemstones from the ocean floor, in an ambitious project to explore between the high water mark and the continental shelf worldwide. Within not so many years, mining the ocean floor may be as commonplace for a range of metals and minerals as mountaintop mining today.

Then there are unexplored regions. The next frontier is likely to be the Arctic, generally perceived to be a treasure chest of minerals and resources. Indeed, explorers have sought treasure from the Arctic for many centuries. Early explorers to the Americas who were not in search of South America's Eldorado were seeking the Northwest Passage to India but were also looking for gold. The area is not without challenges, most obviously the fact that the region is covered in thick ice for most of the year, making exploration difficult and expensive. It is known that there are large reserves of gas underneath the ice, estimated by the U.S. Geological Survey at nearly 1.7 trillion cubic feet. But pumping these reserves out and then building the thousands of miles of pipelines, in inhospitable terrain and weather, may prove a daunting task for the foreseeable future. (See Chapter 17.)

The biggest discovery in the Arctic to date is Russia's huge Shtokman gas field. Discovered in 1988, it is one of the world's largest gas fields and may start to flow in 2013. Greenland is also opening up to exploration for various minerals, and exploration in Canada is slowly pushing northward. But the wholesale exploration of the Arctic region may be some time in the future. After that, the next frontier will be the exploitation of the mineral wealth of the moon. However difficult some of these frontier regions may be, we know that there are minerals to be discovered at some point in the future.

The Social Costs of Producing Resources

Both copper and iron ore have inferred reserves for over 100 years at the present rates of consumption, according to Simon Haley in a Capital Economics 2006 study, but much of these reserves are not profitable with the current technology. Nor of course will rates of consumption remain at today's level. But it makes the point that we are not about to run out of resources.

As for oil, though we are not discovering as much as we are consuming, discoveries last a long time, and current production does not all come from recent discoveries. There is 40 years' worth of proven reserves of oil at today's consumption rates, though how reliable some of those reserves will prove to be, particularly the major Saudi fields, is another question. Similarly, horizontal drilling techniques have increased new gas discoveries, while coal-bed methane makes more sources available. Shale gas is an important new source of supply, particularly in the United States, but we are now seeing shale exploration accelerate internationally. Moreover, there are known sources of gas offshore California and Florida, and in national parks (particularly the infamous ANWAR, which President Bush wanted to drill), but these are environmentally sensitive areas. The issue is not whether the resources exist but at what cost—financial, environmental, social—they can be produced ... and are we willing to pay that cost? The Deepwater Horizon disaster in the Gulf of Mexico in April 2010 highlighted the risk for offshore drilling, and will likely increase opposition to expansion of such exploration.

So again, we are not in danger of running out of most resources soon. What needs emphasizing, however, is that for many resources, there are not sufficiently known resources in politically friendly jurisdictions that can be produced economically at today's prices to meet anticipated demand. Absent new technologies and alternative supplies—and even with them—this means significantly higher prices, both to make more deposits economic and to ration limited supplies.

Resources work in long cycles, as we've seen. Since they are the earliest part of the production cycle, signals of an increase in demand for finished goods take time to work back up the production stream to the raw material producers. And there are typically long lag times between decisions to change production and the resulting changes, exacerbated by political and environmental considerations. This alone makes for volatile prices over long periods.

But now there is a new factor: the massive step up in demand, on a sustained basis for a long period of time, albeit with its own ups and downs along the way. But the demand is likely to be higher in the decade or two ahead than over the last few decades. The resources are simply not available, now or on the horizon, to meet that demand without significantly higher prices.

CHAPTER 4

Control

The looming shortages have led to growing battles for control of dwindling supplies of resources. Just as mining companies have increasingly turned to acquiring other companies to ensure continued production, so too are countries attempting to lock up supplies. This could have critical implications for geopolitics in the years ahead; wars will be fought over tight supplies of essential resources, as they have been in the past. It is clear that despite the $32 billion that China spent last year on acquiring overseas resources, it has not finished yet. China is if anything stepping up its hunt and believes there are many opportunities for mergers and acquisitions ahead.

It's Ours and You Can't Have It

To begin with, many countries are increasingly taking steps to ensure that resources inside their territory are available for its internal uses. And part of this involves restricting the export of essential resources. Most notably, China, which produces almost 95 percent of the world's total production of so-called rare earths, and currently consumes over 50 percent, has successively tightened export quotas over three years, limiting exports to just 35,000 tonnes per year. Some, particularly "heavy rare earths," such as terbium (used as a stabilizer of fuel cells, as well as an activator of green phosphors in color televisions) and yttrium (strengthening agent in steel, and used in portable x-ray machines), are prohibited from export all together. There are reports that the country may increase the number of rare earths to which such bans pertain, focusing on rare earths where its own domestic demand might outstrip supply in the near future, though China has denied this.

Beyond limiting export of a country's deposits, there is a growing move for gaining control of resources around the world, again led by China. This involves everything from buying deposits and mining them, to making strategic investments or alliances with other companies or countries.

You Can't Always Switch

The move is particularly acute for metals for which there are no reasonable substitutes, as well as metals and other resources for which China has a growing need but lack of its own supplies. For most resources for most uses there are substitutes, even if they are not perfect or inexpensive. No wheat? Eat rice. Oil too expensive? Switch to gas. Platinum scarce? Use palladium. Of course, it's not that simple, partly because it's not always easy to adapt machinery and plants and end products for one metal rather than another. And importantly, resources with similar characteristics are often found together (e.g., platinum and palladium), and prices frequently move together over the long term. But certainly, when gas is expensive relative to oil, and the outlook appears to suggest a continuance of the trend, then there will be some substitution, and new demand will tend to favor gas. The market thus tends to return to some equilibrium over time. But such factors become much less important if there is a large and growing demand over a 10- or 20-year period during which both resources are likely to be in short supply.

Of course, it is all the more critical for resources for which there are no realistic substitutes. Consider uranium. There is a growing recognition around the world of the need for nuclear power as an answer to the looming energy shortage, as a low-cost, clean, and efficient power source. The first new reactor in Europe in 20 years was recently built in Norway. France, long a champion of nuclear power, continues to move forward toward greater use. Britain is now committed to reactivating its suspended nuclear program. The United States, of course, is building new nuclear plants with a growing awareness of the essential role nuclear power can and should play in any comprehensive energy program.

China's Challenge

But it is China and the rest of the emerging world where the rapid growth lays. China alone has 11 nuclear power reactors in commercial operation, with more on the drawing board, enough to give a sixfold boost to capacity by 2020, and more beyond that. India, too, is stepping up its nuclear program with large numbers. Altogether, realistic forecasts of the amount of uranium required range from 115 mm lbs to 286 mm lbs by 2030.

Nuclear plants to produce energy are capital intensive, particularly compared with other sources of energy, including coal-fired or oil plans. But they have relatively low operating costs once built. Moreover, uranium is a small component of the overall cost, yet it is absolutely essential. Unlike coal and gas, one can't switch from one input source to another. So once a nuclear plant, with its huge capital costs, has been built, a company will buy uranium to feed it almost regardless of the price in order to keep running, providing there is demand for energy. Mothballing is hardly an option.

Uranium is by no means the most abundant or widely distributed resource. It is fairly concentrated, in fact, with 60 percent of current supply from three countries (Canada, Kazakhstan, and Australia), and equally about 60 percent of production from just four companies (Rio Tinto, Cameco, Areva, and KazAtomProm). As we will discuss further in Chapter 20, it is not the easiest resource to find (often being in highly concentrated deposits), nor, not surprisingly, the easiest to permit and gain permission to mine. Increasingly, in-situ mines are being developed, though these tend to be relatively small.

All forecasts point to a significant supply deficit by 2020 that will only get worse thereafter. Given the long lead times to bring uranium mines into production, this is rapidly becoming a critical issue.

Again, for China, whose long-range energy program relies on a growing nuclear component, the availability of uranium supply is more important than the price. In its latest move to lock in supplies, China offered over $71 million for control of an Australian uranium project, which would supply at least some of its needs.

Domestic Supplies Are Not Matching Demand

The reliability of supply is more important than the price one must pay for a broad range of resources, but particularly for those countries that do not have potential supplies sufficient for their own growing needs. As time and development progress, this becomes true of more and more different resources. China, for example, used to be completely energy independent and export both oil and coal, but now it is a major importer of both commodities. China's oil consumption has tripled in the last two decades, leading China to now import about half its consumption. And that amount will only increase, as China continues to consume more just as production from its major oil field of Daqing, which peaked in 1997, rapidly declines. The International Energy Agency estimates that China will consume over 16 million barrels per day by 2030, up from 7 last year, and further, that of that number, it will have to import over 13 million barrels per day. When you realize that that amount is more than the total output from Saudi Arabia, then the size of China's challenge becomes apparent. (See Table 4.1.)

   · The reverse phenomenon has occurred with steel, of which, despite its enormous demand for infrastructure projects, China is now

Table 4.1   China's Share of World Production, 2005

Commodity	Percentage	Rank
Industrial minerals:		
Cement	45	1
Fluorspar	51	1
Rare earths	96	1
Metals:		
Aluminum	24	1
Antimony	86	1
Copper	16	2
Gold	9	4
Lead	32	1
Magnesium	75	1
Molybdenum	22	3
Silver	12	3
Steel, crude	31	1
Tin	35	1
Tungsten	87	1
Zinc	26	1

As China's economy grows, domestic consumption will take a larger share of the production of these minerals.
Source: U.S. Geologic Survey.

an exporter. Of course, steel is a manufactured product; in order to produce steel, one requires raw materials, including iron ore, of which China is both a dominant consumer and importer. But the country's low labor costs, light environmental regulations, and its own demand have led to a large steel industry that now competes aggressively with other producers.

The key, however, is to buy things China needs and does not have, or not enough of. As writer Christopher Mayer puts it in his *Capital & Crisis* letter, "Buy what China has to buy." Dr. Marc Faber poses the rhetorical question "For which commodities will demand *not* collapse?" I shall return to this theme in later chapters.

For those commodities that China needs and does not have, at least in sufficient quantities, it has increasingly sought to gain control of supplies elsewhere. Many end users have long done this, locking in long-term supply contracts rather than buying in the spot market. But China is taking this a giant step or two further, by forging strategic alliances with producers and in many cases buying deposits or major producers outright. This is ostensibly a more dependable method, though a more controversial one as well.

China's Investment and Trade Influence Is Growing

China is not alone in such moves, but given its enormous and growing appetite, and its massive dollar reserves (the largest by far in the world), it has led the way. Working in many diverse ways, China has sought to gain influence beyond its geographic sphere of influence by increasing trade and making loans. It seems that every week brings a new headline: "Chinese Seek Huge Stake in Nigeria Oil"; "China Makes Big New Bet on Kazakhstan's Oil"; "Yanzhou Bids $3.5 Billion for Coal Producer"; and so on.

China's "whole package" approach has been particularly true in Latin America and Africa, including through the China Development Bank that has provided capital to help finance new projects, often more readily than the World Bank or International Finance Corporation. China readily lent Jamaica $138 million to avoid a debt default, a relatively small investment with a major impact for a small country that happens to have large bauxite reserves. Such loans have led to a growing dependence of countries on China.

Though the country's trade with Latin America represents only 10 percent of the total, it is growing, while the U.S. share is declining.

Indeed, China's trade with Latin America has grown at an average rate of 40 percent per year since 2003, a staggering rate of growth over such a period. Partly because of the economic downturn in the United States curtailing imports, in the first half of 2009 China became Brazil's largest single trading partner, supplanting the United States, which had been dominant for half a century. But this was not just caused by U.S. economic weakness. Trade between Brazil and China has grown from just over $2 billion in 2000 to over $36 billion in 2009. A decade ago, exports to China were slightly higher than imports from that country, whereas last year, exports were 30 percent higher than imports. And while Brazil imports a variety of goods from China, its exports are virtually exclusively in resources. For many countries, including Argentina and Chile, exports to China have jumped, as a percentage of total exports, from low single digits throughout the 1990s to the teens, rapidly becoming one of the most important trading partners for many countries.

Latin America might seem a long way for Asia to go to trade, but trade between the two has a long history. As early as 1560, Spanish galleons made annual voyages from Mexico to Manila carrying silver and returning with silks, porcelains, and other specialized and highly sought-after goods.

In addition to trade, China has been able to gain access to its needed resources through loans. A $20 billion loan to Venezuela in April 2010 followed the previous year's $25 billion loan to Russia, as well as smaller ones in recent years, including two of $10 billion each to Brazil and Kazakhstan, all to oil-producing countries. China provides the loan in return for oil or access to oil developmental projects.

China's Focus: Resources

The trade tends to focus on a narrow group of products, particularly with regard to exports from Latin America. Today, these exports are almost entirely composed of raw materials and tend to be highly focused. For Brazil, soy beans and iron ore account for two-thirds of the country's exports to China; oil adds another 10 percent.

The same concentration holds true for China's investments throughout Latin America. One of China's first investments in the region, from the early 1980s, was a joint venture with Brazil to build communications satellites. Since then, however, virtually all major investments have been in resource development or associated infrastructure. China is upgrading and completing the 1,100-km Inter-Oceanic Highway, from Brazil to Peru, crossing remote Peruvian provinces in the Andes down to the coast. The road is not, from China's viewpoint, intended to help the local inhabitants of these remote areas but rather to enable resource exports to move quickly and efficiently to Pacific ports, and thence to China.

Some other countries also want resources but invest more broadly. India's investments in the continent, for example, include software, in which it specializes, and also a wide range of manufacturing. Other countries, notably Russia and Iran, are also heavily involved in investments and trade with Latin America, though the former emphasizes arms sales while for the latter there is a heavy ideological component.

The opening for all these countries was partly because the United States, under President Bush, was perceived to have neglected Latin America (somewhat ironic given decades of calls of "Yanqui go home!"). Nonetheless, the opportunity for other important trade partners enables Latin countries to assert more independence.

China's activities in Latin America have garnered more attention than its activities elsewhere, though to date China has actually made much larger investments in Africa. These have proven more controversial partly because China is often the only foreign investor in a region, which is not the case for Latin America. Its treatment of locals has proven more controversial in Africa, even though it has been involved there for a longer period and has also made a more diverse range of investments, including infrastructure projects of various types in addition to more direct investments in the resource industry, including direct purchases of mines. (See Figure 4.1.)

In the 1960s and 1970s, China provided aid to Africa on largely ideological grounds, to combat U.S. and Western influence, but today, the exchange is on a purely commercial basis. As in the earlier period, when China built a railroad from Dar Es Salaam, on Tanzania's Indian Ocean, to Zambia's copper belt, China is opening up the heart of Africa, exemplified by its massive $9 billion package with the Congo, signed in spring of 2008. This included a pledge of a $6 billion investment in the Congo's infrastructure, including roads, railroads, clinics, and schools, an amount equivalent to half of the country's gross domestic product, and equal to 10 times the aid that western countries had promised the Congo on an annual basis. The

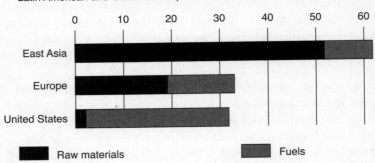

Figure 4.1   China Takes Most of Latin America's Exports
Source: World Bank.

Congolese government hailed the deal as "Congo's Marshall Plan." In return, China has the right to mine copper and cobalt of the same value.

In addition, in contrast to activities in Latin America that are almost entirely by the large state-owned enterprises and businesses, in wilder Africa, there are numerous independent Chinese businessmen trying to strike it rich. These independents might be middlemen, buying from the multitude of illegal wildcat miners and selling to small refiners, often also owned by Chinese companies. It is estimated that about half of the copper smelters operating in the Congo's mining belt are owned by Chinese companies. The Congo has been ranked by the World Bank as the worst place in the world to do business, so it is no surprise that the intrepid Chinese, with fat wallets, can achieve what more refined Western companies often find more difficult. Criticism of the Chinese government for helping its companies gain concessions is rather laughable given that Western governments routinely do likewise. Some can't get used to losing.

China is now the second-largest trading partner for all of Africa, and narrowing the gap with number one, the United States. Already, the continent is supplying China with many crucial resources, about 30 percent of its oil, making it that country's top supplier. For the most part, China is simply buying resources at market price, since many of the continent's resources have already been locked up by companies from other countries. China, for example, produces no oil in Africa. But it is buying arable land and looking to Africa for timber, food, and specialty metals, such as cobalt from the Congo.

It is locking in long-term contracts, often by getting the projects built. China will offer complete packages, not only the capital for, let's say, the mine, but roads, dams, and a refinery. So they are boosting the infrastructure in a way that has not been done for decades. Negotiations are underway for China to build a $3.5 billion port facility in Kenya after Qatar dropped out. "The Chinese offer the full package," said the Prime Minister Raila Odinga, including the technical expertise in addition to financing, plus railroad facilities to Kenya's borders. China needs the port to facilitate export of oil. Kenya does not have the proven resources other countries do, though a Chinese company is now prospecting for oil in the north of the country. But the attraction is as a suitable location for a port facility to export oil from neighboring countries, including Sudan. At the same time, there is growing concern that China's hunger for certain resources, if not activities of Chinese entrepreneurs themselves, are encouraging slash-and-burn farming and logging that will severely harm the long-term productivity of many of these areas.

You Scratch My Back . . .

Beyond such broad trade and finance activities, which buy China influence and a privileged seat at the table, the country and its companies have sought more direct control of resources through financing development of specific projects in return for an equity stake or long-term supply contracts; by buying mines themselves; by buying stakes in companies, often when they are in need of capital; and by taking over entire companies.

A typical straightforward deal is the one between the Chinese government's metals supplier Minmetals and Chile's state-owned major copper producer, Codelco. Minmetals made a $440 million advance purchase agreement for copper production. Such a transaction is win-win. China locks in dependable supplies, while for Codelco, the deal represents very low-cost and low-risk financing. Such a transaction has little risk for a large company such as Codelco producing a commodity, copper, with a very deep market. There are higher risks for smaller companies where such transactions would lead to dependence on a single consumer.

China has been very ready to provide amounts that are huge by the recipient's standards. We have already mentioned the deal with Congo, representing half that country's gross domestic product. Angola actually received so much investment from China that in 2006 it told the International Monetary Fund it didn't need its money, with all the strings attached. It is little wonder that by opening its checkbook, China can gain ready access to the resources for which it hungers.

Originally, deals tended to be in underdeveloped countries, but now the transactions are all around the world and are getting bigger, as well as in developed countries including Australia and Canada. In the early years of this century, for example, Chinese oil companies China National Petroleum Corp. and CNOOC paid $4.2 billion and $3.7 billion, respectively, for shares of PetroKazakhstan and Russia's Udmurtneft. More recently, the two companies teamed up for a proposed $17 billion acquisition of Repsol's stake in YPF, the largest oil company in Argentina. Given that YPF is the largest upstream (producer) and downstream (seller) company in the country, it is a sensitive matter. There was controversy enough when the Spanish company first made its purchase in 1999. When the Chinese purchase was first mooted, there were concerns about possible undue influence on pricing of gasoline as well as long-term supplies. As in many countries, the government of Argentina, while owning no equity, has a veto over change in control.

Softly, Softly

More recent transactions show how China is responding to the concerns, legitimate or otherwise, raised by its investments. One approach is to make investments in smaller and less sensitive companies. Two recent acquisitions in Australia show this. Yanzhou Coal, whose own mine output is falling, acquired Felix Resources, a smaller Australian coal miner, in a $3 billion deal. Yanzhou is a unit of Yankuang Group, the only Chinese coal miner listed in New York.

Another approach is to make investments in specific projects rather than the companies themselves, and not as purely financial investments. China lent Brazil's Petrobras $1 billion to help develop its very capital-intensive deep-sea oil fields. In return, China can buy up to 200,000 barrels per day from the fields for the next 10 years. Similarly, PetroChina invested $1.7 billion for 60 percent stakes in two of Athabasca Oil Sands' projects. Oil sands tend to be more difficult to develop than conventional oil and also require higher prices to be economic. This deal, therefore, underscores China's long-term thinking as it acquires long-term strategic reserves in various resources around the world.

The move into oil sands is typical, a move into an out-of-favor subsector that requires significantly higher oil prices to meet its potential, in an amount considerably more than any other recent investments in the area. However, the investment translates to only 1 percent of PetroChina's output, and thus also underscores the company's—and China's—fundamental problem: how to replace reserves and grow. Most of China's recent investments have been similarly modest and all over the map: some gas fields in Kazakhstan and a refinery in Singapore. Transactions that could have a significant impact are politically contentious, such as the bid for Argentina's YPF and an attempt to buy large properties in Libya.

Another innovative move was made in response to the lock on iron ore supplies and pricing by the big three, Rio Tinto, BHP Billiton, and Vale. Benchmark prices for iron ore used to be set in a series of annual negotiations between these companies and major consumers, but China has balked both at the prices demanded and the pricing system. Chinalco's failed bid for Rio was an attempt to break into the big three.

Now, Chinese institutions, including the China Iron & Steel Association, have negotiated an innovative accord where the Chinese lenders will lend $6 billion for a smaller Australian producer Fortescue in return for the right to buy a steady stream of iron ore at slightly below the world-negotiated price. The amounts of iron ore themselves are small, representing initially only 7 percent of China's iron ore imports. But with China's capital, the company will be in the position to expand more rapidly, while China also hoped its tweaking of the big three would lead to more flexible pricing discussions. This move was successful and the benchmark system is now a thing of the past (see Chapter 16).

Fortescue has certainly seen impressive growth under CEO Andrew Forrest, but when he first announced plans earlier this decade to build an iron ore operation, Australia's mining community was skeptical, partly because of Forrest's controversial time at a nickel company, from which he was eventually forced out and partly because the location of his mine in Western Australia's desert meant high shipping costs to port. But he aggressively and successfully built the mine, helped by a more-than-doubling of iron ore prices in recent years. For Fortescue, of course, the transaction is not without risk; since all its production is sold to China, there may come louder calls for larger price discounts in the future. So far, however, here as elsewhere, China is acting the model citizen in its overseas investments as it steadily garners control of a reliable supply of essential resources from around the world. In 2007, China became Australia's largest trading partner, dislodging Japan. As such, it still accounts for less than 15 percent of Australia's total exports, a significant amount but not an overwhelming threat to independence.

Pragmatism Rules

This growing influence and investment by China in resources around the world has proven controversial. Fully aware of the potential for backlash, China has been very pragmatic and not at all ideological in its dealings, even with countries such as Venezuela where anti-American rhetoric is pronounced. This contrasts with countries such as Iran that deliberately target countries where they can gain anti-American allies. China's own political consideration seems limited to whether a host country recognizes Taiwan as an integral part of the People's Republic.

More accurate is the criticism that by its very pragmatism, China is giving aid and comfort to corrupt and repressive regimes, such as in Sudan. Given the West's sanctions against Sudan, China has been able to acquire much larger stakes in bigger oil fields than it can elsewhere; Sudan now accounts for 10 percent of China's oil imports. China's money comes with no strings attached, so while the country is not helping Venezuela or Bolivia or Sudan politically, nonetheless its aid and assistance makes it more difficult for the United States to counter leftist or repressive governments. Indeed, Chinese investment and trade was originally welcomed throughout Latin America, since it was seen as a fellow developing country and a counterweight to the United States, which they viewed as arrogant.

China Provokes a Backlash

A growing nationalist backlash, even in Canada and Australia, has led China to downplay corporate takeovers, particularly of iconic companies, but focus more on strategic relationships, particularly where the target or partner is in financial difficulty. That makes criticism of China more difficult to sustain. China's pragmatic approach is not always matched by other countries, however. For Australia, concern at Chinese investments has been compounded by political tensions over dissidents living in Australia or specific incidents such as its detention of Rio Tinto employees accused of espionage.

But more recently, Australians have welcomed China's investments as needed capital and jobs. In several recent cases, Chinese companies have stepped in after Australian companies have announced plans to close an operation. The quick response of many major mining companies to the decline in commodity prices and lack of access to credit, following Lehman's collapse at the end of 2008—a response we discussed in an earlier chapter—may have been necessary to prevent the markets being flooded and driving prices down further (and losing money for the companies). But China's ability to come in with large amounts of cash and appear as more long-term and stable operators has helped their image tremendously. For many towns, where the mine may be the only source of employment, they have been welcomed. The mayor of a cluster of small mining-dependent towns in Tasmania, Darryl Gaerrity, said he thought Chinese companies would not be "at the whims of the world market" and would make the towns "not as vulnerable as we were."

Some concern is much more general, such as U.S. Secretary of State Hillary Clinton's comment that China was making "disturbing" gains in Latin America, disturbing no doubt only for America and the loss of influence this represents.

In truth, sometimes hostility to Chinese investments is little more than raw populist or racist emotion, such as when the U.S. Congress rejected China National Offshore Oil's proposed takeover of Unocal oil company for vague "national security" reasons, or the hostility generated by Chinalco's $19 billion unsuccessful bid for an investment in troubled Rio Tinto. (Chinalco had already purchased a $14.3 billion stake in the company in 2008, at that time, the largest single Chinese foreign investment of a resource firm. The new investment, precisely to avoid concerns about a takeover, would have formed a strategic alliance whereby the two companies would have held joint venture various projects around the world.) Even in Canada, there is growing concern at "giving away" the country's wealth, directed not only at China. One of the largest acquisitions of a Canadian company has been the takeover by Brazil's Vale of Canada's iconic Inco.

There are other concerns elsewhere. In Latin America, China was originally insensitive to local needs but learned quickly, in its typical pragmatic way. This is clearly illustrated by its history in Peru. Its first major investment in that country was in 1992, when Shougang acquired an iron ore mine. The company brought in 350 Chinese staff and there were constant clashes with the local workers. A more recent major investment, in the Toromocho mines, has only three Chinese employees, while the CEO is Canadian. More broadly, however, particularly among intellectuals, there is growing discussion of China as a "neocolonial" power, out for a landgrab.

In Africa, Chinese managers have generated much criticism as arrogant and for their alleged cruel treatment of local workers. The situation is aggravated by the often corrupt and inefficient governments' interest in policing abuses, as well as the fact that many independent entrepreneurs operate in the continent. Like the characters from Europe who tried to strike it rich in Africa or Asia a century or two ago, they are often completely unaware of environmental or social niceties, but give "Chinese" generally a poor name. The opposition candidate in Zambia's 2006 presidential election made great play by attacking the Chinese presence.

In general, even the largest Chinese companies are regarded as weak on soft issues, such as people and social and environmental issues, says Hanjing Xu, an executive director of Sino Gold in Australia before it was acquired by Eldorado. But he notes they are generally very strong on analysis and numbers.

China has also generated resentment in particular in Africa with its emphasis on agriculture. The lavish China-Africa Summit of 2006 emphasized agriculture, but land is a very emotive issue on that continent, and Chinese companies buying land produced a backlash. China has recently downplayed that area.

There are also economic concerns that result from consequences of China's heavy investment and trade activities. Such rapid growth in demand for exports has led to strengthening local currencies that, governments fear, will make other exports less competitive. And China's trade patterns have led to a renewed focus on resource development, after a period of industrialization, which some nationalist economists deem negative for a country's development. Chinese exports have caused severe problems for many nascent manufacturing industries in different countries, unable to compete with China's lower costs. Not surprisingly, concern about China's involvement in Latin America is highest in countries with relatively low commodity exports and where Chinese goods, most notably textiles, directly compete with Latin exports. This has been pronounced in Mexico, for example. Other countries, to date, are generally happy to have Chinese investment.

India Moves More Cautiously

Besides China, many other countries have also sought strategic supplies, including Korea buying into liquefied natural gas operations, but none has come close to China's scale. Coming up on the heels of the Chinese in recent years, however, have been the Indians.

In the Indian plan to develop by the export of finished goods, much the same as has China, it is short some key raw materials, particularly coal and iron ore. India is more likely to be somewhat more selective in where it does deals, probably wanting to transact with more stable or salubrious regimes. It likely won't throw its money around in quite the way the Chinese have done, although there are plans to establish a sovereign wealth fund specifically to compete with China for global energy assets. India is also less likely to insist on bringing in a local workforce en masse, as have the Chinese, or insist that certain purchases are from the home country, and perhaps be more attuned to local sensitivities.

India seems to be focusing on Africa, at least for now, but selectively, on more stable and pragmatic regimes such as Malawai and Botswana. It helps that India has English as a native language and, in its dealings with other former British colonies, shares a legal system. In many countries, there is also an established population base already. Though India's gross domestic product (GDP) per capita is half of its rival's, the population is not far behind (1.17 billion versus 1.33 billion) with a much younger demographic. As India develops, therefore, its demand for raw materials will likely become just as powerful as that of China, and arguably will eventually overtake them.

With a large and growing demand and with clear constraints on supply in many resources around the world, we can expect China, India, and other countries to all step up their efforts to gain control of sources of supply to ensure their long-term development. No doubt in the years to come, there will be struggles over export of essential materials; whatever agreements are in place today, will local populations like to see "their" resources exported halfway across the globe? There will probably even be armed conflicts over essential raw materials as there have been many times in the past. But either way, for us as investors, it all points to growing shortages and higher prices.

CHAPTER 5

Economy

The big picture for resources over the next decade or so is clear: a massive step up in demand from China and other emerging economies and a lack of available, accessible, economically viable supplies will lead to higher prices. This is the super cycle.

Economic Forces Affecting Commodity Prices

Overlaying this super cycle, however, will be economic forces, both long and short term, that will affect prices of commodities, individually and as a group. The main economic determinants on commodity prices are the following.

- *Economic growth.* Clearly, more growth leads to higher demand.
- *Interest rates.* Rates that are low in absolute terms or relative to inflation lower the cost of financing, making more projects economically viable; for investors, they make other investments less attractive, "essentially (forcing) investors to do something," as Dr. Marc Faber puts it. Low rates also encourage leverage, which leads to greater volatility and higher prices.
- *The dollar.* Since most commodities are priced in terms of the dollar, any movement in the dollar is reflected in the price. A weaker dollar also tends to encourage investment in hard assets rather than paper currencies.
- *Inflation.* Similarly, higher inflation, often accompanied by higher nominal growth, encourages demand and also leads more investors to seek haven in hard assets.

Reasons for Volatility

Commodities tend to be far more volatile than most other asset classes, and for fundamental reasons. Their demand is extremely sensitive to changes in economic activity, and yet it can take time for supply to respond. I have discussed reasons for this: Companies want to be sure of the change in demand before committing high capital costs required for new projects; having sunk capital, they are reluctant to close facilities when demand slows, even as margins shrink; and it takes time to find, develop, and obtain approvals for new projects.

Stocks of companies that produce commodities are even more volatile, leveraged to the underlying commodity. A company, for example, that produces gold at a cost of $700 has a $200 profit at $900. With an 11 percent increase in the price of bullion to $1,000, the company's profit—other things being equal—jumps 50 percent. The same works in reverse, of course; relatively small price changes in underlying commodities can turn a company's profit into a loss. Moreover, as prices move, investor sentiment changes rapidly, again increasing the volatility of commodity stocks.

In recent years, volatility in most asset classes, and not only commodities, has increased, and a large part of the blame for this lies with the Federal Reserve's easy money policies. One might argue that by mid-2006, the CRB Index, the benchmark for commodities, reflected fundamental supply and demand at that time. Commodity prices peaked and started to decline. Then the Federal Reserve aggressively lowered interest rates and all asset prices reflected this, fueled by speculative money on the back of easy money and low rates. Easy money encourages speculation by making low-risk short-term debt instruments and bank deposits unattractive, and encourages leverage by reducing the cost. Commodities tend to be particularly sensitive to such moves for the reasons I have already discussed. Thus, the CRB reversed, and in mid-2008, just before the onset of the credit crisis, they were clearly ahead of themselves, needing further infusions of easy money to keep going. Commodities tend to fall sharply, just as they tend to rally sharply, and fall they did. But thanks to the infusion of easy money around the world after Lehman Brothers went bankrupt, including stimulus programs in China, commodity prices came roaring back.

A Drop in Prices Is a Long-Term Opportunity

Prices won't continue to go up without sharp volatility in the years ahead. Indeed, one problem with easy money stimuli is that it requires ever greater infusions to have the same impact. In China, resource buying has soared well above current use, despite an increase in usage from new infrastructure projects and legitimate restocking as prices move. But buying of resources appears to have well exceeded both current use and rational restocking, setting the scene for a suspension of buying and sharp drop in prices. There are also concerns that China's economy may suffer a sharp, albeit temporary, setback as the renewed speculation gets out of hand.

Indeed, this may have already occurred by the time you read these words. The critical thing for investors to realize and remember is that, even within a super cycle, there will be setbacks and these setbacks can be very sharp. Rather than let such corrections cause panic, you should use them as opportunities. It may be hackneyed but oft-quoted that the Mandarin word for *crisis* combines the characters for danger and opportunity. We should use the crisis as an opportunity. (In fact, this is a popular misconception. Rather than "opportunity," the Chinese character means "critical point," but that is equally apt. How you respond to a critical point will help determine whether you take full advantage of the commodity super cycle.)

We discuss investment strategies in much greater detail in later chapters. For now, never forget that corrections for resource prices during bull markets can be very sharp. One example suffices. We think of the 1970s as a bull market for gold. After the price rose from the government-mandated price of $35 an ounce in 1969 to $180 by early 1974, it fell by almost 50 percent over the next 18 months, to just over $100. Many gold stocks fell by considerably more. That was a scary time for gold investors, and gold didn't exceed that previous peak until late 1977, nearly four years after the correction started, on its way to that famous peak over $800 an ounce.

Short-term forecasting is a mug's game. As analyst and good friend Paul van Eeden put it to me, "Our ability to predict the future is dismal." Paul advises investors to spend less time worrying about the economy and trying to predict the future, and more time on the fundamental analysis of companies. As Paul notes, "Companies are generally inexpensive when economic conditions are bad and

generally expensive when conditions are good." Investors who focus
on the economy, he says, are tempted to buy when conditions are
good and sell when they are bad. Investors who focus on fundamental analysis of companies will tend to do the opposite. Successful
investors do not try to time the market. But by focusing on value,
and buying when things are cheap and selling when they are expensive, they in effect become timers. "A well-run, well-capitalized
company that can withstand swings in the business cycle and economic volatility is best bought when economic conditions are bad and
sold when times are good," says Paul. "Being a contrarian is simple,
but hard," simple in theory but difficult in practice.

Economic Outlook Is Favorable

When we consider the four main economic factors that affect the
price of commodities—economic growth, interest rates, the dollar,
and inflation—at least three are very favorable for higher prices.

Certainly, the United States and Europe will likely remain very
sluggish for an extended period, and a robust global economy would
be the ideal scenario for higher commodity prices. But the decline in
demand from these sources will be more than offset by the increase in
China, Asia, and other emerging economies. Other economic factors
are likely to exaggerate the moves in prices, particularly the decline
in the dollar and accelerating inflation. My essential thesis for high
prices is not predicated on a lower dollar and higher inflation and
certainly is not dependent on them. But they are likely to lead to
exaggerated moves, particularly as the cycle develops.

Commodity prices and interest rates tend to move in tandem over
long cycles. Both bottomed in the 1920s and 1930s and rose through
the subsequent decades, peaking in the 1970s. They then fell to the
beginning of this decade, though rates remain low. Although it is
difficult to imagine the Fed raising rates in any meaningful way in
the near term—the economy is too weak and the government debt
burden too high—over time, rates will have to move up from these
exaggerated lows in order to attract demand for the huge and growing debt offerings from governments. If the economy continues to
be weak, deficits will increase (due to lower tax receipts) and the response will be to print more money. More money, more government
spending, and low interest rates will lead to acceleration in inflation.

Even if rates do rise, if they lag inflation, that's still positive for gold especially and other commodities.

Moving Out of the Dollar

The U.S. dollar is a fundamentally weak currency, with high budget and trade deficits. Over time, such deficits lead to weaker economies, particularly if interest rates are not high enough to attract international investors. Given the sluggish economy, the troubled consumer, and large government financing requirements, we do not believe it is realistic to expect significantly higher interest rates in the near term. The Federal Reserve, like the good politicians they are, will favor easy-money policies to support the economy, even at the risk of a weaker dollar and higher inflation.

The dollar is going to continue its long-term slide for the foreseeable future, with the ever-present possibility of a sudden collapse. The long-term reasons for the dollar decline and its implications are discussed more fully in the Chapter 6.

Easy Money and More Debt

In response to the U.S.-bred global credit crisis, the United States aggressively eased money, led by Federal Reserve Chairman Ben Bernanke who once famously declared he would drop dollar bills out of helicopters if that's what was required to stop a recession. "Helicopter Ben" has done the modern equivalent of that, more than doubling the monetary base in the six months after the onset of the crisis in September 2008, in an unprecedented move.

The administration is doing its best to help Ben destroy the purchasing value of the dollar by its staggering spending plans, with estimates of a $9 trillion deficit within a few years. And that's without some of the largest spending plans; already, government spending on health care (through Medicare, Medicaid, and the Scopps children's program) accounts for 5 percent of total GDP. The health care legislation of 2010 could vastly increase that over the years. Together with Social Security, these programs will lead to a rapid increase in debt. Within two decades, interest payments on debt will consume 30 percent of the government budget, considered a tipping point. It's very difficult to claw back from such a high level of interest payments. This can be met either by the government reneging on its bonds—unlikely—or by increased inflation and a decline in the dollar.

Other countries see this, and don't like it. Even China has lectured the United States on the need for more monetary discipline. It only serves to accelerate thoughts on the need to diversify.

So all the evidence points in the years ahead to a declining dollar and accelerating inflation, and these together form the ideal economic backdrop for higher commodity prices. Again, they are not required for higher prices; increased demand and restrained supply will take care of that, but they will exaggerate moves, particularly toward the end of the cycle. Before it's all over, expect a mania in commodities, perhaps even greater than the manias in U.S. housing or Internet stocks before that. Astute investors will have made fortunes.

PART

II

GOLD: IN GOOD AND BAD TIMES

CHAPTER 6

Reasons for Gold to Go Up

Gold is the asset of choice for the next few years, above even other resources. Most of the positive factors that will drive resources apply to gold, and a few more besides. Yet gold is not subject to the major downside. Other resources may well perform better than gold; indeed, I suspect some will. But gold is not subject to the major risk associated with the resource complex, namely slowing demand from a major recession. Gold will perform well in more than one scenario. So gold is the foundation of our resource portfolio.

Gold Will Do Well Whatever the Outlook

Gold is the single best asset to protect against monetary and other forms of instability. It is an insurance policy. It can also benefit from economic growth with strong jewelry demand, but, as the last couple of years have demonstrated, it doesn't depend on this. As Marc Faber explained in his book *Tomorrow's Gold*, on the rise of Asia, gold and silver can do well in bleak economic circumstances because of *fear*, not greed. Resources typically do not do so well when fear dominates the economic landscape. For gold, unlike other resources, the investor is a significant and indeed essential part of the demand structure.

The last couple of years have also amply demonstrated the need for insurance, something the world had apparently forgotten.

Any asset, any market, any individual stock has various factors, positive and negative, that could affect it at any time. As investors, we must sort through these various factors, attempt to weigh them, and assess a risk and reward profile. For gold right now, the factors that could affect its future price are overwhelmingly positive. They include both macroeconomic and industry-specific factors.

14 Reasons for Gold to Go Up

As with any asset, gold's price is affected by the overall economic environment. Right now, that environment is overwhelmingly bullish for the metal.

1. Monetary Instability.   The instability in the world's monetary system over the past couple of years, exposing its fragility, has caused a rush into gold. This period has highlighted the main function of gold, namely to preserve assets and to act as an insurance on other assets, including financial markets and currencies. Gold has performed this task admirably, as indeed it has throughout history. The monetary system remains unstable; nothing has changed and the need for insurance is as strong as ever. Interestingly, the rush into physical gold in 2008 and 2009 was far from a mania, and buyers tended to be reasonably price conscious, waiting for pullbacks to buy more.

In 2010, a new fear has come to the fore, the risk of sovereign debt defaults. Greece's government debt is rated as "junk," and there are concerns it may be forced to default. But other countries, with equally high debt levels, are lined up behind it. In such an environment, gold is the clear asset of choice. This suggests the market has further to go, and indeed we know there are many buyers on the sidelines who are waiting for a correction to buy. And those who bought for insurance tend to be long-term holders.

2. Geopolitical Instability. Geopolitical or military crises have tended to boost the price of gold, often with short-term moves as crises flare; these impacts are typically more extreme when gold is already going up. We saw this most clearly perhaps with the Iranian hostage crisis at the end of the 1970s. An underlying tension in world affairs, with occasional flare-ups, also tends to put support under gold. With nuclear programs in North Korea and Iran, U.S. troops on active duty in Afghanistan and Iraq, overall tension in the Middle East, nuclear Pakistan increasingly unstable, and much more besides, it would be difficult to argue that the world is a safer, quieter place today than it was a decade ago.

3. Reflation Policies.   Governments of the world seem to know only one answer to a slowing economy, and that is to pump the economy with easy money: lots of money and low interest rates. This is especially true of the United States. Since the collapse of Lehman in September 2008, over the next year, the administration stepped up spending to the tune of around $10 trillion while the Fed ran the printing presses overtime, doubling the money supply in the space of four short months. Interest rates were dropped to artificially low levels, so that the average money market fund actually returned a miniscule 0.16 percent for all of 2009.

Whether all this easy money helped the economy or simply, as in the 1930s, prolonged the downturn is a subject outside the scope of this book. What we can say, however, is that excess money and artificially low interest rates are positive for gold. In particular, a period of negative interest rates (when short-term rates are below the rate of inflation) is always a very positive indicator of future gains for gold. Rates were negative for most of the 1970s, from 1973 to the advent of Paul Volcker as Federal Reserve Chairman at the end of the decade. For all of the 1980s and 1990s, with only a couple of brief and minor exceptions, rates were positive (sometimes very much so), while again in the 2000s, rates have been negative for much of the time.

Though little of this new money has actually got into the real economy (to date), it is going to be very difficult for the Federal Reserve, and other banks around the world, to exit these stimulus programs without provoking inflation. The growing concern about future inflation is one reason that gold has been going up.

4. A Weaker Dollar.   The most important economic factor affecting gold so far in this bull market has been the weakness in the dollar. Though gold has recently been moving up in terms of all currencies, the expectation of further weakness in the dollar can only be positive for the metal.

Gold has been going up recently in terms of all currencies, and that is a prerequisite to a strong bull market. This bull market is not an antidollar move; there are concerns in varying degrees about all fiat (paper) currencies. However, since gold is quoted in U.S. dollars, then clearly, other things being equal, a lower dollar means a higher dollar gold price. It is concern about the dollar that has sparked much of the move into gold. Notwithstanding the sharp declines in the dollar already in the past few years—in the past five years, it had fallen by almost 40 percent against the Euro, before the recent collapse in the Euro amid the Greek debt crisis—the dollar is set to continue this slide for some time to come.

The twin deficits of the United States—the budget deficit and trade deficit—are both at what has traditionally been crisis levels for a country's currency. This has long been recognized, but the U.S. dollar's reserve status delayed the inevitable slide. Well known, too, is the massive money creation over the past couple of years particularly, though it goes back farther than that. The money supply has more than quadrupled over the past quarter century, much more than the growth in the size of the economy. As with any commodity, more supply leads to a lower price.

The most significant development affecting the dollar is the shift in central bank attitudes. The world today has a higher level of central bank reserves than ever before, and over 70 percent of total foreign reserves of all countries are held in U.S. dollars. Some of the largest reserves have been amassed by newly developing countries who built their reserves while the dollar reigned supreme. At the same time, there was little in the way of alternatives. Central banks used to hold some German marks, a "hard" currency, but with the advent of the Euro, the strength of the mark was diluted by the drachma, peseta, and lira. The pound has been weak and too volatile, the Japanese economy weak, and other currencies lack the depth necessary for substantial holdings in bank reserves. Until recently, gold was completely out of favor. So the dollar it was.

Worried about Too Many Dollars.   But now there is growing concern about both the dollar's stability and the prudence of holding such a high proportion of reserves in a single asset, all the more so given the highly indebted U.S. economy. Some smaller banks (UAE and Sweden among them) have started to swap some dollars in their reserves. Among the larger dollar holders, China's premier Wen Jiabao has publicly said he is "worried" about holding so many dollars. A widely publicized article in the Chinese *People's Daily* in 2009 called for a "new financial and currency order that is no longer dependent on the United States and the dollar," and said "the world urgently needs to create a diversified currency system." Russia has said many times that it wants to diversify, and has been buying both Euros and Canadian dollars, as well as gold, for its reserves. In not-a-few cases, this concern has been tinged with a degree of political antagonism (including Russia and smaller, mostly Islamic countries). Malaysia has long called for a gold-backed *dinar* for trade among Muslim countries. There is always the risk of a country or two aggressively selling dollars at some stage to make a point.

But even apart from that, central banks and governments are realizing the need for some diversification. A significant first-time meeting in 2009 of the heads of the four BRIC countries, scandalously underreported in the U.S. media, was a watershed event. Brazil, Russia, India, and China called for a new global reserve currency to replace the dollar, arguing for a basket of currencies not dissimilar to the old IMF "special drawing rights." China later suggested the basket could include gold. More recently, the United Nations has taken up the issue, calling for a global reserve bank to issue the currency. While a global bank controlled by the UN may not be such a good idea, there is no disputing that the move for a new reserve currency and reduced role for the dollar is gaining ground.

With over $4 trillion in U.S. paper held by the world's central banks—at least half of it by those who are not necessarily friendly with the United States (OPEC, Russia, arguably even China)—a move to become "less dependent" on the dollar is not to be taken lightly.

Most of the large holders do not want, nor can they afford, to sell U.S. dollars. That would only hurt their remaining dollar holdings, and there are not enough suitable alternatives available right now. Who wants to hold the Euro as insurance? Much more likely, however, is that slowly, over time countries will diversify their bank reserves by not adding to their dollar holdings with new central bank reserves.

China recently, for example, put almost half a trillion from its reserves into a "sovereign investment fund" with the goal of making strategic investments around the world. At the time, this represented virtually half of the country's reserves. The new fund has the objective of boosting returns on that portion of the reserves, and the fund has been making investments in companies and directly into business ventures around the world, including most notably in resources. Whatever the stated intention, though, one aim and certainly result of this move has been to diversify reserves out of the dollar.

These moves to diversify come as China has been buying significantly less U.S. debt, increasingly far, far less than its trade deficit with the United States. In other words, it is no longer recycling the dollars it earns from exporting to the United States by buying U.S. Treasuries. From a peak in 2006, when it purchased almost half of all U.S. Treasuries issued that year, China purchased less than 5 percent in 2009, culminating in a large sale in December. That sale reduced China's dominance of foreign Treasury holdings, with Japan now neck-and-neck with China as the largest holders of U.S. debt. How long before China becomes a net seller on an extended basis?

Over time, foreign banks will diversify their dollar holdings for prudence, for safety, if not for political concerns. This will have the effect of reducing the value of the dollar. This may not come all at once, in a sudden wholesale exit from the dollar, but inexorably, one country after another will shift, buying fewer dollars, selling some, perhaps at an accelerating pace, driving the dollar down over the next several years. Such a decline in the dollar's value does not require that any country sell its dollars, but rather that, over time, they buy fewer, thus reducing the percentage of reserves in dollars. We are already witnessing this trend.

A Long-Term Slide.   The situation faced by the United States today is not unlike the situation Britain faced at the end of World War II—and the results may not be dissimilar. Britain had long held military and economic supremacy, and the British pound was the world's main reserve currency. Britain was leader among nations; Britannia ruled the waves. But by the end of the war, Britain had an overstretched military that it could not afford. It was hugely indebted, in Britain's case, from the burden of acting as policeman to the world and specifically the debts it took on to fight the war. (Roosevelt extracted a tough price for U.S. aid.) Foreigners no longer trusted the pound.

The United States took over as the world's leading power and with it the dollar became the world's reserve currency. The indebted pound fell from five-to-one in 1946 to parity four decades later when Britain had to go begging ingloriously to the IMF for aid.

The world's leading power with an overstretched military, an indebted economy, and a reserve currency people no longer trust: Does that sound familiar? The problem is that having the world's reserve currency enables a country to borrow more than it should, more than it could otherwise. But when foreign banks no longer want to hold your currency, all the paper that's been created over the decades still remains. The result is a weaker currency as the economy declines.

In the case of Britain, there was an obvious substitute, America and the American dollar, to take its place (just as Britain and the British pound had taken the place of Spain with its New World gold). But even without an obvious substitute—China is not ready yet—over time, the dollar will lose its reserve status and the dollar will continue to slide. Gold will most definitely gain from a long-term decline in the purchasing power of the dollar but will also likely be a beneficiary of central bank diversification.

5. Central Bank Diversification.   We have already alluded to one consequence of dollar weakness, and that is that holders of much of the world's supply of dollars—the central banks—are looking elsewhere to store their reserves. Gold is a clear beneficiary of this move.

The need for central banks to diversify their reserves out of the heavy concentration in U.S. dollars is one reason that the dollar will continue its long-term slide. But this need for diversification is also a reason that gold will appreciate. Gold has long been the traditional cornerstone of central bank reserves, and it is the ideal asset for that purpose, since it is the only financial asset that is no one else's liability. If China has over $3 trillion in U.S. dollars in its central bank reserves, it is beholden to the United States. Remember that old joke "If you owe the bank $1 million and can't pay, you have a problem, but owe the bank $1 billion and can't pay, and they've got a problem." (Numbers updated for inflation!) Gold has also proven its ability to preserve purchasing power over the years.

As discussed, many of the largest cash hordes in central bank reserves have been built up only in the last couple of decades by the newly emerging countries, particularly in Asia. Until relatively recently, this was a period when gold was out of favor, and it was also a period of global growth when financial assets were appreciating. No wonder that the countries with the largest absolute foreign reserves, built up over the past quarter century or so, tend to have the lowest percentage of gold. (See Table 6.1.)

But this is changing. China recently announced that it had increased its gold reserves over the past few years by 75 percent. Most of that gold appears to have been acquired from domestic mines, but that still helped move the price up since it kept gold off the world market. Russia has also been a steady new buyer, and bank officials have stated clearly that future surpluses will be put into gold.

Table 6.1   Newly Rich Asia Holds Less Gold

	Bullion (Tonnes)	% of reserves
United States	8,133.0	70.5
Germany	3,406.0	66.1
Italy	2,451.0	64.9
France	2,435.0	65.7
Switzerland	1,040.1	27.1
Russia	641.0	5.1
Brazil	33.6	0.5
China	1,054.0	1.6
Japan	765.2	2.5
India	557.7	6.9
Taiwan	423.6	4.1
Singapore	127.4	2.3
Malaysia	36.4	1.3
IMF	3,005.3	n/a
All countries[1]	27,030.4	10.0

Data as of January 2010.
[1] Excludes IMF holdings.
Source: International Monetary Fund, World Gold Council, January 2010.

Despite this boost in buying, however, China, the sixth-largest gold holder in the world, still has well under 2 percent of its reserves in gold, among the lowest in the world. All of China's actions suggest it will continue accumulating gold.

When the International Monetary Fund (IMF) announced it was selling 400 metric tons of gold from its reserves, many commentators wrote of doom for gold. But dramatically and significantly, the Indian central bank purchased half of that in one transaction. That single purchase, 200 tons or 6.4 million ounces for $6.7 billion, a truly significant amount of gold, boosted India's gold holdings by about 50 percent in one fell scoop. Yet its gold holdings went to about 6 percent of total reserves, still well below the global average, let alone the amount of gold held by "legacy" central banks (Germany, France, and Italy, as well as the United States, each hold well over 70 percent of their reserves in gold). This transaction removed the fear of overhang; a truly significant amount of bullion was able to be purchased by a single bank in one transaction, without it stretching in any way.

The amount of gold in reserves for the eight largest Asian bank reserves, plus Brazil, range from 5 percent to zero (with India the new exception following its IMF purchase). To boost these reserves to just 10 percent—again, to emphasize, less than the global average—would require the purchase of over 11 metric tons. To put that in perspective, that's nearly 40 percent more than all the gold held by the United States, which is the largest horde of gold around. Put another way, it represents about five years' worth of production.

Of course, we are not suggesting that all these banks will rush out one day to boost their gold holdings to 10 percent of total reserves. Of course not; that could not be done without extraordinary dislocation of the market. But it likely means that they will be steady buyers, driving the price slowly higher; that large sales of gold can be readily acquired; and that there is significant support under the market.

It was widely reported that China's national bank approached the IMF to acquire the 400 tonnes it had for sale, but wanted to do it at a price below the market. Despite the lip service paid to fears of a gold bubble by a central bank official in December, China's sovereign wealth fund continued to buy gold, including $145 million in the Spider gold ETF (GLD). At the same time, they bought shares in several mines, including Gold Fields and Freeport. China stands, along with others, as potential large buyers waiting in the wings. This limits gold's downside.

6. Change in Bank Attitudes.   These large purchases in recent years by China and India, among others, are but a reflection of a changing attitude toward gold by the world's central banks. For the last three quarters of 2009, central banks became net buyers in aggregate, rather than the sellers they had been for the past 20 years. In addition to this new surge in buying has come a corresponding reduction in selling. For the past decade, the legacy central banks, mostly in Europe, which have the highest allocations of gold (outside the United States) agreed to annual ceilings of the amount of gold they could, in aggregate, sell. (See Figure 6.1.)

In the early years, there was sometimes an unseemly rush to sell ahead of other banks subject to the limit, and even in the middle years of the decade, there was a step up of selling ahead of the annual expiration deadline. But for the last four years, the banks have failed to sell their annual limit, and in 2008–2009 (the agreement runs

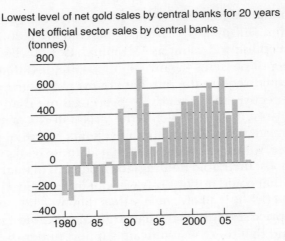

Lowest level of net gold sales by central banks for 20 years

Net official sector sales by central banks
(tonnes)

Figure 6.1   Central Bank Selling Falls
Source: World Gold Council, GFMS.

September to September), they sold little more than 20 percent of the permissible amount. Bank attitudes have clearly changed.

In addition, of course, the banks most likely to be sellers have already sold. Banks such as the Bundesbank or Banque de Franc have an affinity for gold as an insurance against unstable money and are less likely to sell substantial amounts from their reserves. Both Germany and France have seen inflations and significant currency depreciations over the past century and neither wants to repeat the experience. (France could sell some of its stockpile, but we do not expect huge sales. The European Central Bank could sell some of its gold as well.) Swiss National Bank, which was a large seller at the beginning of the decade and in the 1990s, has made it clear it has no intentions of selling gold any time soon; it remains one of the world's top 10 holders of the metal.

Central banks have proved remarkably poor judges of the gold market. The Bank of England infamously sold close to half its gold reserves in 1999 at a 23-year low for gold; within weeks, the low was hit and gold proceeded to move up, more than quadrupling over the ensuing decade, without even coming close to the Bank's selling price again. Of course, the Bank of England, under Gordon Brown at the Treasury, conducted its sales by announcing in advance to the market that it planned to sell. Not unexpectedly, others rushed to sell ahead of the bank, driving price down yet farther. The conspiracy buffs had a field day with this, but conspiracy or stupidity, we can state categorically that the sales were not conducted in a manner designed to maximize the sales price.

Recent bank purchases have also had a significant psychological impact on the market. India is the largest gold jewelry market in the world, with gold the traditional dowry at weddings and a sign of the wealth of the family. But Indians also tend to be price-conscious buyers. When gold moved first over $1,000, they drew back, with gold imports dropping by 50 percent in 2008. Most of 2009 was weak as well. But when the national bank announced its purchase of IMF gold, imports into India surged.

7. Absence of Large Sellers.   During the 1990s, there were two sellers of large amounts of gold, the central banks and the gold mining companies themselves, not with the gold they mined but sales of future production through hedging. These both weighed on the gold price, not only through the increase in actual physical supply but through the potential sales, the psychological overhang that weighed constantly on the market.

Not only are central banks no longer large and consistent sellers, so too the last of the big hedgers have finally closed their hedges. Despite assurances to the contrary, as the price of gold started to accelerate upward during the 2000s, miners who hedged started to take substantial hits to earnings. No longer were these simply accounting charges, but real reductions in earnings. Net hedging turned to de-hedging, as hedges expired and fewer companies did new hedging while others started to buy back old hedges actively. The last hold-out hedgers were forced to sell gold at $300 or $400 while the price moved toward the $1,000 mark, and they too finally conceded victory. (See Figure 6.2.)

Hedging will continue. It is something that banks require when they lend the significant amounts of cash necessary to build a new facility and bring a new mine into production. It varies, of course, but a bank might require, say, 30 percent of its planned production for the next three years to be sold forward. This kind of hedging is of less concern to the market, both in a practical sense, for the amount of ounces involved, but also because there is a legitimate business rational for the forward sales.

Speculative hedging, on the other hand, not only involved large volumes of ounces, but it was also an overhang since one never quite

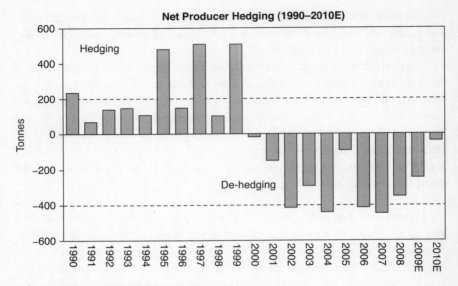

Figure 6.2   Producers Hedge Less

Source: National Bank Financial.

knew when one of these companies could sell another batch of gold. It served as an anchor on higher prices, because, as in a game of whac-a-mole, every time gold moved up, some company would sell a bunch of gold forward. It also had a depressing psychological impact on gold investors since it gave the signal that even the gold mining companies did not really believe in the future of gold. The fact that companies have been forced to stop hedging because of higher gold prices has similarly had an important positive impact on psychology.

8. Increase in Demand from Emerging Countries.   It is not only governments and large institutions that are buying gold but also individuals, everyone from the peasant in rural India to the sophisticate in Zurich or London. We have already discussed in detail the increase in demand for resources arising from the growth in economies of China and other emerging countries. This applies to gold as well. China, for example, was the only major economy to experience an increase in gold jewelry buying in 2009, with demand growing by 25 to 30 percent. Since 2007, China has in fact been the second-largest gold jewelry market in the world, behind only India. Moreover, these countries tend to have an affinity for gold that is not seen in the United States and many other parts of the developed world.

Significantly, half of the growth in gold buying from China in recent years has come from private buying, now encouraged by the government.

It should be emphasized that jewelry demand in much of Asia, as in the Middle East, is more than simple adornment. In China, again as elsewhere, most gold jewelry is 24-carat, not 18-carat that we see in the West. This makes it more difficult to fashion into exquisite designs. Gold jewelry tends to be cruder and sells at a modest markup over the gold content. (In Cartier or Tiffany, the price of a gold necklace is usually a multiple over the value of the gold it contains.) Gold jewelry is more than adornment; it is savings and a store of wealth. When people don't trust their banking system, or their currency, they want their wealth in something recognizable, some indestructible. Gold jewelry is a way of storing as well as displaying wealth.

The demand for gold in China was pent up for many years, when all gold had to be sold directly to the Bank of China and individuals were prohibited from buying gold. Throughout the 2000s, the gold market in China was deregulated until, today, the price of gold in China is essentially the world market price, and individuals have many ways to buy gold, including gold deposit accounts at banks. From restricting access to gold, the Chinese authorities are now actively encouraging Chinese individuals to buy gold and store their growing wealth in this form.

For most developed countries, including the United States, per-capita annual gold consumption is slightly over 1 gram. In only a handful of less-developed countries (Saudi Arabia, Hong Kong, and Turkey) is above 1 gram per year. Despite the historical affinity for gold, Chinese buy only half of that, as do other Asian countries, including Indonesia, Vietnam, and Japan. (See Figure 6.3.) Gold is not some barbarous relic that only people in backward countries buy. On the contrary, as economies develop and people get richer, the per-capita consumption of gold, as with other resources, increases.

9. Increase in Investor Demand.   But for gold, the increase in demand goes far beyond increasing demand from China and other emerging economies, however significant that is. Investment demand doubled in the years from 2005 to 2008, and has continued to increase as concern about fiat currencies increases.

The most important contributor to the increase in demand for gold in recent years has probably been the advent of gold exchange-traded funds (ETFs), which are funds that hold gold on behalf of

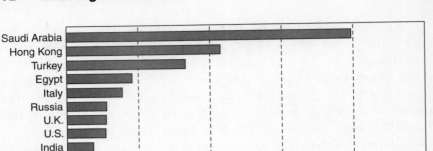

Figure 6.3   Emerging Markets Consume Less Gold

Note: Consumption is for four quarters ended Q2/09.
Source: International Monetary Fund.

investors who can buy and sell the shares on an exchange. The largest of these, the Spider Gold Trust (GLD) sponsored by the World Gold Council, started trading at the end of 2004. From holdings of just over 300 tonnes in 2004 and 2005 for all gold ETFs and similar vehicles combined, they now hold over 2,000 tonnes, over 1,300 tonnes of that in the Gold Trust, an astonishing growth in demand for gold. The gold ETFs make it easy for smaller investors to buy and sell gold in small quantities. They also open up the gold market to various institutional investors, such as pension funds, who had been prohibited from holding gold itself. (See Figure 6.4.)

There have also been recent significant purchases by well-known investors, including George Soros (who doubled his GLD holdings in December) and John Paulson (who launched a new gold fund in addition to the 10 percent gold and GLD holdings he already has in his main fund). These are two of the biggest hedge fund managers who are more likely than not to add to holdings.

Some observers have questioned whether investors would continue to buy gold if the dollar were to rally. Of course, a rally in one currency is necessarily offset by declines in others. A rally in the dollar would most likely be only temporary, in any event, and an opportunity to take advantage of the relative strength to move out into other assets. Moreover, even if the dollar were to rally, that would not mean

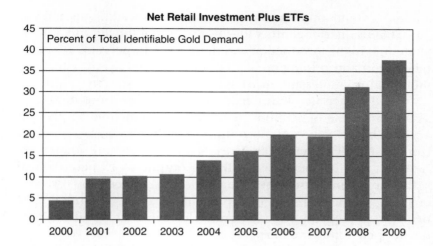

Figure 6.4   Investor Demand Up
Source: World Gold Council.

that all the other reasons investors are turning to gold would have gone away. On the contrary, buying would likely continue, and at minimum, given the current fragile monetary situation, investors seem reluctant to sell. When the Greek debt situation made headlines, European investors fled the Euro and bought gold. When the yen rose sharply last year, so that the price of gold in yen terms actually declined, Japanese investors did not sell, even though they were selling most other assets, and even though they could have locked in profits by selling their gold.

10. Constrained New Supply.   Normally, a market would respond to a favorable macroeconomic environment and new buyers by increasing supply, but the gold market is not boosting supply meaningfully, whether through new mine production or secondary sales. The reasons for this suggest that supply will continue to lag increased demand. We discussed in Chapter 4 the difficulty of finding significant new ore bodies. Even if every government in the world encouraged exploration and mining, removing all the roadblocks put in their way, we should still find that the supply of newly mined gold would not increase to meet demand. As it is, new mine supply declined each year this millennium, until 2009, though it remains well below the production (of 85 million ounces) in 2001. Ironically, that all-time production high came when gold was trading just a few dollars from its quarter-century low; by the end of the decade, with gold at all-time highs, production was down over 10 percent. Despite the new mines and mining areas that have opened up in recent years, more mature mines and districts are falling inexorably.

Finally, after nearly a decade of declines in output, 2009 saw a small increase of around 4 percent in production. Partly, this is attributable to a recovery in output from Indonesia, up 55 percent from a sharply lower 2008. More significant for the longer term, however, was the increase in Chinese output, at 13 percent, which is the largest increase other than Indonesia's exceptional recovery, enabling China to retain its top positions again. China's output is nearly 50 percent above that of Australia (second highest); its output has jumped by well over 65 percent in the past four years, an unrivaled improvement. Both South Africa and the United States, the third- and fourth-highest world producers, respectively, saw further declines in output. Though we may see future increases, it is unlikely that they will be meaningful on a sustained basis.

South Africa, for example, the world's leading gold country for a century, still produced well over half the world's new gold as late as 1975. (See Figure 6.5.) Then the decline in output at its mature and deep mines set in. South African mines went from being the world's

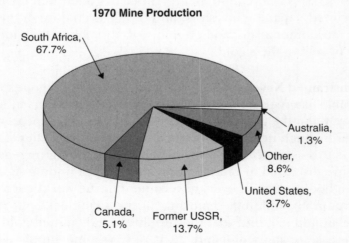

1970 Mine Production

South Africa, 67.7%

Australia, 1.3%

Other, 8.6%

United States, 3.7%

Canada, 5.1%

Former USSR, 13.7%

Figure 6.5   South Africa Use to Dominate Production (1970)
Source: Goldsheetlink.com.

2008 Mine Production

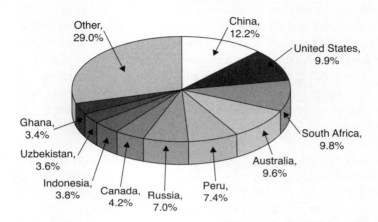

Figure 6.6   The New Producers Take over from South Africa (2008)
Source: Goldsheetlink.com.

lowest-cost mines to among the most expensive, and output dropped. In 2008, South Africa produced less than 10 percent of the world's gold after the largest drop in gold production there since the Boer War. (See Figure 6.6.)

But the decline is more widespread than just one country. Of the largest gold-producing countries in the world, three of the top four saw declines in 2008 over the prior year, as did five of the top eight. And the declines were larger than the increases. Part of the reason for the drop in ounces mined is the decline in grade; this applies both to ounces mined but also significantly to replacement grades. This does not augur well for the future.

Though we do not expect the decline in world output to continue at its recent pace, we do not expect a dramatic reversal. For the past decade, as the price of gold has more than quadrupled, as exploration spending has quintupled, output has fallen and the number of new discoveries of significance has also declined. Even if all projects currently in the pipeline were accelerated and became mines, though output would increase, it would not be by much, not on a sustained basis. It is becoming more difficult and more expensive to find and develop significant gold resources, even without the roadblocks that governments and environmentalists put up.

Some analysts even talk of "peak gold" and the parallels are there. In 2008, companies around the world found fewer ounces than they mined, despite the decline in production. So if ounces found today form the basis for production a few years down the road, the outlook does not look promising for a recovery in production. Where reserves have increased, it is by and large only because of the higher price of gold, making previously uneconomic ore now potentially profitable. Thus, the gold price must stay up and increase in order for reserves to increase.

11. Other Supply Down.   Every ounce of gold that has ever been mined still exists, much of it held in bank vaults. As the wag said, you dig gold out of one hole in the ground only to put it back in another. Unlike, say, copper or oil, it is not consumed and destroyed. After all, gold's indestructibility is one of the attributes that makes it so attractive, particularly for money. The amount of new gold mined each year is overwhelmed by the total amount of gold in the world, and therefore theoretically available for sale.

Throughout history, about 3.822 billion ounces of gold had been produced (according to numbers by the CPM Group, a New York consulting organization, which I've updated). Approximately 90 percent of that amount was mined since 1900. Of the historical total, about 1.3 billion ounces have been used for jewelry; of the rest, about 1 billion is held by central banks and 1.2 billion ounces held by private investors. This is a reversal of the historical division between government and privately held gold. For most of the decades from 1950 through 1980, central banks held three or four times as much gold as was privately held. A slow decline in bank gold, combined with a dramatic increase in private gold, saw the lines cross in 2005. Private forces are creating a de-facto gold standard.

I have discussed why I do not expect significant bank selling in the years ahead; indeed, quite the contrary. So too is forward selling by producers, wherein someone else's gold is borrowed and sold, unlikely to be a major factor in the near future. Nor is selling by investors, whether retail or institutional, who have purchased gold in recent years as an insurance against the decline in purchasing value of paper currencies, as a hedge on monetary instability and financial assets. For those who bought gold in 2008 or 2009 or more recently, the very reasons for their buying gold remain.

Gold Investors Hold, Rarely Sell.   Some of this gold is more available for sale than others; the retail investor in Kansas who bought 500 shares of the Spider Gold Trust, for example, can readily become a seller, forcing the trust to liquidate some of its bullion. But the Californian businessman who purchased 10 kilo bars and is storing them in a Swiss bank vault is certainly a "stickier" holder. Interestingly, though new purchases of gold by private investors slowed in the long bear market of the 1980s and 1990s, investors in aggregate did not sell the gold they accumulated during the 1970s. Once bought, the gold tends to be held. But there is no incentive for either the Kansas investor or the Californian businessman to turn seller in the current environment.

Similarly, the millions of ordinary people throughout Asia and the Middle East who buy gold jewelry as a store of wealth as well as adornment are unlikely to become sellers any time soon. We saw a huge increase in such secondary selling during the Asian crisis in 1997. There was some logic to this. Apart from the fact that it was proclaimed the patriotic thing to do—selling gold to earn much needed hard currency—gold was performing its function as a crisis hedge. Here was precisely the kind of sudden and deep crisis against that gold had been purchased. But in 2008, there was a weak economy around the world, and rather than sell gold, investors turned to the yellow metal.

Scrap, whether from old rings or from candlesticks and other adornments, is always a component in the supply equation. Scrap supplies have increased in the last few years as the price has increased, but by no means dramatically. In the late 1970s, there was a surge of scrap selling, as individuals everywhere searched their attics for bits of gold to sell. That period cleaned out a lot of old gold ornaments and potential supply; it will require a significantly higher price to bring out another round in unwanted gold pieces.

12. Government Debt.   There has also been a surge in government deficits over the past decade and more, primarily in the United States. Gold tends to do well when the deficit is increasing. Frank Holmes, CEO of Global Investors mutual funds in San Antonio, notes the "significant relationship" between federal deficit spending and the performance of gold stocks going back to 1971. When the deficit increases, gold stocks tend to outperform the market.

Countries throughout the developed world have built up massive debt obligations over the past several decades, as well as huge future obligations, including social spending on medicine and old-age benefits. As populations age, particularly in Japan and Europe, the cost of these benefits will rise dramatically while the proportion of the populations that are working, and paying to support the spending, will decline. In some countries, including Japan and European countries like Italy, it will be an absolute decline in working populations.

This has serious implications: Government will be forced to renege on their obligations and significantly increase tax revenue from a smaller base or inflate their way out of the problem. Though we may see a multitude of limitations on benefit spending (raising the age before old-age pensions take full effect, reducing benefits for those with other income, and so on) as well as numerous tax increases (such as we are seeing in numerous Obama administration proposals), the two lines—projected spending and projected revenues—remain miles apart. The clear answer for governments, the only politically feasible answer, is to inflate and destroy the purchasing value of their currencies. If governments around the world are all in a race to devalue their currencies, the winner will be the one form of money that is no one else's obligation, namely gold. As industry leader Pierre Lassonde, chairman of Franco-Nevada Corporation, recently put it in a speech to the Prospectors and Developers of Canada Conference, in March 2010, all countries will devalue their currencies "against the one currency that can't be devalued."

Before the crisis in social spending hits us, we expect the possibility of the defaults by various governments in the developed world, including state governments (California?) and EU member states (Greece, Spain). Certainly, in general, government finances in the developed world are in much poorer state than those in the larger emerging countries. A default by a major country would surely put a firecracker under gold.

13. Gold Is Cheap.   Even when conditions are favorable, investors must always be alert to price. Fortunately, gold passes this test, too. Despite the quadrupling of the dollar gold price over the past decade, gold remains fundamentally undervalued on any metric one chooses. We concede that it can be difficult to analyze gold, to put a value on it. Certainly, one cannot analyze gold bullion the way one might value a stock or bond. After all, it earns nothing (never will) and yields nothing (never will). James Grant, the erudite editor of *Interest Rate Observer*, calls it "a valuation cipher." He notes, "You could talk yourself into some fancy bullion prices." At $1,100 an ounce, all the gold in the world is worth $5.5 trillion, compared with global financial assets valued at over $200 trillion. Investor holdings of gold amount to only $1.3 trillion. Certainly, only a relatively small shift in funds from financial assets to gold would see gold move up smartly. But when would it become overvalued?

Let's look at various ways of putting a valuation on gold; we find that if there can be valid debate about the precise assumptions to be used, gold appears still fundamentally undervalued by all measures.

- *Gold's price on an inflation-adjusted basis.* We know that gold's much-proclaimed top of $850 was a passing flicker on a computer screen somewhere; let's take $650 as a more realistic top, the level gold achieved for more than a few weeks, to make the comparison fairer. Adjusting for inflation over the past three decades, that price would work out to a little less than $2,000 an ounce.

- *Gold versus money supply.* Under the gold standard, paper money would have to be backed by gold. Were we to return to that standard, with the dollars in existence today (using the narrow M2 definition), gold would be valued at $2,214. And I would bet the production of dollars will continue to increase faster than the production of gold.

- *Gold versus stocks.* One can look at the price of gold against the level of equities, since over the long run, they are frequently bought and sold in contradiction to each other. Investors buy equities when they are optimistic on the economy and the future, gold when they are fearful. The Dow Jones gold ratio has moved in very long swings, going up as the stock market has risen (or gold declined), and falling when gold rises and the stock market stumbles. (See Figure 6.7.)

  Over the past century, the Dow gold ratio has returned to nearly 1:1 three times. At the most recent peak, in 1999, when gold was at the bottom of its 20-year bear market and just before the tech stock market bubble burst, the ratio stood at 45:1. That is, it would have taken 45 ounces of gold to buy one "unit" of the Dow. At the beginning of 2010, the ratio stands at 9.3:1. This dramatic collapse in the ratio shows the

The Dow Priced in Gold

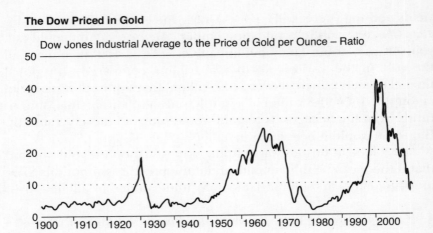

Dow Jones Industrial Average to the Price of Gold per Ounce – Ratio

Figure 6.7   Gold: Further to Go

Source: Sharelynx.com.

relative overperformance of gold against stocks; indeed, the Dow at the onset of the new decade in 2010 is actually below its level at the end of the 1990s.

Before gold's bull market is over, we expect to see the ratio under two, and perhaps closer to one, where each previous decline in the ratio has ended. Stocks could rise but gold faster, or gold decline but stocks more so. With a static stock market, this would imply a gold price of $5,000 to $10,000.

- *Gold relative to oil and other commodities.* Except that gold is money, there is no absolute reason why the ratio of gold and oil prices should be around 14 any more than the price of platinum to wheat should be at a ratio around 2.8. But by comparing the price of gold with a range of commodities—and oil is the major commodity most commonly used—we can see that gold is relatively inexpensive. Over the past 30 years, the ratio has been below 8 and more than 30 in enormous swings. We might say that 16 is an average ratio; using that historically typical ratio, the price of gold should be somewhat higher than it is, around $1,280. If oil goes back up to $150 a barrel, then the price of gold would be around $2,400.

Though one can't analyze gold on a discounted cash flow basis, or net asset value, one can look at gold relative to other assets, as well as to itself and to money. This produces a range of possible prices. We can say that on each valuation method, gold is undervalued, sometimes considerably so. Analyst Ian McAvity in his *Deliberations* letter, March 2010, puts it this way: Gold is 32 percent above its 1980 peak, while the total credit market in the United States is 21 times its 1980 level, U.S. money supply is nine times, and the S&P 17 times. Gold has much further to go to catch up.

14. This Is Not a Top. Some observers are concerned about the possibility of a speculative top for gold. George Soros at the World Economic Forum in Davos, Switzerland, in February, loudly proclaimed gold to be "the biggest bubble of all"; at the same time, his fund was quietly building a position in the gold ETF. Despite these increases in demand and in the price of gold, we are a long way from a manic peak. Previous tops in gold have ended when the bullish consensus on gold is virtually unanimous, well over 90 percent, and we are not there yet. Bullish consensus numbers are typically high, frequently over 80 percent, but tops do not arrive until the numbers are much higher. Nor do we see the typical signs of mania, with long lines outside coin dealers, standing room only at gold seminars, daily headlines about gold, and ridiculous prices on gold stocks. John Paulson, one of the most astute fund managers around, who made fortunes for himself and his investors betting against subprime mortgages, has had difficulty getting investors interested in gold. He has raised just $90 million for his new gold hedge fund, far less than the $250 million he himself put into the fund and a fraction of the $20 billion his investors made in profits from his prior hedge fund. This is not a mania! When will it be a top? There will be signs; you will know it, even if you ignore them and get caught up in the mania. But in the cool light of day, we can say that, notwithstanding the gold vending machines in the United Arab Emirates, the signs are not in evidence today.

What Could Go Wrong?

Any market, any asset, has bullish and bearish factors weighing on it at any given time. As an investor, one must assess these factors, weigh them and go with the preponderance. Today, the factors are overwhelmingly bullish for gold. Nonetheless, there are some potential negatives one must bear in mind.

- *A global depression.* Gold certainly performed well during the last global depression, as we have discussed. But a serious economic slowdown would further reduce the demand for jewelry. It would raise the possibility that investors would return to the dollar as a safe haven, and that they would use their gold as liquidity of last resort. One can counter this by looking at gold's experience in the last global depression, and by looking at how the price of gold has held up despite the recent drop in jewelry demand, as well as how investors around the world turned to gold, rather than the dollar, during the 2008–2009 economic crisis. The dollar seems to be valued less as a safe haven asset than in years prior; with the effective default of Dubai at the end of 2009, for example, the price of gold moved up whereas the dollar hardly budged. (It was, quite logically, the downgrade of Greece that saw Euro selling and dollar buying.)

- *Interest rates could go up.* Interest rates around the world are so low that there is only one direction for them to go—up. Gold typically does not do well in a period of rising interest rates, but specifically when short-term rates are positive and increasingly so, that is, when interest rates are above the level of inflation. So if rates increase, but lag the rise in inflation, gold would not necessarily decline. Though rates are likely to increase over the next decade—some countries, such as Australia, have already been raising local rates—they will rise slowly. If we look at the Japanese experience, rates collapsed after the asset bubbles burst in 1990, but they have remained at virtually zero for the past two decades.

  In the United States, given the state of the economy and particularly the perilous nature of rate-sensitive sectors such as residential mortgages and commercial property, it will be very difficult for the Federal Reserve to increase short-term interest rates in any meaningful way any time soon. So rates are likely to remain low for some time, and any increase is likely to be slow and lag inflation.

- *Central bank stockpiles.* Though we have discussed the shift in central bank sentiment, and that central banks became net buyers in 2009 for the first time, there is no guarantee that this will remain so. It could be that Asian and other emerging nations continue to buy gold, but that legacy banks resume selling. After all, they have massive obligations that need paying, and their gold bullion is one asset they still have. Likewise, the IMF could step up selling of its gold; this would be one source of revenue for the bank that its cash-strapped members may prefer over further boosts in cash contributions.

Less remote but potentially more damaging would be a decision to sell U.S. gold. As we have stated, the U.S. government holds the largest single pool of gold, over 8,000 tonnes, compared with 1,000 tonnes each for Switzerland and China, significantly less for Japan, Russia, and other countries. (All the countries in the Euro Zone combined hold nearly 11,000 tonnes, but this is under the control of individual countries.) There is no suggestion that the United States has plans to sell its gold, but one can certainly paint a scenario when it might be suggested. It would certainly not occur without a vicious political battle. Most likely, if it were ever seriously mooted to sell U.S. gold, it would be because the state of government finances had deteriorated to the point where the demand for gold would match any selling. But it is a potential to bear in mind.

In sum, though, the positive attributes overwhelm the negative ones, and there are good answers to each negative argument. We believe, therefore, that gold will continue to increase over the next few years at least; we are a long way in terms of price and time from any peak.

CHAPTER 7

Gold and Resources in Deflation

Perhaps the biggest concern many have about gold is that the United States and the world economy will enter a long-term deflation. And as we all know, inflation is what's good for gold.

Recent Experience Forms an Association

Certainly, until recently, at any rate, American investors in particular thought of gold essentially as an inflation hedge. And they associate deflations with depressions. It is not so in other countries, nor was it so in other periods of history. The association with inflation has taken hold, however, because, until the current gold market, the only recent experience of gold appreciating was during an inflation. The bull market of the 2000s, which has seen gold quadruple with only modest *price* inflation, to be sure has diminished the force of this association, though many nonetheless suggest that gold is appreciating at least partly because of concern about future inflation.

The association of gold with inflation is reinforced by the mere fact that in an inflation, the nominal price of everything, including gold, moves up. A price rise, say from $100 to $850 in four years (as we saw in the late 1970s), has more resonance than gold holding its price flat, even while everything else is down.

Note also I referred to *price* inflation. But inflation is an expansion of credit, and an increase in prices is simply the symptom. Credit expansion can result in higher consumer prices or indeed in higher asset prices, in stocks, real estate, and gold. There is little argument

105

that the "noughties" were a period of as much credit inflation as the 1970s.

When we think of deflation, we tend to think of depression, again because the most recent experience of deflation in the United States was during the Great Depression. Indeed, most deflations in U.S. history have been during periods of declining economic activity. But it does not have to be that way. If inflation is a period of too much money chasing too few goods, then a deflation is simply a period of too little money chasing too many goods. The price of goods declines while the price of money appreciates.

Good and Bad Deflations

Such does not have to indicate a period of declining economic activity. Indeed, the "ideal" economic scenario would be one of moderate deflation, where goods get cheaper for consumers, money holds its value, and businessmen make money by innovation and productivity gains. The entire century in Great Britain, from the end of the Napoleonic Wars in 1815 to the onset of the First World War in 1914, was both a period of deflation and a period of unprecedented economic expansion. (There was not deflation in every year, of course, and there were some brief periods of relatively sharp inflation, but the overall period was a period of stable money and declining prices.)

In a deflation, by definition, the value of money goes up; people save and hoard rather than consume. And people tend to save the best credits, which means gold rather than paper. Gold is nobody's liability, unlike paper money, and the preferred choice of saving in deflations. Gold can also have an extra boost during deflations when they are accompanied, as they often are, by monetary crisis. But it is inherent in a deflation for money to appreciate and gold remains the purest form of money.

This is not necessarily true of other resources, which lack gold's monetary status. As prices of all assets decline during deflations, by definition, then the prices of resources tend to fall. Since deflations are often accompanied by economic weakness and retrenchment, the demand for raw materials would be expected to decline and with it their prices. However, the prices of commodities can appreciate, albeit modestly, during positive deflations (such as England during the nineteenth century), as we shall see. And other factors, such as a new surge in demand from a newly emerging economy, can overwhelm the deflationary impact from other countries. At best, the picture is mixed.

Gold during U.S. and Foreign Deflations

The historical record for gold, however, is clearer. In the United States, there have been seven deflationary periods of varying duration. Each was preceded by a boom that led to speculative excess (land speculation and the railroad boom in the early nineteenth century, to stock market speculation in the last pre-deflation boom); and each had a panic at or near the onset of deflation. In the earlier deflations, the credit quality of bank issuers deteriorated and caused the exchange of notes for gold; while in later deflations there was concern at the excessive debt of the federal government. Whether there was concern at the potential default of the note issuer, there was always concern that the value of the notes might deteriorate. Hence, gold was preferred as a store of value, for savings. (This is an illustration of Gresham's Law, that bad money drives out good; bad was spent and good money was driven out of the system to be hoarded.)

Gold was saved after the market crash of 1929, but in great volumes especially in 1931, on fear of a devaluation of the dollar after Roosevelt's election. In each of these periods, however, gold was convertible, which muddies the argument of gold holding its value in a deflation and is often used as an argument by gold's detractors against that proposition. We shall return to that shortly.

Each of the deflationary periods in U.S. history was also accompanied by a panic and crisis situation, which itself could be viewed as positive for gold. We can look at deflationary periods outside of the United States, however, and avoid this problem. In England's great deflation, the price of gold held steady (indeed, appreciated modestly, depending on the start and end dates selected). Most other commodities, notwithstanding periods of volatility, were flat (itself a positive achievement during a deflation), as was silver, which is both a monetary and industrial metal.

If we examine nineteenth-century Britain in more detail, we find that although gold held its value in terms of purchasing power throughout the entire deflation, it had spurts of appreciation during periods of crisis, most notably in the second half of the 1840s, with the Corn Laws crisis and the threat of revolution), and again during the

Table 7.1   Gold Holds Its Value over Time

The Index of Purchasing Power of Gold

England 1600–1970 (1930 = 100.0)

Year	Index	Year	Index
1600	124.8	1790	103.1
1610	120.4	1800	66.9
1620	129.0	1810	71.3
1630	119.7	1820	80.2
1640	109.7	1830	97.7
1650	97.6	1840	90.2
1660	105.2	1850	125.7
1670	121.6	1860	97.7
1680	117.5	1870	100.8
1690	109.1	1880	110.0
1700	123.1	1890	134.5
1710	103.4	1900	129.2
1720	115.7	1910	124.1
1730	111.4	1920	51.4
1740	99.4	1930	100.0
1750	112.7	1940	N/A
1760	110.8	1950	128.7
1770	110.7	1960	74.6
1780	112.7	1970	63.5

Since 1970, when the price was still suppressed by the government, gold has gone up from $35 an ounce to over $1,100, holding its value well against declining currencies.
Source: Copyright © *The Golden Constant: The English and American Experience, 1560–1976*, Roy Jastram, John Wiley & Sons, 1978.

great deflation commencing in 1875, which saw a decline in prices over the following 20 years that was unprecedented in its breadth and depth. During that period, prices fell by more than 50 percent and gold correspondingly increased in value.

The same holds true for gold during earlier periods of deflation. The original work on this was undertaken by Professor Roy Jastram in his classic *The Golden Constant*, long out of print but recently revised and updated by the World Gold Council.[1] (See Table 7.1.) Jastram

---

[1] Roy Jastram, *The Golden Constant: The English and American Experience, 1560–1976* (John Wiley & Sons, 1978).

undertook a detailed analysis of prices in England from 1560 to the 1970s, in addition to the United States from 1800. He also looked at the previous three centuries in England. In broad terms, he showed a steady appreciation in the purchasing power of gold from as early as the mid-1300s until the start of the eighteenth century, with a stable price for the next 230 years, during the period of the gold standard, followed by "utter instability in the price of gold, quite unprecedented in recorded history." Of course, the utter instability in the price of gold was more a period of instability in the value of paper money.

The purchasing value of gold more than doubled in the two centuries following the start of this period, then declined steadily following the discovery of gold in the New World and its importation back into Europe, via Spain. This is to be expected, since this new supply of gold greatly increased the extant supply.

Inflation versus Deflation

Jastram studied in particular the period from 1600 on, when statistics become more reliable. He identified five periods of multiyear deflation over that period. In each of those five periods, lasting from 11 years (1658–1669) to as long as 38 years (1813–1851), the purchasing power of gold appreciated significantly. These gains in the purchasing power of gold range from 42 percent in the 11 years after 1658 to 82 percent in the 20 years after 1873 and 251 percent in the period from 1920 to 1933; this latter was a period of deflation in Britain, despite the roaring 1920s inflationary boom in the United States.

In each of the seven identified inflationary periods, however, lasting as long as 35 years (1623–1658), and the last, from 1934 to 1980, the purchasing power of gold declined, even where the price in nominal terms went up by double digits in each period, as much as 67 percent in the boom years from the end of the nineteenth century to 1920. The extreme period from 1971—and particularly 1976 to 1980—was only the finale to a long period of inflation and was exceptional for gold because its price had been artificially held down by government dictate for so long. (See Table 7.2.)

Much of gold's appreciation in the 1970s was catch up. One should emphasize, however, that even though gold loses purchasing power in long periods of inflation, it holds its value from peak inflation to the next peak inflation, as Jastram pointed out. Over long

Table 7.2   Gold Performs Better in Deflations

	Inflation		Deflation	
	Prices (%)	Purchasing Power of Gold (%)	Prices (%)	Purchasing Power of Gold (%)
1623–1658	+51	−34		
1658–1669			−21	+42
1675–1695	+27	−21		
1702–1723	+25	−22		
1752–1776	+27	−21		
1792–1813	+92	−27		
1813–1851			−58	+70
1873–1896			−45	+82
1897–1920	+305	−67		
1920–1933			−69	+251
1933–1976	+1434	−25		

Source: Copyright © *The Golden Constant: The English and American Experience,* 1560–1976, Roy Jastram, John Wiley & Sons, 1978.

periods of time, gold holds its purchasing value and is indeed, the "golden constant."

Historical Record Is Clear

In the period before Jastram's detailed analysis, we see periods of deflation starting with the Black Death (1348) and decline in population and economic activity thereafter, as well as the period of civil war in England known as the War of the Roses, for the 30 years starting in 1455. In both periods, the purchasing power of gold appreciated rapidly (in the first, from under 17 to 20 on the index, and in the second from 20 to 28).

Clearly, the earlier one looks, the less reliable are the statistics, as well as conditions more different, though in the case of England, records are remarkably good over the past nearly seven centuries and the value of gold well defined. The period began with the stable 50-year reign of King Edward III. (Lord Beveridge was able to publish in 1939 a groundbreaking piece of research on *Price and Wages in England from the Twelfth Century to the Nineteenth Century,* with annual prices for nearly 170 different commodities.) For this broad sweep, two main sources are used, and from 1560 to the current, a single source, which, as Jastram points out, is essential for sound statistical analysis across time. Earlier periods, using different sources, can however add support to the argument. Looking at deflationary periods in ancient Greece and Rome, and the period following the fall of Rome (the so-called Dark Ages), one again finds gold appears to have held its value. Not only the price sources but also the precise value of gold are less reliable, but the very broad trend seems to hold.

Answering the Critics

There are difficulties with such analyses, however, beyond the reliability of statistics, or lack thereof. Critics, looking primarily at the last two centuries, also point to the relatively few examples of deflation studied and to the fact that gold was convertible during these periods; if the value of money went up, then so too did the value of gold, which was simply an extension of the monetary unit. As for the 1930s, well of course gold went up; Roosevelt fixed the price higher. What does this tell us about future deflations, critics ask, when gold is not tied to a currency? Critics point out that gold fell during the deflationary period following 1980, suggesting that, without convertibility, the price of gold would fall in deflations. I would address these criticisms in several ways.

1. There are indeed multiple examples of deflation over the past two millennia, as we have shown, and though the reliability of evidence varies, the conclusions are always similar. These various periods of deflation took place in widely differing economies, some agrarian, some where barter was common, some with global trade dominant, some with political turmoils, and so on.

   To see a common thread, that of a rising purchasing power for gold during every period, is quite staggering, though it clearly fits with the theory as well as the historical evidence.

2. Gold may have been convertible in the last few centuries—though not during the Dark Ages or Black Death—yet a government can no more put a value on something by fiat than can my cat. It can enforce it by sword and prison, but that doesn't make the value so.

Thus, in many of these examples gold traded *above* its conversion price on the black market, as Sam Hewitt of Sun Valley Gold in his 1996 study showed.[2] An example would be during the 1930s. This was a global deflationary period, and U.S. $20 Gold Eagles traded for as much as $30 in France, where a huge minimum for gold convertibility was in force. (The U.S. and France were the only two countries still on the gold standard by 1932.) The ban on private ownership of gold held down the price of gold, rather than the opposite.

3. The theory of money certainly suggests that the value of gold, which is pure money, should appreciate during deflations, so theory supports historical evidence.

4. As for the 1980s, that was not a deflation. It also followed an extreme peak for gold, when, in truth the price of gold rose above any theoretical level of value. It was also a period when the credit worthiness of the United States was going up, so people saw less need for a hedge against the dollar.

In any example, there are also extraneous factors, positive or negative, that can affect the outcome. This is true for inflationary as well as deflationary periods, of course, and sometimes these extraneous factors overwhelm the underlying monetary phenomenon. To see gold consistently appreciate during deflations, over two millennia, whatever the other circumstances, would surely seem to suggest that we should rely on gold during any future deflationary period.

Where Are We Today?

How does this analysis fit into today's scenario? In a deflation, credit is relatively scarce and the value of money (including gold) goes up. Money and gold appreciate because they are relatively scarce; the value of the scarcest hoarding asset, usually gold, appreciates even more than paper money, which may be distrusted for one reason or another. Today, though currency is certainly anything but scarce, credit in the real economy is restricted. Gold is most emphatically scarcer than paper money, which is certainly distrusted. Though not

---

[2]Sam Hewitt, *The Behavior of Gold under Deflation* (Sun Valley Gold Company, 1996).

a strict deflation, this period has deflationary overtones, and gold is appreciating as a scarcer, more trusted form of money.

Today, again as critics of the "barbarous relic" like to remind us, there are alternative forms of monetary protection; it is no longer simply a matter of putting paper money under the mattress or gold in a hole in the backyard. Today, we have insured bank deposits (insurance means little if the value of the insured deposit declines); and sophisticated hedging tools like over-the-counter derivatives and collateralized and securitized debt obligations (some comfort).

It is true of course that it is easier today for ordinary investors to buy foreign currencies as well as other assets, including collectibles that may cushion the blow of currency instability. The extent to which foreign currencies can help depends on the extent to which the monetary instability is global or restricted to one country. Certainly, other assets can hold value during monetary instability (more often in inflations), including real estate, the aforementioned collectibles, and even some food such as rice or coffee. These can take the edge off the extent to which gold might rise, but they do not override gold's propensity to hold its value in a period of instability.

In America, gold is viewed with some suspicion. There is some association with extremists or survivalists, or at the very least it is not considered mainstream. It is an "alternative asset." In many other countries, this is not true. In Europe as well as Asia, gold is part of the culture, and gold has indeed protected populations many times, whether during the French Revolution or the Weimer hyperinflation of the 1920, whether Jews fleeing Nazi Germany or South Vietnamese clinging to U.S. army helicopters after the fall of Saigon. The mental association with gold is more favorable, and Asians are as likely to put excess savings into gold as into a bank.

Gold can indeed appreciate in periods of inflation, but it can also appreciate in periods of deflation. It is monetary instability and crisis more than anything that cause gold to go up.

Resources and Deflation

Resources, however, act differently from gold during deflations. This is to be expected, since most resources are not monetary assets. In the nineteenth century, the broad commodity index was very volatile, but around a mean, and ended the period not far from where it began. There are overlaying factors. Over time, as we have discussed, commodity prices tend to decline when:

- Usage becomes more efficient;
- Demand from mature economies slows down; or
- Technology increases supply, through better exploration or extraction techniques.

But there can be long and significant countertrends, such as when there is a step up in demand from a new source (industrial revolution in Britain, growth of the United States' economy, and today the emergence of Asian economies) or a decline in available supplies (whether from the long steady decline of major ore bodies or disruption from civil wars) overlaid with shorter-term disruptions from war or other civil unrest.

In a deflation accompanied by a weakening economy, we should expect the price of resources generally to decline, notwithstanding the possibility of short countermoves caused by the previously mentioned factors. In a deflation accompanied by an expanding economy, we would expect the price of resources (again other factors being equal) to appreciate on growing demand. This is what was seen during expansionary periods of the nineteenth century (with sharp increases in the years 1812–1820, 1861–1866, 1900–1905, and again 1915–1918).

The conclusions are clear, however. Most resources do best in periods of economic growth, whether inflationary or deflationary. However, during deflations, when money increases in value, particularly during periods of monetary instability, gold can be depended on to not only hold its value but appreciate in purchasing power terms.

CHAPTER 8

When to Buy

To everything, there is a season." For gold, as with other assets, there are better times to buy, both on a long-term and short-term basis. We've already discussed gold's long-term cycles. Even if you understand and are in accord with the long-term view of higher prices for gold, it can still be discouraging to buy gold (or any asset) and see it promptly decline in price. So when should you buy?

Contrarians Win

Certainly, it usually proves a better time to buy when others are selling, or better yet, ignoring or laughing at the asset.

At the end of 1997, the mining reporter for the *Financial Times* (FT) had an article with the headline "The Death of Gold" (note the lack even of a question mark). In the spring of 1999, governments and populace wanted little to do with gold. First, the Swiss, of all people, voted in a referendum to sever a 100-year link of the franc with gold, which allowed sales of bullion by the national bank, and then Britain Chancellor of the Exchequer Gordon Brown announced the sale of over half of Britain's gold reserve. Before Britain could complete the sale, as many as seven other central banks rushed forward to dump their gold. In June, long-time bear Andy Smith said at the *Financial Times* World Gold Conference that "it shouldn't take two days to discuss the demise of gold."

Within two months of the FT conference, three months from Brown's announcement, gold hit its low of $252.

And between the aforementioned FT article and the FT conference, in June 1998, the Tocqueville Asset Management group in New York established a gold mutual fund. Ever the contrarian, manager John Hathaway noted, "We see great opportunity in gold . . . (it) has lost all investment credibility." In the opposite corner was *The Wall Street Journal*'s top-rated precious metals analyst, from Lehman Brothers, who said, "Gold is a relic of the past." James Grant, to whom thanks for these anecdotes,[1] dryly notes, "Now Lehman is gone and gold is flying."

Certainly without doubt, in hindsight we can say that the end of the 1990s was the time to be bullish on the asset hardly anyone wanted.

Better Times to Buy Gold

Over the past 20 years and more, any time would have been a good time to buy gold. Some times were clearly better than others, of course. Gold does well when interest rates are low and lagging inflation. It is also strong during periods of particularly acute monetary instability. In addition, there are seasonal patterns to gold, which have not only held up over the years but are grounded on sound reasons.

Historically, gold tends to be strong from September through January, and weaker from February through August; March, June, and July, as well as November (between Diwali and Christmas) are often the weakest months. This matches the main holidays throughout the world, holidays when gold purchases tend to increase. Starting with the Islamic holiday of Ramadan in September, there is the Hindu festival of Diwali in October, then Christmas of course, followed by the Chinese New Year (usually at the end of January or early February). (See Figure 8.1.)

As central banks have turned net buyers and, more important, private investing in gold has surged, while jewelry sales declined, the seasonal patterns have become a little more discreet. February, for example, historically a weak month (after the Chinese New Year), has been a positive month in recent years, as has November. But the very broad pattern of rising strength in July and August, followed by appreciation through to February remains intact.

---

[1] "Cool thoughts on a molten metal," *Grant's Interest Rate Observer*, November 27, 2009.

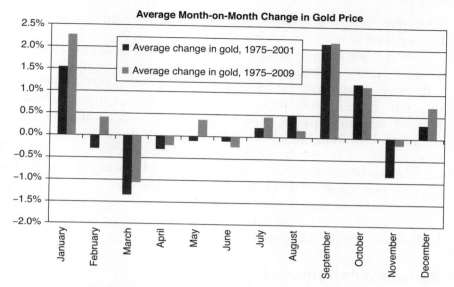

Figure 8.1   Seasonal Patterns to Gold Price
Source: Kitco.

Times to Buy the Stocks

Similarly, there are good times and not so good times to buy gold stocks. The long-term cycle not surprisingly broadly follows gold itself; again, the end of the 1990s was a good time to follow John Hathaway and buy gold mining stocks. Since then, there have been better times to buy gold stocks, as well as some times to stand aside or even sell.

Gold stocks tend to do well when government spending is increasing (signaling inflation ahead), for example. There has been a surge in government deficits over the past decade and more, primarily in the United States. When the deficit increases, gold stocks tend to outperform the market. Since gold stocks are both gold assets and stocks, they tend to be weak when the overall market is weak, even if they do better than the broad market.

There have been periods when gold has outperformed gold stocks and vice versa. And this is usually clearer to see. One can use a ratio of gold to the gold stock indexes as a rough guide to when one is relatively more or less expensive. The ratio of bullion to the benchmark Philadelphia Gold & Silver Index (commonly called the

XAU) has proven a very good guide, with any number above five being a time to buy gold stocks.

There have been five major bull moves for gold stocks since the low in 2001, and each time the ratio has exceeded five. In the previous bull moves, stocks have moved anywhere from 50 to 100 percent. In the credit crisis of 2008, however, the ratio rose dramatically as gold held its own, after a brief decline, while gold stocks collapsed with the market. Although gold stocks subsequently more than doubled from the October low, the ratio remains high. With the ratio at over seven as we enter 2010, it would appear gold stocks have further appreciation ahead of them if gold does not decline.

Certainly, on most historical measures, gold stocks are inexpensive (as we discussed elsewhere). Relative both to the broad market and to gold bullion, they remain undervalued.

Seasonal Patterns to Gold Stocks

As with gold bullion, there are seasonal patterns to gold stocks. September tends to be the strongest month, with an average return in bull and bear years of over 4 percent; that is followed by May and

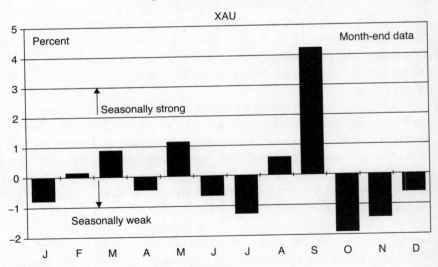

Figure 8.2   Buy in August, Sell Next May

Source: Dundee Wealth Inc., 2010.

March. June and July tend to be weakest, along with October and November. However, the declines in October and November tend to simply take back some of the strength of the prior two months, so buying in August and holding through March or even May would still, historically, have generated positive returns. (See Figure 8.2.)

A general strategy based on seasonal patterns would be to buy in early August, take some profits in early October, and buy back in December, selling in May, though one should avoid trying to be *too* clever in short-term trading.

Seasonal patterns or other guides to short-term timing of purchases are just that, guides. They can be wrong at any given time. And it is more important that the long-term trend is in your favor. Obviously, there's little point in buying gold stocks, say, at the lowest point, in August, if the long-term trend is down. But the opposite holds true. If, as we believe, we are in a long-term bull market for gold and other resources, then you want to ensure you have positions, and use these timing signals as guides to when to lighten up and when to add, never failing to keep an eye on the main direction.

PART

III

INVESTING IN RESOURCES

CHAPTER

9

Ways to Invest

There are two overarching themes to the world of commodities today that are critical for investors. First, we are in the midst of a super cycle, predicated on a massive step up in demand from China and a shortage of new supply sufficient to meet that demand. Second, commodities are by their nature extremely volatile, with massive swings, devastating corrections, and variability even within the sector.

For the investor, this means he must be exposed to the sector . . . and he must be ever vigilant.

Emphasize Commodities in Your Portfolio

Commodities are the place to be for the next decade. U.S. stocks could be sluggish, with an extended period where the broad stock market does very little, similar to the 1968 to 1982 period. Bonds worldwide are hardly attractive, with very low interest rates and the likelihood of a long cycle of rate increases; at minimum, there is little upside left. I expect emerging markets to be a very strong performer, though they share some of the characteristics of resources, namely, they too are very volatile and subject to large corrections and variability within the category.

However, as investors, we most definitely want to overweight the commodity sector. By how much? Very conservative, older investors with the bulk of their assets in cashlike vehicles, might be reasonably comfortable with 10 to 15 percent of their overall portfolio in this sector. For them, this exposure will act as a hedge on the rest of their assets, particularly cash, and provide some opportunities for upside without risking too much. Some aggressive investors, particularly those still earning, might tolerate up to half their portfolios in this sector. This is an individual decision and depends on circumstances, both current and future, as well as risk tolerance, a broad subject beyond the scope of this work.

Crucial, however, is how you respond to volatility and risk. If you choose to invest in the commodity space, you will encounter extreme volatility. And if you invest in junior or exploration companies, you will encounter not only volatility but absolute losses from time to time. There is no way around this. How you deal with this to a very large extent determines how successful you might be, and even whether you should be in this sector at all. Investing in resource stocks but not wanting volatility more or less guarantees losses and an unsatisfactory result.

A Story of Two Investors

In my money management business, I have two clients with similar financial and personal situations (age, obligations, net worth, and so on). One, let's call him Contrarian Charlie, is "glad to see" we have some cash when the market is overheated; he adds money when the stocks are flat on their backs. The other, Panicky Pete, insists his funds are fully invested when the market is hot, even asking me to invest in tiny speculative stocks about which he knows nothing other than their names. But when stocks have declined 30 or 40 percent, he decides he "can't stand any more" and wants to move to cash "until things look better."

It is true that one needs to be a bit of a contrarian in any investing. When everyone is buying, it can't still be cheap, and when everyone is selling, it probably is. This is all the more important in a volatile sector, yet it is also the most difficult thing for any investor. Analyst Paul van Eeden calls being a contrarian "simple yet hard"; the concept is relatively simple but the execution is difficult, but for psychological not practical reasons.

We call Pete our perfect contrarian indicator; by the time he finally gives up, we know it's time to buy. The critical lesson is that ancient Delphic wisdom: Know thyself, and invest accordingly. If you don't have the stomach for it, that might mean using mutual funds or independent managers (though they too can be volatile); it might mean sticking with more conservative vehicles, including bullion itself; or it might mean limiting exposure to the sector.

Managing Your Portfolio

Investors should separate their resource investments into a core port-folio and a trading portfolio. This is a good discipline in any sector or market. The most important distinction is how much you allocate to each portion, based on your personal circumstances. Which in-vestments go where is not necessarily a function of size, but of each investment's characteristics and your goals for each portion of the portfolio. The core is intended to provide exposure to the broad complex for the duration of the super cycle. Here you will buy with less regard to price, hold for the long term, and accept volatility. In the trading portfolio, however, price is more critical, you will hold for shorter periods trying to maximize gains, and you will attempt to use volatility to your benefit. The goals are different: One is intended to provide certain exposure to the sector for the duration of the cycle, so what you own is critical; the other is intended to maximize gains from the sector, so how and when you own is critical.

This is in addition to insurance positions, including cash reserves and gold bullion. The different parts of your pyramid can be looked at in terms of *potential*, of *risk*, or of *time*, with the investments with the highest potential, greatest risk, and shortest time-horizons at the top. They can also be looked at, most important, with regard to their *objective* and their place in your overall portfolio; the rest derives from this key issue.

Investments toward the bottom of your portfolio, the core ex-posure to the resource super cycle, should be purchased for the long term. Once you've decided on employing certain investments in this role, they should be purchased with relatively little regard to short-term price and held through intermediate price fluctuations. These might include common stock of quality global companies and preferred stock. The companies should be substantial and well estab-lished, and you will often be looking for dividends.

At the apex of your pyramid are those investments with the great-est potential, but also the greatest risk. You should put into these speculative investments only money that you can *afford to lose* without it seriously affecting your standard of living. Thus, for many investors, there should be no top segment to the pyramid. Anything with risk of significant loss, including investments in illiquid markets, any use of leverage, short-term trading, including speculations on specific developments (such as so-called *drill-hole plays*), and any time-wasting investments (such as long options), belong here.

Each and every investment decision—to buy or to sell—should be made within the context of your investment pyramid. That is a first, but essential, step toward building a successful investment portfolio. In the core portfolio, you should avoid constantly second-guessing yourself. You should sell only if something fundamental changes with the company, and I don't mean changes in the stock price. In the trading portfolio, however, though you do not *expect* to lose money here, you should be prepared to *cut short any losses* that do occur. Similarly, though you are investing here for a full cycle, you should be prepared to take advantage of any unusual profits that present themselves in the shorter term.

There is no absolute distinction between what specific investment goes where. Indeed, sometimes the very same stock may belong in each portfolio. One of my favorite strategies is to take a long-term position in a favorite stock and then trade around the edges. That may mean buying more on dips and trimming on rallies, while always holding the core position. It could mean selling puts to add, and if we buy more, then selling calls on that extra position. Again, the critical distinction is the purpose for which one buys and holds: Is it long-term certain exposure to the sector, or maximization of gains? Doug Casey has a wonderful metaphor for what goes in each portfolio: He calls them "eating sardines" and "trading sardines." With the latter, as with dead fish, you want to get rid of them before they go stale or start to stink.

Exposure to Commodities

As mentioned previously, there are various ways to gain exposure to commodities. You can invest in the commodities themselves or in the stocks of resource companies. You can invest directly or through mutual funds (or indeed managed accounts that combine some of the benefits of funds with the advantages of investing in individual securities) or through futures or options, which are simply more investment tactics.

If you invest directly in the commodities themselves, you gain direct exposure. You have no upside leverage that comes from buying mining companies, but similarly you have no downside beyond the commodity price. You don't have to worry about the company's management, or balance sheet, or anything to do with running a mining business. It's a pure investment in the commodity itself. On the other side, there are holding costs associated with owning physical commodities, including storage and insurance that can be costly over time.

True, for only a handful of commodities is it feasible for an individual to hold physically: gold, silver, and the other precious metals (platinum and palladium), plus diamonds and other stones. Some, such as copper and lead, are too bulky in any meaningful value. Others, such as uranium, require special handling. And yet others, primarily the agricultural commodities, will rot.

Hedge funds, however, have become particularly innovative and aggressive in buying physical commodities, which certainly offer their investors low-cost and more direct exposure to various commodities. However, increased speculative interest in the sector does present an added risk, at least a short-term price risk. If the hedge funds and speculators for some reason decide to sell—and they frequently move together in one direction—then there is the risk of a sudden price collapse. We saw this at the end of 2008, amid the Lehman collapse, when margin calls and other factors forced hedge funds to dump commodities (as well as many illiquid junior shares), causing prices to collapse beyond any reasonable assessment of their fundamentals.

Physical Gold as Insurance

I strongly recommend that all investors have an insurance position in physical gold itself, ideally held in a secure bank vault outside the country. The Swiss have long held similar views, and Swiss banks specialize in gold storage, though the minimums generally required for an account are high. Most Swiss banks want a minimum of $1 million or more, and many don't want American clients at all (thank the U.S. government for this). Failing physical gold, an investment account indicating segregated gold in your name, or a certificate program (such as the Perth Mint's certificate), is the next best alternative. But clearly, if physical gold is intended as insurance, then you must be absolutely sure of the safety of the counterparty, and ideally you don't want it comingled with other people's, still less held as an asset of the dealer. Storage and insurance fees are the cost of physical ownership.

Coins

Physical gold can also be held in the form of coins. Bullion coins, as their name implies, are an alternative to holding bullion bars; though frequently beautiful, their value is determined almost exclusively by the value of the gold they contain. There are dealer markups, while from time to time, various coins have a market shortage and attract premiums, while during the era of sanctions on South Africa, Kruger-rands sold at a small discount to other coins. Such variances from the value of the bullion content usually are short lived, since investors simply switch to another bullion coin with a lower premium. The Krugerrand, first issued in 1867, was at the time the only coin to contain a full ounce of gold. Today, one-ounce coins, manufactured by the mints in the United States, Canada, Australia, Mexico, Austria, and South Africa are plentiful and can be manufactured to meet demand. Having said that, some government mints were unable to keep up with strong demand in 2008 and 2009.

Semi-numismatic coins have a limited supply and attract a premium over spot (the value of the gold they contain) due to their relative rarity and fluctuating supplies on the market, as well as the demand. These premiums can be anywhere from 20 percent or so to hundreds of percent, but they likewise tend to go up or down with the price of gold. Numismatic coins attract premiums to varying degrees, based on the rarity of the coin as well as its collectability (a rare date in a coin set will often attract a higher price than a "similar" one-off coin, just as rare). The value of these coins depends primarily on their rarity and value as collectibles rather than their intrinsic gold value. Though a strong gold market will generally increase demand for numismatics, there is no absolute relationship. In a strong market, however, carefully chosen numismatics will appreciate several times more than gold itself. Numismatics are a valid and attractive investment, and a lot of wealth can be contained in a small package.

However, this is an area rife with ignorance and worse. Many investors have wondered why the numismatic coins they purchased 20 or 30 years ago are worth so much less today than they paid. Frequently, they blame the dealer who provides the appraisal today, whereas, most often, the error was in the original purchase. So know and understand what you are buying, and use a dealer who is knowledgeable and trustworthy.

ETFs and Funds

Beyond owning actual physical commodities, the next most direct investment would be a share in an exchange-traded fund (ETF), an exchange traded note (ETN), or a closed-end fund that tracks one or more commodities. There is now a proliferation of ETFs investing in the commodity complex; at last count, more than 100 existed in the United States alone. Some invest in one commodity, others in a basket. Some are long, some are short, while yet more promise to double or even triple the unleveraged returns of the underlying commodity. They work in varying degrees and can be a suitable substitute if you don't want to pay the costs associated with physical ownership or physical ownership is impractical, but there are pitfalls.

Best are the pure, unleveraged ETFs that hold the physical commodity itself. There are about a dozen available for gold and silver, platinum and palladium, even uranium. The oldest and largest is the Spider Gold Trust, established by the World Gold Council, which holds gold bullion in bank vaults in London to match the investment in the trust. The price of the trust (symbol GLD), therefore, hardly varies at all from the price of gold itself. (One share of the trust equals one-tenth of an ounce.) Each share of the silver ETF (symbol SLV) represents one ounce of the metal. Both trade on the New York Stock Exchange. The ETFs purchase (or sell) physical gold or silver to match holdings with the demand.

The Gold Trust is now the third-largest ETF of any type in the United States, with nearly $40 billion in gold bullion as of the end of 2009. These are the old and largest precious metals ETFs. Their success led other ETF sponsors to bring out their own competing funds, and there are now five gold funds, four silver funds, two platinum funds, and another two that invest in all the precious metals. The newer funds are considerably smaller, however; compare the Gold Trust's $40 billion in bullion with about $2.4 billion for the Comex Gold Trust, and less than $100 million for the Physical Swiss Gold Shares.

Some of these other funds attempt to capitalize on suggestions that the Gold Trust does not really own the gold it claims, though these rumors are normally put about by interested parties. There is no credible reason to believe the trust does not own sufficient gold to match its assets, which gold is held independently and audited regularly. For large quantities, trust holders can demand to take delivery of their gold, though that is an expensive and cumbersome procedure. One real drawback to the gold (and other) ETFs, however, is that the tax rules are unfavorable. As with owning physical gold itself, a shareholding in the ETF is treated as ownership of a collectible, meaning sales of shares are taxed at rates higher than capital gains: at ordinary rates for shares held less than one year and at 28 percent for shares held more than that. However, bullion ETFs generally are exempted from the prohibition on ownership of collectibles inside IRAs.

Closed-End Funds

An alternative to the ETF is a closed-end fund. Although a closed-end fund trades on an exchange and can be bought and sold just like an ETF (or any other shares), a closed-end fund has issued a fixed number of shares and can trade at a premium or discount to its underlying value. In addition, the assets may be managed. Generally, such variations from the underlying value do not become too large nor stay there for a long period, if only because in cases of a premium, the fund will often issue new shares to capture that premium, while with a discount, arbitragers will buy the shares and sell the underlying asset to capture the difference.

One attractive closed-end precious metals fund is the Central Fund of Canada, which trades on the New York Stock Exchange (symbol CEF) as well as in Canada. It holds both gold and silver, 1.2 million ounces of gold and 62.1 million ounces of silver stored on a fully segregated basis in Canada; has low operating expenses; and avoids the negative ETF taxation issues. From time to time, it issues new shares, but since these are issued at net asset value (NAV) or a premium, there is no dilution to existing shareholders.

Other than funds holding the precious metals, however, the only current fund holding a *physical* commodity itself is the Canadian Uranium Participation Certificate (symbol U on Toronto), which holds uranium in different forms. Because storage of uranium is more complex than storage of metals, the administrative costs tend to be a little higher. This trades like a closed-end fund, that is, at discounts or premiums to its NAV. As with other similar funds, of course, the fund tends to trade at a premium when the market is hot and the price rising. For investors interested in exposure to uranium, this is a good direct play, particularly attractive given the paucity of solid investments in this resource (which we discuss in Chapter 20).

Commodity Funds Have Problems

Most of the commodity ETFs, however, use futures rather than hold the physical commodity. And therein lie the problems. Typically, the funds purchase short-term contracts (to match more closely spot prices) and roll them over on a continuous basis. First, this adds costs, by the continuous buying and selling of contracts.

But that is the least of our problems. Future prices of commodities can be either higher or lower than spot prices. If they are higher, the difference between the spot price and future price is called the *contango*. When futures prices are lower, the commodity is said to be in *backwardation*. This typically occurs when there is a short-term physical shortage and customers push up the spot price for immediate delivery. More often, prices carry a contango, which is a carrying charge. Thus, the ETF, in continually rolling over contracts, is forced to sell contracts and replace them at a higher price. Over time, this can act as a not-insignificant drag on the returns vis-à-vis the appreciation in the spot price. Of course, ETFs offer convenience at a low cost and can certainly be a valid way to invest in the commodities.

The most damning drawback affects those commodity ETFs that offer leveraged returns by promising two or three times the unlevered returns. The problem here is that the returns are on a daily basis, so a short-term spell against the longer-term trend can wreak havoc on the returns. Investors have often found, to their frustration, that they were correct in selecting a particular commodity for a particular period but their returns from the leveraged ETF did not measure up to expectations.

Another drawback to commodity funds is the way they are taxed. As mentioned, gold bullion funds are taxed at a special—higher—capital gains rate for collectibles. Taxation for commodity ETFs is complex and higher than normal gains rates. One example is that the Internal Revenue (IRS) requires open futures contracts to be marked to market at year end. This means that the investor can owe taxes even if the fund has not sold its positions—let alone whether he has sold his shares in the fund. Worse, these phantom profits are taxed at a blend of short-term and long-term rates, currently 23 percent. Besides the actual tax, the instructions for preparing returns will flummox many tax preparers, in addition to giving investors an unwelcome surprise.

What Do You Own?

Perhaps the most critical thing for investors (as always) is to know what you are buying. The PowerShares Agricultural Fund (symbol DBA), for example, is intended to track the Deutsche Bank Liquid Commodity Index-Optimum Yield Agriculture Excess Return Index. Whew! That's a mouthful. But do you have any idea which specific commodities it tracks? Nor do I! Is it beef or corn? And after exhaustive research, all I can discover is that it includes "contracts on some of the most liquid and widely traded agricultural commodities." The opaqueness is compounded since many of these multicommodity funds can change their allocation, so you may not own what you thought you bought.

Because the ETFs are buying futures contracts, they are subject to the commodity exchanges' various "limit up" rules or size limitations, meaning that the funds sometimes cannot purchase sufficient contracts to match an inflow of shares. The commodity ETF market is in a state of flux at present, with ongoing proposals to limit investment in various commodities. The Commodity Futures Trading Commission (CFTC) has enforced maximum daily limits for various commodities, including many agricultural commodities, and is considering imposing absolute caps on investment in a range of commodities. The CFTC is particularly concerned when a single investor (which includes a fund) holds positions that breach certain overall levels.

The rules already enforced as well as fear of further restrictions have already led some funds to stop issuing new shares; Barclays stopped creating new shares for several of its funds, including broad-based ones like the iShares Commodity–Indexed Trust and narrower ones like the iPath Natural Gas ETN. It certainly makes difficult the concept of an ETF, whereby there is continual issuance or redemption of shares to meet demand, with shares trading at NAV.

To avoid some of these problems, many of the commodity ETFs have moved to offshore locations where they can buy foreign commodity contracts, or if they are multiple commodity ETFs, have altered the composition of their funds as one or other contract reaches the limit. This, however, makes it difficult for the investor to know what he owns, as well as increases tax consequences. Despite these drawbacks, however, for many investors, these ETFs represent the only feasible way to invest in various commodities. If you know what you are buying, and understand the characteristics and risks, then commodity ETFs offer a convenience and low-cost way of investing in these assets.

Of course, individual investors can buy futures contracts themselves, and although they will be subject to the limit and size rules, they are likely to be less of a concern to most individual investors than to a fund. By doing it yourself, you can select the commodities in which you want to invest and in what ratios; and you can select the term of the contract. Commodities futures have a bad name among investors as being highly risky, but that is only because of the high levels of leverage that are available. You do have the flexibility if you so desire of putting up more cash even 100 percent, so you would have an unleveraged exposure to the commodity for the duration of the contract or contracts. Futures are simply just another investment vehicle, neither more nor less risky than buying stocks.

Broad Diversification for a Long Period

Perhaps a better long-term solution is to buy a fund with investments across the entire commodity spectrum, such as the Elements Rogers Total Return Fund (RJI), knowing that it will include individual commodities on which you may not be so bullish at any given time, and will not involve the precise balance that you seek, but will give you broad exposure to the entire complex. And we are, after all, bullish on the entire complex over time. Note, however, that this, like many of the other funds, is an ETN, not strictly a fund. A note is issued and backed by a specific issuer (in this case, the Swedish Export Credit Corp.) and though they are not comingled assets of the corporation and there are normally reasonable safeguards, it is important to know who is backing the note.

Moreover, notes have a maturity date, and frequently notes are sold to investors with very short-term lives. You may well be betting, therefore, not only on being right but being right within a short time period. At maturity, the issuer may well offer another similar note, but you will have the high initial selling fees to pay each time you "roll over." I avoid notes with short maturities. All-too-frequently, the maturity date will come at an inopportune time to be selling the underlying asset, but unlike a fund or a company share, you do not have the luxury of deciding not to sell when the maturity date rolls around.

The Elements Rogers Fund matures in October 2022, so that allows plenty of time for the commodities super cycle to develop as well as provides plenty of time for you to choose your own exit point. You should also be aware that exchange-traded vehicles frequently do not match the returns of the underlying index they are intended to track because of fees and costs. The Elements Fund, for example, has underperformed by a little over one percentage point in the two years since inception, which, while not an extraordinary amount, is something of which you should be aware. The fund is linked to the Rogers International Commodity Index, which is broadly exposed to the entire spectrum of commodities, as shown in Figure 9.1 and Table 9.1. You should also be aware that, although the fund is not actively managed, the allocation does change, usually as a particular commodity becomes overweight. For example, at the end of 2007, crude oil represented almost 48 percent of the fund. This was when oil was on its way over $100. At the end of 2009, the allocation to oil was less than half that.

There are also Elements notes designed to track various Rogers subindices, namely the agriculture, energy, and metals indices. These indices are designed to market-weight the various individual components. The agriculture index (RJA) provides a very broad exposure to the commodities complex, 21 different commodities, everything from canola to rapeseed and azuki beans. The metals index (RJZ)

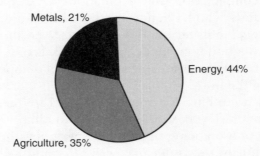

Figure 9.1   Energy Dominates Commodities ETF
Source: RICA Handbook.

Table 9.1   Commodities Diversification across the Board

The Index Weights are:

Crude Oil	21.00%	Platinum	1.80%
Brent	14.00%	Gas Oil	1.20%
Wheat (CBOT)[1]	6.00%	Cocoa	1.00%
Corn	4.75%	Lean Hogs	1.00%
Cotton	4.20%	Lumber	1.00%
Aluminium	4.00%	Nickel	1.00%
Copper	4.00%	Rubber	1.00%
Soybeans	3.35%	Tin	1.00%
Gold	3.00%	Wheat (KCBT)[3]	1.00%
Natural Gas	3.00%	Canola[4]	0.75%
RBOB Gasoline	3.00%	Soybean Meal	0.75%
Soybean Oil[2]	2.00%	Orange Juice[5]	0.60%
Coffee	2.00%	Oats	0.50%
Lead	2.00%	Rice	0.50%
Live Cattle	2.00%	Palladium	0.30%
Silver	2.00%	Rapeseed[6]	0.25%
Sugar	2.00%	Azuki Beans	0.15%
Zinc	2.00%	Greasy Wool	0.10%
Heating Oil	1.80%		
		Total	100.00%

January 2010.
[1] Current weight of Wheat (CBOT) is 7.00%. The weight will be decreased by 1.00% and allocated to Wheat (KCBT) during the January 2010 roll period.
[2] Current weight of Soybean Oil is 2.17%. The weight will be decreased by 0.17% during the January 2010 roll period.
[3] Wheat (KCBT) will be added at 1.00%, allocated from Wheat (CBOT), during the January 2010 roll period.
[4] Current weight of Canola is 0.77%. The weight will be decreased by 0.02% during the January 2010 roll period.
[5] Current weight of Orange Juice is 0.66%. The weight will be reduced by 0.06% during the January 2010 roll period.
[6] Rapeseed will be added at 0.25% during the January 2010 roll period.
Source: RICA Handbook.

currently has 10 different precious and base metals, though the energy index (RJN) is less diversified, with almost 90 percent in various oil contracts, with the rest in gas and gasoline.

The Rogers series of funds offer broad diversification, even in a single area such as the metals, and have a reasonably long holding period. All ETNs, ETFs, and commodity futures aim to offer investors the opportunity to make as close to a direct investment in the commodities as is feasible, where physical ownership is not practical. Many investors, however, prefer to buy shares in companies involved in the resource area, especially mining and exploration companies, since they offer leverage to the underlying commodity, as well as their own risks. I shall discuss these investments in the next few chapters.

CHAPTER

10

Investing in Companies

Investing in mining companies offers the potential for exaggerated returns. It is a very rough rule of thumb that when an underlying commodity moves, the large producing companies move two to three times as much, while the junior companies can move five times as much or more. When gold moved up in 2002 and again from 2004 to early 2006, the gold stocks outperformed bullion, with several of the better producers returning two to three times as much as gold even in those brief periods. Similarly, however, when gold fell in the second half of 2006, by about 13 percent, some of the very same gold producers fell 30 percent or more. Over both the short term when gold appreciates, and over the longer period of an entire bull market, however, the gold stocks tend to outperform gold bullion.

Gold or Gold Stocks?

There can also be periods when gold appreciates but the stocks lag. First, we should not forget that gold stocks are gold assets but also stocks, meaning that they are influenced by overall stock market patterns as well as the gold price. I shall have more to say about this later. Sometimes, in unusual periods, gold stocks can actually fall even though the price of gold is moving up. This was most certainly the case in the aftermath of the collapse of Lehman Brothers, in September 2008, when access to credit tightened and the broad stock market fell. Such periods typically do not last long, and certainly gold stocks roared back the following year when the broad stock market recovered.

For the exploration companies, so much depends on their success, of course, but returns of 10-to-1 are not so uncommon, and even 100-to-1 not so rare, when a company makes a discovery in a strong market. And that, of course, is the reason why investors move away from a straight investment in a resource into the shares of companies that produce, own, or search for those resources. There are pitfalls, however, and I shall discuss those—as well as ways to avoid or minimize them—in the next chapter, Chapter 11.

Risks in Shares

For now, let me just catalog some of the major risks and look at different ways in which the investor can participate in this area. An obvious risk derives from this leverage that mining companies have to the underlying commodity, and that is that the leverage works both ways. So the stocks of mining companies, and especially the juniors and exploration companies, tend to be extremely volatile. In a bad market, declines of 90 to 95 percent among the thinly traded exploration stocks are not unknown.

Another major risk is selection, again even more critical in the exploration companies than with the producers. But clearly, not all major producers are made equal. Over both the long term and short term, returns can vary considerably. In the bull market of the new millennium, many underperformed, including major hedgers, such as Barrick (hedging, or selling gold forward, limits the upside) as well as the major South African companies (because of maturing mines as well as political risk). The best-performing companies have been those with a strong growth component (such as Goldcorp or Yamana).

With the exploration companies, the task is even more daunting than selection of seniors, since there are over 1,000 exploration companies in Canada alone. No individual investor can be expected to sift through that number of companies. A certain amount of knowledge is required to understand the meaning of exploration results: Is this flashy drill hole an indication that the deposit may realistically get much bigger, or was it perhaps simply a twin of a known hole that tells us nothing we did not already know? Does the stock price already reflect the upside?

There was a point in the Bre-X stock scam of the late 1990s when the market cap of Bre-X exceeded that of Freeport Copper & Gold, which had a *real* operation in Indonesia. That's all you needed to know. Even if Bre-X had not been a scam and the property genuinely was a major discovery, it still would have been without production and with costly development ahead of it, with all the uncertainty that involved. Freeport, on the other hand, owned a mine that was both the world's largest gold mine, as well as one of the world's largest copper mines; it was already producing and making money. Clearly, at the very minimum, we could say that one was undervalued relative to the other . . . and it wasn't Bre-X!

Today, there's a high flyer exploring in Colombia, and though it has indeed seen some very impressive drill results (with no suggestion for a second that it's not real), the market cap is over $1 billion . . . and it has yet to develop a resource for the property. This may well develop into one of the largest gold mines of the last decade . . . it may well eventually justify that enormous price tag. In such cases, I always ask, however, "What else could I buy for $1 billion?" Right next door to this exploration property is a property with a 15-million-ounce resource *and* a lower market cap. Given what is known, one could probably buy many things with a better risk and reward for one's $1 billion than this company.

Even with adequate knowledge, it takes an enormous amount of time to follow these companies, particularly the exploration companies where a single piece of news can mean the difference between success and failure, between a stock price that doubles or falls in half. And never forget that, as Peter Bianco of GLS Capital puts it, "Someone's always got a bigger junkyard dog," meaning no matter how knowledgeable you are, how much work you do, how closely you follow the company, there's always someone better equipped than you, and that person will be first out of the door when something goes wrong.

Funds: Not So Simple

For the investor wishing to go beyond investing in the commodities themselves in one form or another, and invest in the companies involved in the sector, there are, as with other sectors, three broad choices: You can invest in funds; you can do-it-yourself; or, you can hire a manager. Each has benefits as well as potential drawbacks.

Funds can be either open end or closed end. Open-end funds (usually called mutual funds), as the name suggests, continually issue or redeem shares, depending on investor buying or selling every day. When you invest $1,000 in the Great Potential Gold Fund, you are adding $1,000 to the assets of the fund, just as when you redeem your shares, the assets decline by that amount. You buy or sell each day at that day's net asset value (plus or minus usually modest sales or redemption charges). When investors buy more shares, the fund can invest in more stocks, just as it must sell stocks when it has net redemptions. Mutual funds can be purchased directly from the fund company or, increasingly, from brokerages in your normal account.

A closed-end fund, on the other hand—again, as the name implies—issues a fixed number of shares, which then trade on an exchange. When you buy shares, you must do so from an existing shareholder who is selling, and vice versa. The price is determined not solely by the net asset price of the fund's holdings but by the price a willing buyer and willing seller can agree on. Thus, shares often trade at premiums or discounts to the net asset value (NAV). In reality, the variance from net asset value rarely grows very large—10 percent would be high—nor stays there for long, since when the premium grows too large, investors eschew the fund and buy another fund (or individual securities), while conversely a large discount attracts bargain hunters. With large, liquid funds, the arbitrageurs may come in and short a high-premium fund against purchases of securities the fund owns.

There is no shortage of gold and resource funds. Bloomberg lists 1,649 gold funds, plus another 314 precious metals funds. It lists 1,355 commodity funds and another 828 resource funds. Most major fund families in the United States include at least one gold or resource fund (usually more), while a company like U.S. Global specializes in the sector. Funds offer the obvious benefits of diversification and professional management (most gold funds beat the indices more often than not, for example), and they do this at low cost. These advantages are obvious and do not much need to be explained, yet they are very powerful factors for most individual investors.

Drawbacks to Funds

The disadvantages can be more subtle. As with all funds, there is a lack of control. A fund may emphasize gas when you want to be in oil. It may have investments in Africa, which you consider too risky. It may not emphasize exploration companies sufficiently. And so on.

Of course, with so many funds to choose from, you should be able to select those that match your wants and needs. But you won't know about changes until after the fact.

Lack of control, however, also means you do not get to choose when to sell. Again, as with all funds, once you are a fund owner, you are responsible for your share in the gains generated. When a fund sells a big winner the day after you buy the shares, you still pay tax on your share of the gains, and that's even if the fund shares you bought have declined in price!

More nuanced is the major disadvantage, that you do not pick the time when your assets are bought or sold. Sure, you buy shares at a time you believe them to be inexpensive and about to appreciate. But suppose you are alone in your belief. Shares continue to be weak for a little while and more and more existing shareholders give up and sell. What does the fund manager do? He sells the shares in companies he loves, at rock-bottom prices, because he has to. Similarly, as the sector moves up and up, more and more investors decide to invest and buy the fund shares, forcing the fund manager to buy shares at ever higher prices. As shares go down, and fund holders redeem, he must sell; when they go up and investors buy fund shares, he must buy. This produces a constant drag on performance that the manager can do little to mitigate. And it affects all fund shareholders.

This effect is most pronounced in narrow-interest funds, particularly those that invest in volatile sectors, such as gold and resources. Your astute timing in picking very close to the bottom has not produced quite as dramatic a result as you expected. Mutual funds are not the best vehicle for the contrarian. Nonetheless, for many investors, in a field that requires a lot of expertise and discipline, professional fund management can help you avoid the pitfalls and stay focused.

Buying closed-end mutual funds has some of the advantages of open-end funds in that you gain the experience of a professional manager while the fees tend to be low. Closed-end funds trade at both premiums and discounts, which can be an advantage or a drawback. Certainly, in a hot market it will usually mean paying up for what you want to own.

But unlike mutual funds, you are not disadvantaged by the selling of others. Sure, in a weak market, the NAV of a closed-end fund or the value of managed accounts will decline. If there is a wave of selling of a closed-end fund, however, the fund manager is not required to sell any shares at all, unlike with a mutual fund. If sellers overwhelm buyers, the shares go to a discount which tends to be self-correcting. You can hold on if you think shares will recover, or even buy more. So you do not get hurt by the decisions of others, unless you chose to sell when everyone is selling.

Top Funds

Different funds perform well at different times, though fund investors must avoid the error of performance chasing. More important than a quarter's outperformance is a good track record over time, as well as an approach that matches your own. Do you prefer more consistent performance at the cost of lower absolute returns? Or are you trying to maximize returns over the long run and can accept higher volatility? And so on.

Though there are many good quality funds, I have narrowed my selection to three. The First Eagle Gold Fund (SGGDX, formerly the SoGen Gold Fund) is managed by the same group that manages the conservative First Eagle global funds. It is perhaps the most conservative of the gold funds, holding significant amounts of bullion and fewer exploration stocks than other funds. Its returns have matched the performance of major gold indices, though arguably at considerably less risk. First Eagle will not usually be at the top of performance rankings, but it will rarely be near the bottom. This is a suitable choice for more conservative investors who want exposure to gold, as well as for long-term holdings.

More aggressive is The Tocqueville Gold Fund (TGLDX), which will frequently appear at the top of fund listings. It has outperformed the benchmark indices by an appreciable margin, though this comes at the cost of greater volatility (compared with First Eagle, but still less than the entire gold fund group). Manager John Hathaway holds many of the major gold producers but is not afraid to take big bets on up-and-coming companies. His top five holdings account for about 30 percent of the fund (compared with about 12 percent for First Eagle, whose 10 largest holdings are still a smaller proportion of the fund than Tocqueville's five largest).

Though U.S. Global Investors, like Tocqueville and First Eagle, offers several broad-based funds (global, American value, and so on), it is best known for its resource funds. It offers a fund that focuses on gold producers (Gold and Precious Metals Fund), another with a greater emphasis on juniors (World Precious Metals Fund), and a third on energy and basic materials (Global Resource Fund). U.S. Global, headed by Canadian ex-pat Frank Holmes, is more willing to make investments in early-stage companies, those that often produce the great returns, and you will frequently find one or other of the U.S. Global resource funds at the top of the performance pack. Like Tocqueville, U.S. Global is a no-load family of funds.

Going Alone Means a Lot of Work

Doing it yourself certainly means you are in control, of what you buy and when, of when you take gains or generate tax losses, and so on. But, as discussed, it requires an enormous amount of work and expertise to select and track companies. It also requires a special psychological skill set, in being patient and disciplined in both buying and selling. Not every investor is suited, either by skill or psychology, for such a specialized and volatile sector.

An individual managed account combines many of the advantages of do-it-yourself and fund investing. You have the benefit of professional management, while your account can be tailored to your own risk profile, and take account of your needs regarding income and taxes and so forth. Please note that when I discuss individual managed accounts, I am not referring to managers who pool your assets with those of others (though that can be legitimate). I am referring to situations where your money is held in a segregated manner, in your own name, with an independent custodian, with the manager holding a limited power of attorney to manage your account. The main drawbacks to individual accounts are the normally high minimums and fees that can be relatively high (managers, because of the total size of funds they manage, can usually negotiate lower fees and commissions from custodian and brokerage firms than individuals pay, but still higher than funds).

Professional, separate account managers are subject to the same herd mentality that affects mutual funds in that more people want to open accounts at the top and want to cash out at the bottom. One should point out that managers usually have a closer relationship with individual investors than do fund managers. Investors and managers tend to be better matches in terms of thought processes, and managers are better able to inform investors who likewise are better able to ask individual questions. The major difference is that the impact of other people's decisions on you, the astute contrarian, need not be as pronounced.

With an individual account, in a weak market, many investors may panic and instruct the manager to liquidate their accounts (though, as mentioned, managers tend to have educated their investors as to expectations so separate account managers tend not to get as many redemptions as do funds). This forces him to sell his favorite shares (which presumably other clients own) and push down the prices of his major holdings. It affects the performance *averages* he may report. But it does not affect *your* account. The manager is not required to sell *your* shares (as he does with a mutual fund). And you can hold on, knowing that corrections are inevitable. So again, your individual account is not subject to this "herd drag" on performance. The manager does not sell *your* shares at the bottom, nor buy them at the top (at least he does not have to).

Figure 10.1 summarizes the benefits and drawbacks to the main investment approaches, though many of these are nuanced and need not apply at all times. Whether your own account, if managed by

	Self	Fund	Manager
Professional management	?	✓	✓
Independent advice	x	x	✓
Diversification	?	✓	✓
Fees	x	✓	✓
Time	x	✓	✓
Individualized	✓	x	✓
Tax efficiency	✓	x	✓
No negative surprises	✓	x	✓
No dilution effect	✓	x	✓

Figure 10.1   Managed Accounts vs. Funds vs. Self
Source: Adrian Day Asset Management.

yourself, is diversified, for example, depends on how large your gold or resource portfolio may be.

If you choose to go alone, you are in for a wild ride. Gold and resources generally are volatile, both in the short and long term, and the stocks even more so. To be successful requires expertise, insight, and discipline. You need to have the courage to buy when stocks are depressed; the patience to hold and the ruthlessness to sell when appropriate, and the wisdom to know when to do either; and the control to sell when things are expensive. These traits are critical to success in any investment area, but all the more so in a volatile sector. Many, whatever their knowledge may be, simply lack the appropriate emotional temperament. Such traits as discipline, patience, and the ability to remain cool under pressure are every bit as important in investing as technical skills or knowledge.

Wrong-Way Corrigan

One former client added funds in the spring of 2007, close to the top; he insisted I buy stocks whose names he barely knew. By early 2008, he queried why I held any cash in the account; but a year later, he liquidated his account, with the famous words, "I can't stand it anymore." This was all against my strong urging. I knew we were close to a bottom. He sold 50 percent lower than he had bought just a year earlier, and he missed out on a 70 to 80 percent rally in the ensuing 10 months. He wasn't stupid; he simply had his timing all wrong because he got caught up in the emotional excitement of a rising market and he panicked on falling markets.

Often, such emotional responses arise from being overcommitted to the market in general or a particular sector. If you invest only what you can afford, if you commit to a volatile sector only what you can be comfortable with, then you can afford—financially as well as psychologically—to ride out the inevitable downturns. If, however, you stretch to invest and overcommit to a sector, it is not surprising that you might panic. This is true of any sector or market, and indeed of the market overall. Rule #1, therefore, is to invest only up to your comfort level. If you are losing sleep over market gyrations, you need to sell down to your level of comfort and reduce your risk.

Know What You Are Buying

The second most important factor is to understand what you know and what you don't know. By *know*, I mean both knowledge and understanding. With more than 1,000 exploration companies on the Toronto exchange, the individual cannot be expected to have deep insight into more than a small proportion. All too often, this lack of knowledge (and discipline) makes investors chase high-fliers, or worse, respond to promotions. It never fails to stagger me when investors buy stocks simply on the basis of an unsolicited promotion.

The lack of knowledge and experience in the sector makes investors more susceptible to promotions or worse. Many can't tell the difference between an objective report by a knowledgeable analyst and a one-sided hype by a writer paid by the company. Many of the unsolicited "newsletters" dropping through your mail slot are paid for by the companies they recommend. Oh yes, they normally tell you this in the small print, but an experienced investor can tell the difference without reading the tiny disclaimer. Outright frauds are relatively rare in the gold and resource business, although they do occur. But all too common are the exaggerations, the hypes, the paid promotions.

Any sector where sharp returns over a short period are possible attracts the fraudsters and promoters. Some companies are little more than promotions and some newsletters are little more than paid touts. It's the more nuanced deceptions that require more experience and insight, the company that twins a hole with known high-grade mineralization simply to generate a positive press release; or the company with nothing that attempts to trade off a successful company in the same geographic region (known as *close-ology* in the business), even using a similar name. You learn of these deceptions only through years of experience.

The coin market also has its share of deception. A company will buy a supply of coins no one has heard of, write an intriguing report of how the hoard was found in a safe in some out-of-the-way country, describe a fascinating history of how the coins wound up where they did—perhaps all factually accurate—and then sell the coins for three, four or more times what they are worth. When the promotion is long over, the "investor" finds there is no market for his coins.

Whether buying commodities or equities, funds or individual stocks, hiring a professional or doing it yourself, it is important to realize the benefits and limitations of each approach. Match the investment to your objectives as well as circumstances. And take the time to educate yourself. Nothing in investing beats knowledge, understanding, and working with ethical professionals, not even capital.

11

How to Select Gold Companies

The entire global gold mining sector is very small. Even after an extraordinary eight-year bull market, it totals only around $200 billion . . . that's less than the size of Walmart, less than Microsoft, less than Exxon. It is dwarfed by other sectors, just one-twelfth the size of the oil and gas sector. (See Figure 11.1.) Then consider that the gold mining industry is remarkably diffuse, with only a small handful of companies over $2 billion. This is one of the reasons we can experience such extraordinary gains in short periods of time. When the mass of investors wants to buy gold stocks, it will be like "trying to put the Hoover Dam through a garden hose," as speculator Doug Casey puts it.

Big Problem for Big Companies

Gold companies can be divided into three broad categories: the major producers, the junior producers or developmental companies, and the explorers. For investors, the selection criteria and investing tactics should be different for each group. If we start by examining the major producers, we arguably have it backward. After all, in the mine life cycle, exploring comes before finding which comes before developing and finally before producing. Nonetheless, we'll start by looking at the largest companies, then the smaller ones, and put it all into context later.

By any reckoning, there are fewer than two dozen major producers around the world. As we have emphasized before, the major problem facing these companies is simply remaining where they

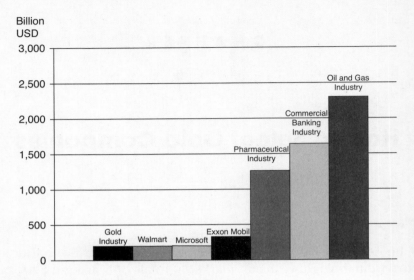

Figure 11.1   The Gold Stock Universe Is Small
Source: Casey Research. Data: Yahoo! Finance.

are. Mines are depleting assets, so every time a company produces 1 million ounces it must replace them with another 1 million of reserves. (Actually, it needs to replace it with more, since in any deposit not every ounce is actually produced.) For the large companies producing 4 or 5 million ounces a year, this is no easy task.

In fact, for the most part, the major companies have grown in recent years largely from acquiring other companies, not from exploring, discovering, and developing ounces. So perhaps the most critical issue for investing in the major producers is where their future ounces are coming from. First, what's the mine life of their existing mines? Second, how robust is the pipeline of future properties? And third, are they in a position (strong balance sheet, expensive shares for stock transactions) to make accretive acquisitions?

Obstacles to Mining

Given that mines owned by major international companies are an easy target for populist governments, it's best for major producers to have operations in multiple jurisdictions, and mostly in safe jurisdictions. For investors also, this diversification is a key attribute in selection criteria. There are exceptions. Freeport Copper, which, prior to its acquisition of Phelps Dodge, had its sole mine in Indonesia. This mine was simultaneously the largest single gold producer and one of the largest copper mines in the world, a truly world-class deposit, with low costs and enormous nearby exploration potential, yet the company and its stocks were highly sensitive to events in Indonesia. During the upheavals of the late 1990s, Freeport's share price lost over 50 percent of its value.

A company like Newmont has major operations in Nevada, Peru, Indonesia, and Australia, as well as small operations in other countries, making it less vulnerable to particular governments and countries. That is not to suggest that it hasn't had its challenges at different times in different countries; it most certainly has. But at no time was the viability of the company threatened.

Margins Get Squeezed Despite High Resource Prices

Costs are another major factor in analyzing producing companies, both the cash costs of mining as well as the all-in costs (including general and administrative [G&A] and amortization). All too often investors look only at cash costs, and this is the way many companies would like you to view costs. But these are only a part of the overall cost of running a mining company. Mining companies have high capital costs to build mines, so the depreciation and amortization of that capital, as well as the reclamation costs at the end of the mine life, need to be added to the cash costs to see if the mine is profitable. In addition, one needs to look at the cost of running the company (G&A costs), as well as interest and taxes, things that apply to all companies, to see if the mine's profitability extends to the company as a whole. (See Figure 11.2.)

There's one more major item for mining companies, however. Because mines are depleting assets and one must add new ounces to replace mined ounces just to hold steady, it is necessary to add to all the money the company spends to find and develop those new ounces. In all, cash costs are typically a little less than half the company's total expenditures. It is important to compare apples with apples in looking at costs across companies. South African companies, for example, typically include more items than the bare bones that North Americans like to report.

Another critical factor looking at costs is to know whether the company is reporting on a by-product or co-product basis. If a gold mine also produces some silver, for example, the price received for

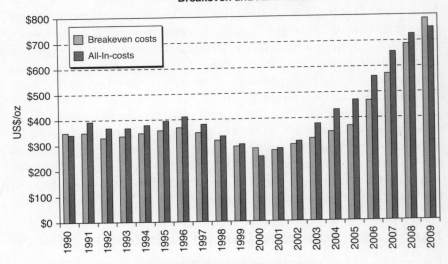

Figure 11.2 **Gold Mining Margins Get Squeezed**

Source: National Bank Financial, February 2010.

that silver can be deducted from cash costs. This can lead to some ridiculous results. I recall Jim Bob Moffett, chairman of Freeport, once somewhat facetiously saying that the company's cost of mining gold was a negative number, using copper as a by-product, while the cost of mining copper, was also negative, with gold as a by-product.

When a company uses the by-product method of stating costs, it is important to know, first of all, how much of the by-product is being produced and then, most important, not to then go ahead and count the by-product production. I have heard companies say they produce, for example, 300,000 ounces of "gold equivalent" (meaning gold and everything else converted into ounces of gold), at a cost of only $150 or whatever (using by-product accounting). Don't let them have it both ways.

I indicated earlier that it's important to look at the company's growth profile (if there is one). Typically, seniors with high-growth profiles, assuming there are no hiccups, tend to have stronger price performance; in the recent past, this would include such companies as Goldcorp and Yamana (both of which still have strong growth outlooks). After all, when gold stocks are trading at 15 times cash flow and 30 or 40 times earnings, with dividends usually less than

1 percent, they are hardly value stocks. Unless there is growth, one is buying such a stock purely on the expectation that the price of their product—gold—will move up enough to justify the high multiples.

How to Value Major Gold Companies

In valuing major producers, there are various valuations metrics, including comparing price to earnings (P/E), cash flow, ounces of production, reserves, resources, and net asset value (NAV). The first three look at valuation on a current income basis, the last three on an asset basis. Given the paucity of earnings of most mining companies, analysts tend to focus on cash flow rather than earnings, and on various asset metrics.

Remember the old saw in mining, however, that "not all ounces are equal." The location is a critical factor (for both political risk and infrastructure); the likely capital cost is another (depending on infrastructure and the type of facilities necessary for the particular ore type, among other factors); and the ongoing costs of mining (the ore type, local costs, and taxes being factors here) is a third. The number of ounces in the ground is only a starting point. Some ounces will never be mined, or not for many years, anyway.

It is noteworthy that, of the top gold producers, most generate all or nearly all of their revenues from the one metal (with Freeport and Rio Tinto being the exceptions). Gold stocks tend to trade at higher multiples than stocks in other sectors, even other resource sectors. The reason is straightforward: Investors buy gold stocks when they believe the price of gold is going up, thus justifying paying higher multiples today. (One doesn't buy a widget manufacturer because the price of widgets is going up.)

This also provides exceptional leverage to the single commodity. Gold stocks, like stocks of other resources, have leverage to the underlying commodity, as we have seen. If, for example, a gold company is producing gold for $800 an ounce when the price is $900, there is a 12.5 percent margin (there's more to it than that, of course, as we shall see). Even a very small increase in the underlying commodity price can have a significant impact on profits; in our example, a 10 percent increase in the gold price would boost profits by 24 percent, more than double. But greater price moves can be even more dramatic. If the price of gold moves to $1,200—a 30 percent increase—the producers' margin *other things being equal* (which they never are) jumps 140 percent. So there are fundamental, logical reasons for the leverage of gold producers over gold, in addition to the increased interest in investing in gold stocks that higher prices cause.

Lots Can Go Wrong

There's an old saying in the mining business that if anything can go wrong, it will; as we have mentioned, wizened miners say that "Murphy works overtime in the mining business." It's just not as simple as the previous examples. As we've seen, major producing companies face several hurdles, including higher costs that generally go along with higher gold prices, and the difficulty of finding new reserves to replace depleting reserves, just to stand still. Basic cash costs have risen from around $170 an ounce in 2001 to around $300 in 2006 to well over $500 today.

Many people simplistically and mistakenly look at the cash cost of production at a mine, say $500 an ounce, and look at the price of gold and assume the company is making "obscene" profits. In reality, the mine site cash cost of producing a marginal ounce is only a part of the overall costs. There are the amortization costs of the capital spent to build the mine, the ongoing capital to expand the mine, the set-aside for eventual safe and environmental shut down of the mine, plus the costs of ongoing exploration to replace the mined ounces. Breakeven costs for mine operations are estimated at over $750 an ounce, and all-in costs over $800.

Given the risks in the mining business, that's not a huge margin. It explains why Newmont, one of North America's largest miners, has a return on assets of only 5 percent, while it's a negative number for many other companies. Returns on equity are even worse: AngloGold has a –12 percent return on equity, Barrick –28 percent. In short, mining is neither an easy nor especially profitable business. It has been a long-term destroyer of capital rather than a creator of value, second only to the airline industry.

One cause of this record is the propensity of the mining industry to continually issue new equity, forever diluting shareholders. Over the course of 2009, for example—not the most propitious period for issuing new equity—most major gold mining companies issued new stock representing from 5 to 20 percent of existing shares outstanding. Given that such equity offerings are a not-infrequent occurrence, the dilution over time can be staggering.

   In addition, mines are not only depleting assets but they are immovable. When the price of commodities goes up, governments around the world look for ways to milk the cow, whether it's increased taxes or even expropriation. We have seen several examples of both in recent years, and not only from unstable third-world governments, as we have discussed. In addition, higher prices generate more exploration activity, which itself generates more opposition from social and environmental groups.

Major Challenge: How to Keep Going

The major hurdle facing mining companies, the one we keep returning to and a major factor in our bullish case for the commodities, is the difficulty of finding new reserves, reserves that are economically viable in politically safe jurisdictions. For a company like Barrick, producing over 7 million ounces a year, this is no easy task. There are few enough new deposits found with that number of ounces, so this often means finding or acquiring more than one deposit in any given year. Newmont, which only a few years ago produced over 7 million ounces, recently gave up that task, and looks to stay at a steady state somewhere over 5 million each year, in itself a major challenge. The truth is that it is difficult to grow organically much above 2 million ounces. But think: a leader in an industry whose product is commanding recording prices in the market sets itself a goal of reducing production and shrinking! Thirteen companies produce over 1 million ounces a year.

Major Gold Producers	
1. Barrick Gold Corporation	7.2 million ounces
2. Newmont Mining Corporation	5.2 million ounces
3. AngloGold Ashanti Ltd.	4.5 million ounces
4. Gold Fields Inc.	3.6 million ounces
5. Freeport Copper & Gold Inc.	2.6 million ounces
6. GoldCorp Inc.	2.4 million ounces
7. Kinross Gold Corporation	2.1 million ounces
8. Harmony	1.5 million ounces
9. Rio Tinto plc	1.2 million ounces
10. Newcrest Mining Ltd.	1.1 million ounces
11. Yamana Gold Inc.	1.1 million ounces
12. Lihir Gold Ltd.	1.0 million ounces
13. Agnico-Eagle Mines Ltd.	1.0 million ounces

There are three ways a company can add to its reserves. First, by expanding reserves at existing mines; second, by discovering new deposits; and third, by acquiring mines or companies with reserves. Expanding around existing mines or deposits (so-called brownfields exploration) is often the easiest and most dependable. For one, the best place to look for gold is where there already is gold. Second, much of the capital cost has already been spent so additional ounces found are cheaper ounces. It is cheaper for a company to explore in the central highlands of Papua New Guinea if it already has a mine operation there than if it didn't, for obvious reasons. And if a new mine eventually comes into being, the existing infrastructure makes mining less expensive than if they had to start afresh.

There is a fourth way that reserves can grow, and that is simply if the price of gold increases. As the price of gold (as with any resource) increases, it makes more ounces viable, ounces that were previously known but not considered economic. The company can then add those to its reserves. Gold has already been discovered but needs a higher price to be mined at a profit. Some mines are very sensitive to the gold price, others less so. This adds ounces cheaply but tends to add only incrementally.

Beyond that, companies need new deposits, which they can either discover or buy. It is usually cheaper and certainly easier for the major companies to acquire reserves than to find them. There is the difficulty of finding significant new deposits, which we have constantly emphasized. Many of the major companies have drastically reduced their greenfields exploration and look to juniors to do the high-risk exploration. Some companies will actively fund such exploration, either through straightforward joint ventures (on specific properties) or through strategic alliances (often covering an entire region). More often than not, however, they will pay the big bucks after a discovery has been made and most of the risk (including the permitting risk) has been removed. They prefer to pay up for a known quantity than take the risk early on. This gives investors potential for enormous profits, by buying stock in potential acquisition candidates, which we'll discuss in our next chapter.

Buying Is Cheaper Than Finding

Acquisitions by a senior company can involve purchasing a specific property or an entire company. The latter can run the gamut from a large company buying a small one to two reasonably similar-sized

companies merging. The last decade has seen a merger and acquisition frenzy, one that has seen many iconic names swallowed up,
including Homestake Mining and Placer Dome (itself the result of a
combination of two major companies). In 1996, the 10 largest companies produced 25 percent of the world's output. A decade later,
the top five alone produced 33 percent, a stunning consolidation.
Part of the process was the change in structure in South Africa,
as the mining houses consolidated individual mines with complete
ownership. There are now three major South African companies,
AngloGold, Goldfields and upstart Harmony, compared with dozens
of individual mines trading separately up to a decade ago.

That's not the entire story, however. The merger frenzy increased
in pace as the decade and the gold bull market progressed. In 2006,
as the price of gold moved over $500 an ounce, the merger went
into a manic phase: Barrick and Goldcorp teamed up to buy Placer
Dome; Goldcorp bought Glamis; Iamgold bought Cambior, and
Kinross Bema, among others. In all, a total of $25 billion was spent
on acquisitions, more than all in the previous five years, and much
more, by a factor of 10, of the money actually spent on exploration.
The mania continued into 2007, when Yamana acquired Meridian
Gold, and other successful juniors such as Arizona Star and Miramar
disappeared.

We can distinguish between acquisitions of major multimine
companies, such as Placer, and acquisitions of juniors, where the major company is typically looking at a single property. It was Arizona's
Cerro Casale deposit high in the Chilean Andes that attracted
Barrick. It was Hope Bay that led Newmont to pay up for Miramar.
Similarly, Cumberland's Meadowbank or Glamis's Penasquito were
the attractions for acquiring companies looking for large deposits
that could be developed reasonably quickly. (Again, there are lessons
for us investors that we'll discuss in our next chapter.)

Whether a company buys just the property or acquires the whole
junior depends on several factors, including what else the junior
might own (seniors usually don't want to pay for a lot of early-
stage "baggage") or the motivation of the management of the target (Virginia sold its Eleonore property to Goldcorp rather than
the entire company because they were motivated to continue exploring many of their other properties and repeating the discovery/
sale process again). This is often different with a junior *producer*,
which will more often be acquired *in toto* than an exploration
company.

Juniors Are Better Explorers

In essence, major producers have outsourced their exploration to the juniors, in much the same way we see in oil or even pharmaceuticals. And it makes sense. Producing and exploring are two different businesses with different skill sets, with smaller companies typically more effective, more mobile, and more motivated than seniors. Motivation? The geologist who forms his own exploration company is amply rewarded if the company makes a discovery through low-priced options. The geologist working for a major company? Maybe he gets a gold watch and corner office. Mobile? A company, such as Virginia, drilling on four of its own properties this year, can quickly adjust budgets if one property looks more promising than another. The vice president of exploration and the CEO discuss the issue and the next day or next week the drills are moving.

In a major company, however, the on-the-ground geologist talks to his regional superior who talks to his divisional boss who brings it up to the vice president of exploration (if there is one), who discusses it in committee and finally takes it to the board. In most cases, it doesn't even get that far, because as each person gets more removed from the field, they are more cautious of asking for more money that may turn out to be a mistake. As with any large organization, people are often more concerned with keeping their jobs, which means not making mistakes, than with taking risks for big rewards. And even if it gets up the chain, the big company will rarely add more funds midway through a program. So money may be added, but next year.

The truth is that exploration is more suited to juniors than to seniors. Most exploration companies never intend mining (if they do, it's often a mistake). Rather, the plan is to find something of value to a senior and cash out.

Acquisitions Can Hurt Buyers

When the senior announces an acquisition, particularly with major acquisitions, the stock of the senior usually underperforms over the ensuing six months or so. There are several reasons for this:

1. The senior pays a premium, often a hefty one, to make the acquisition; sometimes arbitrageurs come in buying the target and selling or short-selling the acquirer, pushing the price down.

2. Often, with a large acquisition, the company will have to undertake an equity offering, if not to complete the acquisition, then later to replenish the treasury. Investors see this coming so wait for the inevitable decline that accompanies equity issues.

3. There are often digestion issues when a large company is acquired, including everything from differences in cultures to incompatible software programs.

4. Synergies and cost savings are often overadvertised; as often as not, the primary purpose of a major merger or acquisition is simply to get bigger. Shareholders usually grumble at the cost of the acquisition, while inevitably there are some shareholders who do not like a particular transaction (when Iamgold acquired Cambior, for example, many shareholders didn't like Cambior's hedging liability).

Avoid the Flawed

Although the exploration end of the chain is where the truly big stock price moves take place, nonetheless the major producers can be attractive investments. After all, if the price of a resource goes up, the stocks of the companies that produce the resource and have large reserves will also go up, and more than the resource itself (as we have seen). Major producers are far more certain gainers in a bull market. Senior companies tend to move much more with the broad gold market, and so a good place to start is by looking at how expensive the gold stocks are relative to gold.

An easy measure is the ratio of the XAU Index to the gold price. Historically, any time this ratio has moved above five times has been a good time to buy gold stocks. Over the last year, the ratio has been at an historic anomaly, moving over nine times at the end of 2008, and remaining high for an extended period. In May 2010, the ratio stood at 6.8 times. This partly reflects the attraction of physical gold as well as broad stock market weakness, which affects gold stocks as well as other stocks. What we can say with certainty is that gold stocks are inexpensive relative to bullion; if gold continues to move up, the stocks have the potential for outsized gains. Gold stocks are also cheap on other measures, which we'll discuss later.

Not all seniors move in lockstep, as we have seen, and they are by no means buy-and-forget investments. We've discussed the ongoing difficulties facing major producers. In addition, they tend to be very sensitive to the broader stock market as well as to the economy and credit markets (as we saw at the end of 2008). Moreover, things change over time. The blue chips of one period can fall from grace, as evidenced by RTZ or Royal Dutch Shell, for example.

The key is to avoid fatal flaws as much as possible. In the gold sector, this includes companies whose output is heavily hedged, companies with a concentration of assets in risky countries, and companies making high-cost acquisitions. Hedgers Barrick and Cambior underperformed as the price of gold rose. The South Africans underperformed as perceived risk in that country rose, as well as higher costs associated with the mature mines there. Until its acquisition of Phelps Dodge, Freeport's stock was highly sensitive to political developments in Indonesia. Newmont's stock collapsed from $55 to $40 after its high-cost purchase of Miramar (equating to $4,600 for each proven ounce of reserves), before the credit crisis took it under $25 per share.

So, avoiding companies with these so-called *fatal flaws*, or moving quickly to sell when things change for the worse, can help investors boost returns in the senior sector.

What to Look For

In looking at seniors, the most important factors to consider are the following:

1. Diversification of properties
2. Political risk of assets
3. Pipeline of future projects
4. Cost of production (including by-products)
5. Balance sheet

We have discussed earlier how by-product production can help a company by showing lower costs. In many ways, it's a bit of a shell game. Nonetheless, if a gold company can lower the cost of producing the gold by crediting proceeds from nongold production, it can help. The downside is when the by-product production becomes too significant a portion of the whole, since gold mines are afforded a higher multiple. (We saw this with the royalty company Franco Nevada, where at one point almost half its revenues were coming from oil and gas, largely a result of dramatically higher oil and gas prices. Nonetheless, gold investors did not like this and gave the company a lower multiple than pure gold royalty companies.) Similarly, an erstwhile high-growth producer can see its multiple cut as it matures into a slower-growth outfit.

No analyst today provides a better guide to the producing companies than John Doody in his *Gold Stock Analyst.* Sometimes called "a Value Line for gold stocks," John provides detailed analysis on all the major producers (gold and silver) around the world, and not a few smaller ones as well. He has a rigorous hurdle for companies, willowing down the universe to his top ten. He also provides monthly commentary on the overall sector. Without a doubt, his service is indispensable to any serious investor in the gold sector.

Gold Stocks Are Inexpensive

The gold stock sector as a whole, as we have seen, is inexpensive relative to bullion. The sector is also cheap on historical valuation metrics. One can look at the sector using the same metrics one uses to value individual stocks by looking at cash flow multiples such as price to production, price to earnings, price to cash flow, and growth to cash flow. Most gold stocks are expensive most of the time on these metrics—no one ever accused gold stocks of being Graham and Dodd value stocks—so it's partly a matter of looking at today's valuations in an historical perspective.

On an historical basis, however, looking at cash flow metrics, gold stocks are inexpensive. (See Figure 11.3.) The price-to-earnings (P/E) multiple of North American stocks today is under 20, the lowest it has been in over the past 20 years. Similarly, with a price-to-cash flow multiple of 12, the gold stocks have not been cheaper in 20 years. In the past, particularly during periods when gold was strong, P/Es have been as high as 50 and cash-flow multiples over 25. Valuations typically expand when the price of gold is high and moving up, so gold stocks today are at a historically anomalous level.

Some analysts prefer to look at major companies on an asset basis, a valid approach if one believes the gold price is going to be in a bull market for several years. Such measures include price to reserves, or to resources, or to NAV. All such measures have drawbacks. As mentioned earlier, not all ounces are equal. An ounce in a capital intensive mine in a high-risk country is certainly not as valuable as an

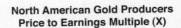

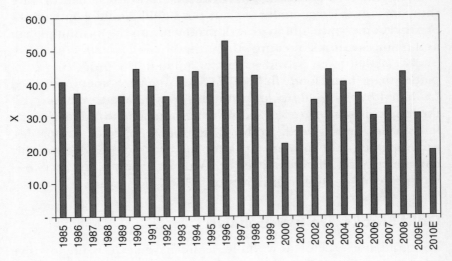

Figure 11.3 **Gold Stocks at Cheapest**

Source: National Bank Financial. February 2010.

ounce in a simple open-pit in Nevada or Chile. An ounce in a mine under construction is more valuable than an ounce in a property that's been put on the shelf for development at some indeterminate point in the future. And so on. Such gauges can only be guides, but together, they can aggregate to something more meaningful.

Significantly, however, while the gold stocks are generally selling at multidecade low valuations on the basis of revenue, income, and earnings, they are not so cheap on the basis of assets. Indeed, stocks today are selling at their 20-year highs based on reserves. And this tells us again the difficulty that companies have increasing reserves, and portends much higher prices in the years ahead.

Political Risk

Mines are geological gifts of God, and unlike a typical business, they can't be moved. This makes mines very attractive targets for populists and rapacious governments everywhere. Of course, though one can't move the deposit, neither the company nor the investor has to put their money there. The most recent clear example of this came when Rio Tino of London, one of the world's giant mining companies, announced it would restart a half-billion-dollar iron ore expansion program in Canada just days after it said Australia's proposal for a "super tax" on mines there would cause investment to shift elsewhere. Other major companies followed suit.

Through some cosmic irony, however, many of the world's worst basket cases are rich in resources (think of Zimbabwe as only one of so many). Different companies, like individual investors, have differing tolerance for risk. Some eschew Russia, others South Africa, most Venezuela and Zimbabwe. Of course, investing for companies as for individuals is a matter of risk and reward. A large enough prize may justify a greater political risk, and different companies are more or less willing to take it.

Freeport Copper, for example, has spent billions of dollars building a copper mine in the Democratic Republic of the Congo, undoubtedly among the worst places on earth to undertake any kind of business, much less a long-term capital intensive one. Yet the prize is Tenke Fungurume, perhaps the richest copper mine brought on stream in the last 20 years. When fully up and running, it will produce nearly 250 million pounds of copper, as well as significant cobalt, each year, with a 40-year mine life, a prize worth going for. Freeport has experience in politically challenging jurisdictions, through its decades in Indonesia, and is more willing to tackle political difficulties than some other companies, and perhaps is better at it.

Other companies are more willing to take political risk, but they seek to mitigate it by broad diversification. Newmont has had significant political problems at many of its mine sites over the year—Uzbekistan expropriated its tailing operation there—but the diversification, including some operations in more political safe jurisdictions like Nevada, meant the company was not destroyed by any of these issues.

Again, individuals must decide on their political risk tolerance. A higher risk may mean buying bigger assets cheaper and reaping greater rewards. But sometimes the risk can mean absolute losses for investors. Crystallex ostensibly had the rights to develop the huge Las Cristinas, one of the largest undeveloped known mine deposits in the world. The company had spent hundreds of millions of dollars over many years developing the property. But Hugo Chavez decided he wanted his Russian buddies to have the mine, and Cystallex share-holders saw their investment plunge from over $5 to 30 cents in one year.

Best Places to Explore and Mine

There is no doubt though that a stable jurisdiction, where there are rules that are obeyed, without the threat of expropriation, violence or corruption, makes exploring and developing properties easier. A jurisdiction with a history of mining more often understands the challenges and does not see foreign mining companies as a goose to be plucked. Quebec and Newfoundland are among the most highly rated areas in which a miner can operate (and two of my all-time favorites, Virginia and Altius, focus on these two provinces respectively). (See Figure 11.4.)

In Latin America, Chile has long rated highly, along with Brazil, Mexico, and Peru. However, in a survey of mining companies by the respected Fraser Institute, whereas Peru's ranking has been increasing in recent years (particularly after the violent Shining Path guerrillas were destroyed), Mexico's ranking, which used to be one of the highest in the world, has been falling quite sharply and more and more companies have been running into permitting and land ownership disputes.

These are, for the most part, different from the main factors we consider in accessing exploration and junior companies. Reality is critical for major producing companies, whether it is cash flow or taxation or future ounces. For exploration companies, hope plays a larger role, though some of these same problems remain, if in an attenuated form.

We can avoid the operational problems all together, however, by investing in a special breed. Neither producer nor explorer, the royalty company owns royalty interests on other companies' mines and exploration properties. These royalties come in various forms, but essentially, they provide that part of the cash flow, or sometimes profits, of a mine go to the royalty holder. Traditionally, royalties were granted by the mining company to the original landowner and subsequently sold to a royalty company. But increasingly, the best of these companies are using the royalty as a financing tool, providing capital to an exploration or development company in return for part of the future cash flow.

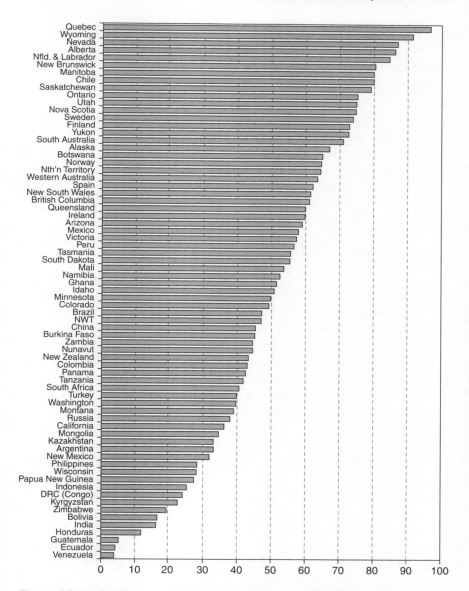

Figure 11.4   Canada and United States among Best Places to Mine

Source: Fred McMahon and Miguel Cervantes, *Fraser Institute Annual Survey of Mining Companies 2008/2009*. Available at www.fraserinstitute.org. Reprinted with permission.

These are among my favorite investments in the mining business. Royalty companies have full exposure to price appreciation and to exploration upside on their royalty land but have various advantages over the mining companies themselves, which are:

- They have no operations and are not responsible for fixing mine site problems that can unexpectedly cut into profits.
- They have reduced exposure to capital, costs, and political problems.
- Overheads are very low, and margins are high; for Franco-Nevada, the largest gold royalty company, 85 percent of revenues are free cash flow.
- Both the companies and the stocks tend to have less downside sensitivity.

Of course, such advantages do not come without a cost. There are essentially two. Just as there is less downside, so too is there less leverage. (However, though gold royalty stocks will not often be the best performer any given week or month, they are likely, over the long term, to be among the best stocks in your portfolio.) And most important, as holder of a royalty rather than owner of the property, others are in control. It may not do the company much good if the mining company on whose land you hold the royalty postpones putting the mine into production. (Sometimes, this risk is mitigated by what are known as *advance royalties*, which provide for some payments after a certain date even if the mine is not in production.)

There are three gold royalty companies, and I like them all. Franco-Nevada (FNV, Toronto) is the largest, with top management and a very solid balance sheet. It also has some oil and gas royalties as well as a royalty on the Stillwater platinum mine. Not much smaller is Royal Gold (RGLD, Nasdaq), which, following an acquisition of a smaller rival, also has a spread of nongold royalties, plus a strong pipeline of gold royalties coming into production. These two should be your first royalty companies, perhaps the foundation of a more conservative gold portfolio. Gold Wheaton (GLW, Toronto) is newer and far smaller, and does not own any royalties but rather similar vehicles called gold streams. (We will discuss these revenue streams fully in Chapter 13.) With only two primary gold streams at present compared with hundreds of royalties for the other two, it is in a different league and far more speculative, but potentially attractive.

Many investors want more excitement than royalty companies are likely to offer, and they turn to exploration companies. And it is to this sector that we turn next.

12

The Mine Cycle and Juniors

You should keep at the forefront of your mind three important facts about the mining business: The odds of a successful discovery are very long; seniors are hungry for new resources; and they will pay up after most of the risk has been taken out. Keeping these facts in mind we can see how huge returns are possible, and at lower risk, for investing selectively in the junior and exploration stocks. It may help prevent you investing too indiscriminately in early stage companies as well as selling too soon when one is successful.

Growing Junior Producers Can Be Attractive

The most attractive target can be a growing mid-tier company, one with several, larger and growing properties. Such a company might have two or three properties in production with a pipeline of developmental properties for future production. Such companies are very attractive targets for seniors since they can add immediate production ounces with the risk out, as well as future growth, but such companies come along only occasionally. They are, however, an attractive win-win for investors: Either a senior buys them or the market rerates them from risky developmental companies to successful producers. They are not without risk, however, since moving from exploration to production is a giant step fraught with risk. Many have stumbled. But once a company has demonstrated an ability to get a property into production successfully—and it is never smooth all the way—then it becomes very attractive.

Earlier in the decade were three successful such companies, known as the "three amigos": Glamis, Meridian, and Agnico Eagle. Two of these were acquired for significant premiums; Agnico has enjoyed a somewhat bumpy ride from the low teens throughout the first half of the decade to prices over $50. Both Agnico and Yamana Gold, which bought Meridian and is a multimine company, could be attractive to a major. In neither case, however, is there any indication that a takeover is in the works or that management is looking for an exit.

Major companies, when they make an acquisition, are more often focused on a single property, particularly with earlier-stage companies. Among those that could be targets—either as a company or for one of their projects—are Allied Nevada, Vista Gold, Esperanza Silver, Nevsun Resources, Sunridge Gold, and Mag Silver. All own one multimillion ounce deposit that would be attractive to a major company. As for earlier-stage exploration companies, Virginia Mines, Midland Exploration, Eurasian Minerals, and Kiska Metals all have good shots at finding something of interest to a major company. (Please note that here, as throughout this book, we are not making active current recommendations to buy. Much can change between the writing and the reading.)

Goal Is to Go Away

Few exploration companies set out to build major mining companies. More often than not, the business plan is to develop one or more properties that can be sold to seniors. As we have mentioned before, perhaps one in 3,000 anomalies ever becomes a mine, so the odds are long. Major companies usually like to see most of the risk taken out by a junior, including the exploration and even permitting risk, before making an acquisition. They prefer to pay up for greater certainty. Sometimes, however, if initial exploration suggests the potential for a truly large discovery, particularly in a good jurisdiction, then a senior might try to buy in early, perhaps through a joint venture in which it funds exploration.

This provides a foot in the door, and access to ongoing information, giving that company an enormous advantage in any eventual sale of the property. Another strategy for seniors, particularly when a company is involved in multiple exploration projects in a new mining environment is to make a strategic alliance. Typically, such an arrangement has the major company funding most of the exploration in return for the right to joint venture a selected number of properties (e.g., Newmont has such an arrangement with Eurasian in Haiti).

Major companies are prepared to pay for known deposits. In the last few years, acquisitions have often been as much as $10,000 to $12,000 per ounce of production, or $200, $300, as much as $1,000 per ounce of reserves. As can be seen, the numbers range all over the map, and it's difficult to generalize at how much reserves are truly worth. Obviously, not every ounce is equal. In looking at production numbers, how many years of production have been proved? How profitable is the mine? What are the growth prospects for future exploration? Reserve numbers can be misleading, since a narrow underground vein deposit, for example, will typically have reserves for only a couple of years ahead of it at any time, yet the mine could go on for decades. (The reason for this is because the work necessary to define reserves in such deposits is nearly as costly as the mining itself. With a disseminated, open-pit mine, however, the mine's potential may be known before mining operations begin.) Unless there is a true synergy, such as an existing adjacent mill with spare capacity for more feed, a major company making an acquisition usually wants at least some growth potential.

Premiums paid over prevailing stock prices can be steep. The average premium over the past few years has been 27 percent, but some have been 100 percent or more, and some just 5 to 15 percent. If the premiums do not seem that attractive, remember that usually stock prices have moved ahead of the takeover announcement, both in the longer and shorter term, on successful mining or exploration results, and later in anticipation of someone making a takeover offer, or even takeover rumors. The level of the premium is determined by many factors: how expensive the stock is prior to the takeover, whether the senior is in a strong position to succeed (existing share ownership, management lockups and so forth), and whether a competing bid is expected. Some properties may be a perfect fit for one particular major company, which perhaps has an existing mine operation nearby with spare mill capacity, for example, but not be so attractive to other companies.

Mine Life Cycle

The cycle of a mine life goes through several stages: exploration, discovery, evaluation, development, operation, closure. The exploration stage can last several years. Many companies never move past this stage. Once a discovery has been made, it can take another year or two for further exploration and evaluation until a feasibility study for a mine is produced. It can take another three to four years before the mine starts production. So from discovery to production can be five to seven years on average. These are only approximate and average times, of course. Occasionally, it is quicker, as in the extraordinary case of Pierina in Peru, which Barrick acquired after only a handful of holes had been drilled and had in production less than three years later. In other cases, extraordinary delays in permitting can go on for many years.

Once a mine is in production, there is no such thing as a typical mine life; mines can last for just a handful of years and still be profitable, or for 100 years. One might expect a major mine to operate for 10 to 15 years. But all mines at some stage reach maturity and start to decline. Typically, production and grade drop, driving up unit costs. By this time (hopefully) all capital costs have been fully amortized and mining can still be profitable. As an example of a large, successful mine, Goldstrike, in Nevada, saw production steadily decline throughout the decade from 2.5 million ounces in 2000, to 1.3 million ounces in 2009, at the same time as grades declined from 0.4 ounces per ton to less than 0.2 ounces per ton.

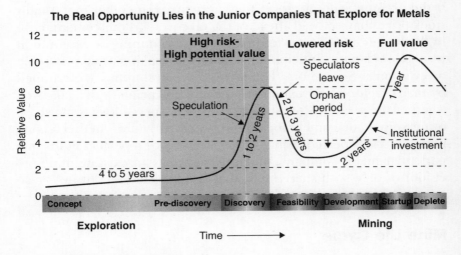

Figure 12.1   The Mining Cycle

Source: Exploration Insights.

Stocks go through a typical pattern throughout this cycle. A much stylized depiction of the life cycle of a mining share is shown. (See Figure 12.1.) You can see there are two main opportunities for big gains: after the discovery hole as the deposit grows and is defined and after a feasibility study until the mine reaches full production. Of course, any number of things can affect the stock price, both relating to the project itself—environmental protests at the site—or extraneous, most notably the price of gold (or the project's main resource). A feasibility study (by outside experts) may be disappointing, financing may prove difficult to obtain, the host government may decide to renegotiate the mining agreement, and so forth. While developing a large copper-gold project in Eritrea, Nevsun Resources saw its stock plunge 27 percent in three days—and that from an already depressed level—after the United Nations Security Council voted limited sanctions on that country. In a two-month period, the stock had collapsed by almost 50 percent.

Discovery!

Some investors like to bet on a discovery. One cannot predict when, or even if, a discovery hole will be made. Ace analyst Brent Cook, who writes *Exploration Insights,* the top advisory focusing on the exploration end of the food chain, puts it this way. On the TSX Venture Exchange (in Toronto), there are about 1,000 listed exploration companies (about half of all the world's junior resource companies). His "rough guesstimate" is that about 5 percent of them on an annual basis "actually *appear*" (Brent's emphasis) to find "something of potential economic interest." He then goes on to say that there is perhaps only a one in 10 chance that any of these properties of interest become economic. So, ever the cynic, Brent concludes that around 900 companies "have nearly nothing of economic value except the geologists, miners, and promoters that are working peddling their favorite piece of moose pasture or jungle to you and me."

One can only say that particular ground is conducive to a discovery and that the people know what they are doing. Now, Brent is an experienced and hard-nosed geologist, so he is able to make assessments of the likelihood of a piece of ground yielding a discovery and eventual economic deposit. As Brent told me when I caught up with him on the way to Senegal following a trip to Colombia, "Geology and the prospectivity of a mineral system are ultimately what counts in exploration."

Of course, without the geology you can't have a discovery. If you are going to play in this sandbox, you had better have the necessary experience and analytic skills, or depend on someone, like Brent, who does. But it is worth noting that even after the initial stock price jump following a particularly good drill hole, there is plenty of time for investors to get in on the play, as the company continues drilling and expands the resource and word gets around.

In a study of 10 discoveries in the first half of 2009 (not all will become mines, of course), Catherine Gignac of NCP Northland Capital Partners, Inc. showed an average double in the stock price *following* initial discovery over the next six weeks. At some stage, there is usually a pullback, as early buyers take their quick profits, and then, she showed, with an average of 10 weeks for the next set of investors to get on board, there was another gain of 60 to 80 percent over the next several weeks. So there is usually lots of time for active investors to buy into a new discovery, albeit at a higher price but with more certain gains. Here we are talking only about the initial stage of the discovery. The stock can continue to climb, though at a less dramatic pace, for the next two to three years as advanced exploration and evaluation takes place. Of course, subsequent drill results may not live up to the expectations of the first exciting discovery hole. (See Figure 12.2.)

At some point, when most exploration is completed and the company sets out to prepare a feasibility study and obtain permitting, the stock slides, often giving up most of the previous gains. This is true even if there is no bad news, but this is also a period when generally there can be little positive news, only potential setbacks. Permits may be delayed, social and environmental opposition comes forward, and so forth. Once the feasibility study has been produced, however, assuming it is positive, then a new group of investors gets involved and there are often even greater gains over a longer period of time until the mine is in production at its full expected rate. Again, in this second stage of profit, things can go wrong, including financing difficulties or cost overruns. The mine then enters a steady state until it matures and starts to deplete (which in some cases could be decades into the future).

And this typical pattern involves one project from start to finish. A company could easily be seeing positive exploration results on a new

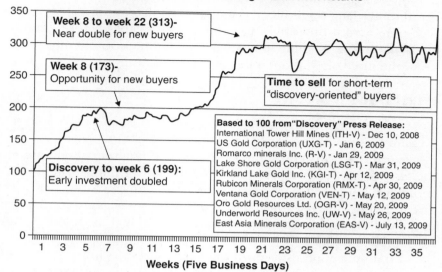

Figure 12.2   Opportunities for Profit after Discovery

Source: Catherine Gignac, NCP Northland Capital Partners Inc., Investing in Gold Equities presentation to the Denver Gold Forum, September 13, 2009, page 17.

property, offsetting the negative price implications of the feasibility and permitting process at its first project. A buyout could come at any stage but is more likely to come after the feasibility has been released. This is when a senior company knows what it is dealing with and how much to pay.

In the earliest age, the grade and size of the drill hole is the most important factor. Investors have to move quickly. As the deposit starts to develop, investors start to evaluate the potential mine: What is the potential size? How remote (or otherwise) is the property? How about the metallurgy? Will this be a high-cost operation? Any political risk? How much dilution will be necessary to move the project forward? And so forth. There is now a little time for serious evaluation before buying. In the second period for big stock gain, after the feasibility study has detailed all these factors, then other factors start to loom larger, including the state of the gold and credit markets.

So investors have time to get on board discoveries. Too often, we look at the stock price and think we've missed out of an opportunity. As more exploration is undertaken and the discovery confirmed, the deposit gets larger and more certain. So one can invest with more certainty at a later stage, albeit at a higher price. Some investors won't buy something if they could have bought it cheaper before, but it's a mistake (reminding me of Oscar Wilde's admonition of those who know the price of everything but the value of nothing).

What Does It Mean?

Now, of course, it's not quite as simple as this, not as simple as investing in any old stock that's jumped 30 percent, 50 percent, or more on a flashy drill hole and proclaimed a discovery, then waiting for it to rise another 50 to 100 percent. It takes a significant amount of geological knowledge and market savvy. Certainly, to invest before a discovery, one must be able to assess whether the rocks are conducive to a discovery and to gauge how much is already discounted in the stock price.

Certainly, a good drill result will excite investors initially, as they focus on the potential. But slowly investors start to consider the various factors mentioned previously, the *risk* as well as the *potential*. Certainly, however, in this stage if you bet on the right horses, there is the potential for enormous gains in short periods of time. Over time, however, dreams give way to reality until the feasibility study is produced—what is known in the business as a "truth event."

One needs to beware of flashy holes that signify nothing. They may be rewarded in the market, perhaps excessively, for a short while, but this is usually a good opportunity to take some money off the table. This could be an exceptional grade over a very short interval, not supported by results from the rest of the drill hole. It could be that the drilling was deliberately engineered to derive a good result, perhaps twinning an old hole or drilling down a known ore shoot (though this can be valid if properly disclosed). It does take some knowledge to be able to interpret results properly, but honest management and full disclosure is a prerequisite. Even if you don't fully understand the results, you still want to see the full data disclosed properly. As reality sets in, the valuation may become more realistic.

So if an exploration stock price jumps after an initial spectacular drill hole, it could be a very good time to jump on board, if real, or could be a gift from heaven to exit. You need knowledge. Chasing good drill results could be as foolish as refusing to buy something after the stock has moved.

What to Look For

Other than the pure geology and results, one must be aware of the company's management and balance sheet and funding needs. Exploration can be very expensive and if a company does not have sufficient funds for the next drill program, it will look to raise funds on any stock rally. I like to see at least 18 months' worth of cash in the bank, and that's a minimum. One of my favorite exploration companies, Miranda Gold, just issued some new equity, even though it has a very solid balance sheet, in order to ensure it has *five* years' worth of expenses in the bank.

Be aware that in some territories, drill programs cannot go year-round (whether because of a rainy season or winter freeze). A long lull in exploration, and lack of news releases, frequently sees stock prices slump. This can be a good time to buy, ahead of the next drill season. One gauge of whether a stock is a good buy is to look at the market cap (the price of the stock multiplied by the number of shares out) and compare it with what else you could buy for the same money. Such a simple test frequently puts highfliers into perspective.

Again, I emphasize that investing around discoveries requires skill and experience, as well as an honest understanding of the limitations of one's apposite skill. Failing this, to play this game, you need access to someone with the relevant skill whom you can trust. There is no shortage of recommendations of tiny exploration stocks on the web and most of them are worth what you pay for the advice (i.e., nothing). Small exploration stocks (like penny stocks in any sector) are a favorite hunting ground of scammers, hucksters, and the plain ignorant. The low market cap and illiquidity of such stocks means they are susceptible to big moves when buying comes in. Some deliberately pump junk in order to dump their own shares into your buying; others naively think they are tremendously clever when stocks move up after their recommendations.

If you want to follow someone with the necessary skill, experience, and honesty in this sector, then take a look at Brent Cook's *Exploration Insights* advisory. As mentioned, his focus is on early-stage exploration, based on geology. He also has a strong nose for the market. Another advisory with a strong track record is John Pugsley's *The Stealth Investor*, which has a broader small-cap focus than Brent's hard-rock emphasis. Pugsley does not pretend to have deep geologic knowledge, but he has the market experience and ethics, and knows who to talk to. (Contact information can be found in the Resource Directory at the end of the book.)

Company Not Property

Another approach to the high-risk exploration sector is to focus on companies rather than properties, companies that have reduced their risk and increased their odds of succeeding. Let's first review the traditional model for an exploration company. It's straightforward. A geologist finds a property that for some reason he believes has promise. He raises money on the back on that assessment and puts the money into the exploration in the ground. (This assumes it's not wasted on vintage wines and promotions.) One way or another, the funds raised are eventually spent, and without any revenue, the company has to go back to market to raise more money to continue its program. If initial exploration was promising, this may be fairly easy and the stock price may even have gone up (assuming favorable broad market conditions). More money is raised and that too goes into the ground, and that too eventually runs out. So the process is repeated.

But the results need to justify more equity raising. Perhaps the biggest risk to exploration companies is always running out of money. Brent Cook concurs. "This is an extremely capital intensive (industry) that relies on the generosity of gamblers and mining companies whose investment decisions are based on metal prices," he says. The problem is that if the exploration company does not have a strong balance sheet, it might want money at precisely the time others don't feel like giving it. (This is also one of the biggest risks for the investor in junior stocks, running out of money. You should never invest so much money that you might be forced to sell a stock to pay a bill, because it will always be at the worst possible time. That's Murphy's Law!)

Even assuming positive results and favorable market conditions all along the way, there is still ongoing dilution. Given the extraordinary odds against success, this is an easy way to lose money.

Why do so many companies follow this path? Overconfidence and the promise of enormous riches. Geologists are, by their nature, optimistic people; they have to be. Why else would a sane adult spend his life slugging across arctic tundra or tropical forests banging on rocks? When a geologist finds something that could be a deposit, the last thing he wants to do is give it up. The truth is that failure or, at best, constant dilution, most likely lies ahead.

There is a better way, a way that minimizes risk and increases the odds of success. This is the business strategy known as the prospect generator business model. This involves a company looking for properties with potential, undertaking initial (inexpensive) exploration, and then bringing in a partner to spend the money. In a typical deal, a partner might agree to spend a certain amount of money on the property in each of, say, four years in order to earn 70 percent of the property.

Whoa. Wait a minute. Why would you want to give away most of the property if you think it has potential? Let's just go back to the odds of making a discovery, and the answer is obvious. Moreover, by preserving its own balance sheet—someone else spends the big exploration dollars—the exploration company can go out and repeat the process, generate another prospect, bring in another partner, and so forth. It's a little like having parts of several perpetual lottery tickets rather than all of one. Again, not only do the odds of being involved in a successful discovery increase tremendously, but equally important, the risk of failure falls dramatically. Over time, there is much less dilution, and the company protects its balance sheet. If a property turns out to be a dud, the company lives to fight another day.

Minimize the Risk

Analyst Dr. Nicole Adshead-Bell notes we should never forget the long odds involved in exploration and want to ask the question, "If this (drill hole program) fails, what's left?" With the prospect generator, one is investing not in a specific drill hole, but in a company and business plan. In brief, one is using other people's money, which is generally a good business strategy! It should be noted, however, that even prospect generator stocks generally do not really move until there is a flagship project, one with real potential. However, before that is apparent, we have lots of opportunities to buy a sound company with several opportunities at a cheap price; and if the flagship fails, we have plenty of potential and opportunities left.

In a good joint venture agreement, the prospect generator will get paid a little upfront for the option on the property and may even get paid to manage the project for the other, usually larger, company.

Thus, a successful prospect generator can build a portfolio of projects, on which other people are spending money, and it is getting paid to do the exploration. Some of these companies have more money at the end of an exploration season than at the beginning because of these fees.

Of course, there are downsides to the model. Most obvious, of course, is that in the event of a major discovery, the exploration company has given away most of the upside. In addition, in a weak market it may be difficult to find partners willing to spend the money on exploration. And, of course, the properties can still turn out to be duds. Perhaps most important of all, the junior is no longer in control of its properties. The joint venture partner may have spent its annual expenditure commitment and not want to be aggressive in following up good results, for example. More often than not, the property is of keener interest to the exploration company than to its joint venture partner, who may have a longer-term (slower) focus.

Prospect generators, and there are now well over a dozen good ones, tend to focus on a particular region or type of deposit. Virginia and Midland, for example, both focus on Quebec, but look at any kind of properties in that province. Another, Miranda, has a strong geological team with experience in Carlin-type sedimentary deposits; they are exploring in two areas known to host such deposits, Nevada and Colombia. There is, or should be, a focus, however.

To help spread the risk, prospect generators like to build portfolios with different minerals, at different stages of exploration, and bring in different partners. All too often, a major company might change its approach, regardless of any success on the ground. Thus, for example, an Australian company might decide that it no longer wants any grassroots exploration in North America. Word comes down from head office, and the joint ventures are terminated. For the prospect generator, it's not all bad; they get the property back, often after millions have been spent, along with the data from the exploration. But most prospect generators would much prefer to have a good partner spending money than keep getting their properties back. This again points to the main downside of this business model: the lack of control.

This business strategy minimizes risk and increases the odds of success, but it does not guarantee it. Indeed, investors in prospect generators need patience because it can be many years before any hint of a discovery as they try over and over again. Some of my favorite prospect generators are listed here:

Almaden Minerals	AAU New York
Cartier Resource	ECR Toronto
Eurasian Minerals	EMX Toronto
Kiska Metals	KSK Toronto
Midland Exploration	MD Toronto
Miranda Gold	MAD Toronto
Riverside Resources	RRI Toronto
Virginia Mines	VGQ Toronto
Altius Minerals	ALS Toronto

Again, remember that any one of these may or may not be a particularly good buy at the time you read this book; it may be simply a matter of a change in the stock price, or it could be a fundamental change: a key property has disappointed, or there's been a management change, or any number of things. However, one might argue that because of the business model, a specific development is less likely to change fundamentally an overall rating of such a company than with a traditional exploration company, which can go from hero to villain overnight.

A stock that is, say, $1 today might be $2 when you read this, but it might be a better value and a better buy then, than had it dropped to 50 cents. I cannot know that ahead of time, of course. But I can say that, provided the companies have not abandoned their business approach, you are unlikely to go seriously wrong over the long run with a basket of these prospect generators.

Minimizing Risk Is the Key

There are many variations on the prospect generator theme, the broad strategy of minimizing exploration risk at the junior end of the market. So let's look in a little detail at my favorite exploration company to see how it goes about maximizing shareholder value while minimizing risk.

Virginia Mines (VGQ, Toronto) grew as a traditional prospect generator, and has been very successful at it, selling its discovery of a major gold deposit at Eleonore to Goldcorp a few years ago in return for shares and a royalty. This transaction was a good example of the way these companies often retain an interest in their projects while replenishing the balance sheet. It is also a good example of the patience that is required with prospect generators (and indeed exploration companies in general). Virginia stock did relatively little for many years until the Eleonore discovery and subsequent property acquisition by Goldcorp, which ultimately generated gains of over 2,000 percent. Now, once again Virginia is returning to its roots, generating prospects and joint venturing them, though prepared—and able—to explore itself if the potential is extraordinary.

Like many prospect generators, Virginia is inexpensive. It has cash and marketable securities (as of the end of 2009) of over $40 million (mostly cash). The royalty it negotiated with Goldcorp on the Eleonore property is very attractive. It is a net smelter royalty (not profits) on a sliding scale, beginning at 2 percent and moving up to 3.5 percent as the price of gold increases. Further, it is an advance royalty, meaning that Goldcorp is now paying even before the property is brought into production. Once in production, this could represent up to $4 million in the first year, with plenty of upside from both the gold price and from exploration potential. Goldcorp recently doubled its estimate of the gold ounces at Eleonore to 9.4 million ounces. With that higher resource and at today's gold price, the royalty has a net asset value (NAV) on a discounted cash-flow basis of over C$200 million.

Together, the royalty and cash exceeds the company's total market cap. That means all the exploration is free! It holds an extensive property portfolio in Quebec, including about 1,000 square kilometers of land in the Eleonore region, with almost half a million ounces of gold in resources at Post Lemoyne and La Grand Sud. It also owns 100 percent of a zinc deposit, Coulon, that it discovered shortly after the sale of Eleonore, and which is ready for a sale or addition exploration when the zinc price market recovers. In addition, there are about half a dozen active projects, in a range of minerals, throughout Quebec. These include the Corvet gold property, originally optioned to Placer Dome, but now because of the latter's acquisition, to Goldcorp. This property portfolio received only modest attention in the last few years after the discovery of Eleonore, since all of the company's focus was on developing that property rapidly. Now that Goldcorp owns it, Virginia can return to developing its other highly prospective properties. Virginia has about a dozen active projects in Quebec, with six drill programs this year. The current budget for exploration is over C$10 million of which Virginia pays just over $3 million. The rest is paid by joint venture partners, and incentive tax grants. Now that's what I call leverage, and it beats the leverage obtained by putting all of one's bank balance into drill holes on a single property. Apart from all this, however, perhaps Virginia's main asset is its people, lead by geological engineer Andre Gaumond, one of the most respected industry leaders in Canada.

Of course, these details may have changed when you read this. But that's the whole point of investing in these companies. Whatever the details at any given time, Virginia has a proven exploration team, lots of ground, multiple exploration and drilling targets, a great balance sheet, and a sound business plan. That all adds up to a recipe for ongoing success.

Companies for General Investors

Investing in these companies requires far less geological knowledge than when investing in pure exploration companies. In these companies, and any junior company trying to build a successful company over the long term, much more important than any single property is the management, the capital, and the plan. I will bet on strong management with capital over a specific prospective property any day. Even geologist Brent Cook says, "Of course, it comes down to people. Incompetent management can ruin a good property."

And good management with capital will eventually find something, or at least, they will give it their best and improve the odds in your favor tremendously. Interestingly, of the various successful juniors I've owned, few if any have been successful on the back of the first property on which they raised their initial capital. If that failed, they had the skill and the means to carry on until they were successful.

Soon after Franco Nevada went public, CEO Pierre Lassonde showed me Hasbrouck Mountain in Nevada, the property on which the company had high hopes. (The company name had no hyphen in its first incarnation.) Franco Nevada of course went on to become one of the most successful companies in the mining industry ever, but Hasbrouck was quietly dropped. (Incidentally, this tour of Carlin took place on the weekend of October 17 and 18, 1987, and we all boarded our early morning flights the next day not knowing the stock market was crashing. My recommendation to my investors to buy Franco

Nevada, typed overnight, must have been one of the few buy recommendations that day!) Interestingly, only now, more than 20 years later, another company, Allied Nevada, is finally drilling Hasbrouck.

Good management involves much: exploration expertise; understanding of a region; management skills; financial, technical, and market savvy; ethics; and ability to relate to and inspire employees, the community and shareholders. A plan includes goals and a focus, as well as a way to minimize risk and take advantage of opportunities. I like to see a junior that is focused, whether it's on a particular metal or a region or a type of deposit. As investors, we should be aware of companies that are constantly changing their stripes according to the latest market fancy, one day a diamond explorer in the Northwest Territories, the next looking for uranium in Saskatchewan, and then rare earths in Wyoming. More often than not, such companies are playing the market rather than trying to build real successful companies.

Small Companies but Better Than Before

We must always remember that exploration stocks, at least until a major discovery develops, are very small, with very few over $200 million market capitalization and most considerably less. Some of my favorites, including some that developed into successful companies, were bought when they had total market caps of only $10 million or even less. These are small companies, and small stocks, with all the risk of volatility and indeed loss that that implies. Equally, of course, these stocks can move dramatically on good news when buying comes in; it doesn't take much to move the stock significantly.

There are far more good-quality, serious exploration stocks today than in previous cycles. They tend to have better managements. Whereas in past cycles, such companies have often been led by finance people (good or bad) and many by stock promoters, today more often than not, the people running the company have geology degrees, and frequently experience with senior companies. Many major producers have downscaled their exploration divisions over the years, and many highly skilled and experienced explorers were let go. Many found their way to juniors. They are also better funded than in the past, when they frequently went from financing to out of money to promotion and another financing. If the financing was not available, the companies were toast. Today, these companies tend to have solid business plans and, though they dislike the dilution that comes from new equity offerings, they are more likely to finance when they can, ahead of running out of money.

Traps to Watch Out For

When investing in an exploration or junior stock, you should emphasize these two aspects, the management and the money. With management, look not only at its experience and its ethics, but also how much ownership they have. It is important that the founders and key players in a junior company have significant ownership, in shares and an option package, so they have an incentive to put all their effort into this company and to try and make it succeed. As for money, the junior should always have cash on hand to survive for at least 18 months without a new equity offering. In addition to cash in the bank, you want to look at other marketable assets, and their "burn rate," which is how much the company has to spend on a regular basis even before any extraordinary expenditures. This tells us how long they could survive if things took a downturn and they scaled by discretionary operations.

The capital structure is also important. You want to know how many warrants are outstanding and at what prices they are exercisable. In a company, for example, that has 10 million shares out and the stock is trading at $2, it has a market cap of $20 million. But if it also has 3 million in-the-money warrants, then its real market cap ("fully diluted") is $26 million. As an investor, it's important to know when these warrants expire. If they are in-the-money, then they will be exercised, and frequently this is accompanied by stock weakness. Often, warrants are held by investors who already own a large number of shares. When they exercise warrants, they will often sell some of their shares in the market to fund the exercise. If the stock is at $2, but they have warrants to buy more shares at $1.70, why not? But it means that the stock price will often retreat around the time of the warrant exercise. We see the same phenomenon if there is a new private placement. Those buying will often sell some of their existing shares to fund the placement, and then, as soon as the restrictions of the private placement are lifted, sell some more, knowing they still have exposure through the warrants that came with the placement. Thus, stocks can pull back four or five months after a placement.

Be Patient but Don't Fall in Love

As an investor in this sector, I do my research and select what I see as the best companies. I get to know management. It is important to be patient to let the plan be executed, remembering it always takes longer than one initially imagines. But it is also important not to fall in love with the stocks. One can like and admire management, and one can like the company, but avoid getting married to the stock. When it's time to sell, either because of disappointments or valuation, then one must bite the bullet. As discussed already, if my concern is only temporary, a short-term disappointment or a stock getting ahead of itself, I might sell only part of my position, keeping exposure to a company I like for the long term. Indeed, if the stock of a company with good people and a good business plan drops on temporary concerns, that might be an opportunity to buy more.

But if there is a fundamental change for the worse, perhaps a deviation from the business plan, or a change in management, or a lack of success at a flagship property, it might be time to move on. I avoid the temptation to market time in this sector, selling a stock I want to own thinking I'll be able to buy it back at a cheaper price. It's easy to be wrong-footed with this exercise. But selling part of a position where the stock is overvalued lets you lock in some profit and retain exposure. Then, by all means if the opportunity to buy at a lower price comes along, you can buy back the shares you sold.

While it's important to take profits in this sector, for profits have a habit of disappearing, I don't advocate the mechanical approach that some people have of selling half when a stock doubles and holding the rest for a free ride. The problem is obvious: One stock that doubles might be worth holding or even still buying while another should be sold completely. Investing involves a strategy of capital allocation: where are the best places for your money at any given time. There are times to be fully invested and times to be cash heavy; you don't have to invest at any time. Similarly, there are times to sell a stock, even of a good company that has served you well.

And you shouldn't be afraid of holding cash. Warren Buffett has a wonderful metaphor for successful investing. He likens it to being a batter in a game of baseball where there are no strikeouts. You can just stand there at bat and wait for the perfect ball. So it is with investing and perhaps nowhere more important than in the junior exploration sector.

It's also critical in this sector, where the volatility can be extreme and patience is key, never to invest more than you can afford. Never invest the rent money. If you are forced to sell on someone else's schedule, it may not be the best time—it probably won't be—to sell any of your stocks. So this money should be set aside for this sector.

Advice from the Masters

The question of the mistakes that many investors make, as well as the keys to being successful in the volatile junior space, is a topic that consumes a lot of time when those of us who invest in this sector get together. There is no magic formula. But there are things that we have learned, often in the school of hard knocks, things to avoid as well as strategies and tactics to employ.

Two of the most successful, each in a different way, have been Paul van Eeden and Robert Bishop. Originally from South Africa, where he grew up among the "big boys" in the mining industry, Paul now lives in Toronto, home to a good number of juniors. He is president of Cranberry Capital, a private Canadian holding company. Robert Bishop wrote the highly successful and respected *Gold Mining Stock Report* for a quarter of a century, before retiring a little over a year ago. He had a series of very profitable recommendations, including Diamondfields (the Voisey's Bay nickel discovery sold to Inco) and the discovery of diamonds in the Northwest Territories. These are but two of many. We recently discussed what makes a successful investor in the junior space, and their advice, from years of experience, is worth passing on.

Avoid Emotions and Know What You're Doing

Paul told me he thought the greatest mistakes came from fear and greed. These come in many forms. To overcome these, he says, one must be a contrarian. But fear and greed are powerful emotions. The investor who jumps on a "hot" stock he knows nothing about is often acting in fear of missing out on potential gains. Not selling a stock that has gone up is often because of the fear of losing out on additional profits. A more disciplined approach can help the investor make more rational decisions and limit losses.

Says Paul, "The antidote to fear is knowledge." If you truly understand a company, then you are more likely to make rational decisions about the stock. Paul says that if he owns a stock and finds that he is afraid it might decline, "I immediately recognize that I don't know enough about the company and therefore should not own the stock in the first place." On the other hand, when you truly understand a company and believe it is good value with good prospects, then if the stock price declines, you welcome the opportunity to buy some more.

There is no question that the more you know about a company and understand it, the less likely you are to make irrational, panicky, or greedy decisions about the stock. And in the exploration sector, this means spending time on the ground with the company's management and geologists. "Unless you are personally doing hands-on due diligence on your mining investments," Paul advised, "I strongly suggest you align yourself with someone who is." Paul recommends Brent Cook, as do I. Investing without adequate knowledge, says Paul, is gambling, "and if you find yourself with a gambling problem, invest more time to learn about the companies you are investing in, or seek help."

Buy Right, Buy Big, and Be Patient

It's not unfair to either of my two friends, both very successful in this sector, to suggest that Paul is probably a little more conservative than Bob Bishop. Though with different emphasis at times, their advice overlaps. After we spoke, Bob took the time to write down some thoughts for me and you, and they are so important, I thought the best thing I could do was pass them along as written.

> There are several (mistakes), and if they can be avoided, one's chances of success are much improved. One of my greatest frustrations was that many investors seem to need to hear a buy recommendation several times before making their purchase. *[If you are paying good money for the advice of someone you trust, then listen to his advice, both to buy and to sell.—AD]* This often means that they are ignoring the timeliness that frequently accompanies a stock recommendation, the thing that makes it a good buy when it is highlighted as one, as opposed to when the investor gets around to acting on it.
>
> One of the truisms of investing is "Don't tell me what to buy; tell me when to buy it," and the investor who requires a multitude

of buy recommendations before acting on one frequently negates the timely nature of a recommendation. Another way to express this is that a stock recommended at $.50 is not necessarily a good buy at $1 or $2; price is a big factor in many recommendations, and this seems to be lost on many who are on the receiving end of that advice. *[The $1 or $2 stock may be an even better buy at the higher price, but that's another story, and one that has nothing to do with the timeliness that Bob is discussing.—AD]*

Just as it sometimes takes investors a long time to act on a recommendation, when they do act, many investors buy in such small quantities that even a big percentage return will not be meaningful in the context of their portfolio. I'm not suggesting that all investors make big wagers in this riskiest of stock sectors, but rather, that as investors gain experience they should also work toward a goal of owning enough to make a difference. In too many cases, those who make insignificant commitments to high-risk stocks are equating mining stocks with gambling, and usually predisposing themselves to a similar outcome: losing money. My strong preference is to regard these stocks as informed speculations—not gambling—and while not all stocks are deserving of a meaningful commitment, correctly assessing when a larger commitment is required is also the formula for attaining big profits.

To be clear, I am not advocating that everyone adopt what I used to term a "Go big or go home" strategy, but that the more experience one gains, the greater the commitment should be to specific—by no means all—stocks. *[Again, we come back to the issue of knowledge. If you are not prepared to make a sufficiently meaningful investment, perhaps it means you do not know enough.—AD]*

How to Make the Big Money. I asked Bob, "How do you make the truly big money in junior resource investing?"

As noted earlier, buying right is important and learning to be disciplined on the buy side is essential. If you can simply learn to be contrary, only buying weakness and only selling strength, this puts an investor on the right side of the trade most of the time, and makes for much greater investor confidence—as opposed to being on the wrong side of the trade from the outset.

Having just advocated owning enough to make a difference, a corollary is to own a stock long enough to make a difference. In recent years especially, with the opportunity to have access to the market at all times, many investors have shortened the length of time they are willing to hold a stock. In most cases, this precludes the possibility of owning stock that produces big gains.

Most of the time when I buy a stock I expect to hold it for at least a year. As times passes, the stock is either living up to my expectations or it is not, and I modify my strategy accordingly. My experience is that investors find it is much easier to buy a stock than to sell it, and too often, the result is an unwieldy collection of stocks, as opposed to an actively managed portfolio. "Pull the weeds and water the garden" is one way to describe the necessity of selling as well as buying, and Dennis Gartman's mantra to "Own more of what's working and less of what's not" is another way of saying the same thing: Stick with what's working; get rid of what is not.

The points just made about money management put the odds in the investor's favor, but the biggest money I've made has almost always been associated with mineral deposits of consequence. As mineral deposits take time to be explored and develop, companies with exposure to big deposit stories also represent the best chance of booking long-term gains. Identifying a big deposit story early, and sticking with it, is where I think the most money gets made (a) because the growing deposit drives the market and (b) because these are also the kind of companies that are most likely to be acquired by major mining companies in search of tomorrow's reserves.

In my experience, investors who can afford to be patient, importantly, when patience is justified, are also the investors who will achieve the greatest profits. While patience may not sound like an investment strategy to some, that's probably because they've never managed to attain large profits; they're unclear on the concept until they prove to themselves that it works. Once the light has gone on, truly large profits become possible.

So making big gains and minimizing risks comes down to a combination of emotion and skill: avoid fear and greed...be a contrarian...learn what you're doing...pay attention to price and value . . . make meaningful investments . . . don't forget to sell . . . and be patient with developing stories. I am not suggesting it's easy, but you can tilt the odds in your favor by taking the advice of these masters.

And stick with the program. Once you have decided on a strategy, don't keep changing your mind. Now, of course, I don't mean you should be stubborn and refuse to sell the stock of a company that is disappointing ("pulling the weeds," as Bob puts it). But don't be a contrarian, until the stock goes down; don't be a long-term investor, until the first minor setback.

So while, like the geologist who dreams of finding the next huge discovery, we can dream of buying a penny stock just before it hits pay dirt. We can also buy shares in companies that employ a risk-minimization strategy and be patient, allowing good managements to build their companies over time.

PART IV

TOP SECTORS

CHAPTER

13

Silver: Poor Man's Gold?

Silver is different from both gold and from base metals in that it is both a precious and an industrial metal. It has unusual, and in some cases unique, attributes that affect supply, demand, and investment.

A Precious and Industrial Metal

Silver has both multiple industrial uses, including growing uses in a modern society, as well as a long history as a precious metal and as money. Though neither as highly regarded nor clearly as valuable as gold—silver is bulky and it tarnishes—it is nonetheless universally recognized as precious and has been widely used in different societies throughout history as money, including most notably by the Indian societies of Latin America as well as, at times, in the United States. The very word *sterling* resonates with meaning; we talk of a person of sterling character.

Silver is also quite different from both gold (and other precious metals, such as the platinum metals) on the one hand and copper, say, on the other: it is usually found in conjunction with other metals not as a pure or even primary silver mine. This attribute affects supply.

And just as there are few pure silver mines, so too are there few pure silver mining companies, and this affects investing in the metal.

Changing Pattern of Demand

Silver is a small market, with less than 1 billion ounces of silver consumed in a year. Demand for silver, however, is much broader

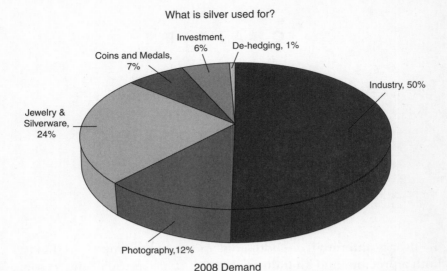

What is silver used for?

Investment, 6%

De-hedging, 1%

Coins and Medals, 7%

Industry, 50%

Jewelry & Silverware, 24%

Photography, 12%

2008 Demand

Figure 13.1   Industry Is Main User of Silver
Source: GFMS.

than for either gold (and other precious metals) or for base metals. About 50 percent of silver is consumed for industrial uses, almost one-quarter for jewelry and silverware, almost one-eighth for photography, and the balance (about 16 percent) for coins, medals, and investment. Industrial usage has grown tremendously over the years, both in the breadth of applications as well as absolute numbers, while photographic demand has steadily declined with the popularity of digital photography. (See Figure 13.1.) Though investment demand has been growing, it is still very modest compared with gold.

Photographic demand not so long ago was the primary use of silver, and many analysts predicted a permanent collapse in silver prices as silverless digital took over from halide film. The pictures are not only taken with silverless digital cameras, but most often, the pictures are not developed (on silver-halide paper) but stored on a computer. There has indeed been a decline, but its impact has not been as signficant as the pessimists predicted. In the years from 1977 to 1989, silver used in photography ranged from about 140 million ounces to a peak of 180 million ounces. In these years there was steady growth from new markets, particularly Japan, while demand from North America and Western Europe held steady. Then along came digital photography, cutting into demand in developed countries. Today, a little more than 100 million ounces is used worldwide; that's a decline, to be sure, but there remains a healthy demand.

The pessimists missed three important factors. They were indeed correct in predicting that digital would completely take over from silver-based film for ordinary consumers in the developed world. But during this period, there has been a huge growth in photography in the emerging world, where many consumers still buy traditional cameras requiring silver-based film for cost reasons (not only are extremely inexpensive film-based cameras available, but they do not require the possession of a computer, which many households do not possess). In addition, there has been a growth in disposable (film-based) cameras in the developed world. Second, and more important, a large part of the photography base still prefers—or must use—silver-based film. Professional photographers prefer it for sharper images, as do hospitals for X-rays, and other high-end users. Although most commercial photographers have switched, fine-art photographers and some top photographers—including, reportedly, Annie Liebovitz—still prefer film.

There is one other very important factor. About half of the silver used in photography returns as scrap; so as the use of silver-based film has declined, so too has the amount of scrap, mitigating the *net* loss of demand. Though there has indeed been a dramatic long-term decline in the demand for silver for photography, its overall impact is less than one might have thought.

Wide Range of Industrial Applications

Offsetting the long-term decline in the use of silver in photography has been the growth in industrial uses for silver. In 2007, silver use in electronics exceeded that in photography for the first time (and electronic use is only one part of overall industrial demand).

Silver has many important properties that, combined with its low unit price, make it the preferred choice in a range of industrial applications. Two important properties are as an electrical conductor (silver does not spark when a current is applied) and as an antimicrobial agent. So silver is used in cell phones, iPods, PDAs, flat-screen

TVs, and so on. In each use, only a small amount of silver is used, meaning both that price is relatively unimportant to demand (price inelastic), but equally important that it is not being recycled. It is being consumed in a way that silver was not when its main use was for photography. As an antibacterial agent, silver is used for water purification, creams for treatment of wounds, in flooring for the food industry, in soaps, and even in toothbrushes. We will likely continue to see silver used in a wide range of health and medical items. Again, most of this is not recycled, so it does not come back to the market.

There is also a wide range of new applications, so much that each year the Silver Institute puts out a publication on new uses of silver. It is used in clothing (as a catalyst for the production of ethylene glycol, a component of polyesters, and in other uses), in solar panels, in batteries, and in biocides. It is the least expensive of reliable components for switches and circuit breakers and is replacing lead-based solders (which are now banned in Europe).

Increasingly, silver has "green" uses replacing lead and other toxic metals. And researchers are continuing to find new uses for silver. Mitsui is working on a silver catalytic converter, initially for diesel farm equipment. But if the silver-based catalytic converter works, then no doubt work will be undertaken on adapting for gasoline-powered vehicles. The incentive is there, given the prices of platinum and palladium (though we like those metals, too). It is worth noting that though some of silver end-products, such as iPods and TVs, are discretionary, much of its industrial use is not. In fact, in 2008, despite the global economic crisis, industrial silver demand dropped just 1.4 percent.

It should be noted that since most silver is produced as a by-product from base metal mines, when the economy slows, base metal production is curtailed, and, consequently, less silver is produced.

However, perhaps the biggest risk facing silver would be a continued economic slump leading to reduced consumer consumption, given over half of silver used today is in industrial applications, many aimed at the consumer market. That's the assessment of Robert Quartermain, a geologist who in his 25 years at the helm built Silver Standard into the billion-dollar-plus dominant player it is today (he recently left the company) and is past president of the Silver Institute. Offsetting that, of course, is the increasing number of new applications, including "green" technologies, that would be more recession-resilient, and, increasingly, many uses of silver have no substitute. Moreover, unlike gold, silver stockpiles are small, so any increased consumption could be reflected in price, Quartermain notes. And there are the other factors we discuss in this chapter.

Silver also is used in jewelry, as always as a less-expensive alternative for gold; it is popular with teenagers and hippies for this reason. But increasingly, given the high price of gold, it is being used in high-end designer jewelry.

Investment Interest in Silver

Silver also has long attracted investors, as "poor man's gold." It is more highly prized as an investment in certain countries, including the United States, whereas in others hardly at all. Though silver has a long history of use in coins—the Romans minted silver coins as early as 269 B.C.—over time it tended to be used for lower-value coins while gold was used for higher-value coins. More recently, as the price of silver appreciated and more importantly, the value of all currencies declined in purchasing power, the value of silver in coins started to move above the face value of the coin. One by one, countries reduced the amount of silver in coins—the United States went from 90 percent silver to 40 percent silver—and eventually stopped using it altogether. The last coin containing silver minted in the United States was the Eisenhower dollar of 1976, containing 40 percent silver. Today, the silver in that dollar is worth well over $6. The 1964 Kennedy half dollar has a silver value over $7, while the last dime containing any silver, minted in 1964, today is worth almost $1.50, just for its silver content. Today, only Mexico still uses silver in its circulating coinage.

Many developing countries used to be on a silver standard, including China. Quartermain thinks this could be important. As the economy grows, "those in the lower income brackets might look to silver as a form of investment," which, he points out, is what we see in parts of India.

It can be bought in physical form for small amounts of money (either through shiny new one-ounce coins like the Maple Leaf or Eagle, or bags of what is known as "junk" silver). "Junk" silver is old U.S. 90 percent silver coin, minted prior to 1965, and frequently selling barely above melt value. (A few silver dimes were minted in 1965, but by mistake, and today they command significant numismatic premiums.) The standard "unit" for junk is a bag with a face value of $1,000; each bag contain 715 ounces of silver. The premium over spot, that is, the premium over the value of the silver in the bag, is currently as low as $1. So "junk" bags are an excellent, low-cost way of investing in silver. There is also now a silver exchange-traded fund (ETF) (iShare Silver Trust, symbol SLV on the New York Stock Exchange), with each share trading at the price of one ounce of silver).

As a precious metal, silver tends to move broadly in line with gold, but in a strong market, frequently outperforms it. It is a very small physical market, though the futures are very active and often influence the physical price. Like gold, silver tends to do well when the dollar is weak, but perhaps more than gold, silver performs well in inflationary periods. For purchases of physical silver, I recommend two dealers in particular, Asset Strategies and Liberty Coins, whose contact details can be found in the back of this book. As always, for high-end numismatics, whether silver or gold, an area where knowledge and integrity is essential, I recommend Van Simmons, at David Hall Coins.

Many countries, however, do not regard silver as money for investment purposes and treat it differently than gold, whose monetary value is implicitly recognized. In Switzerland, for example, gold is bought at bullion prices, whereas buyers of silver must pay the "Value Added Tax" on top, putting silver at a distinct disadvantage. The Silver Institute is looking into lobbying governments to change such discriminatory laws, following the great success the World Gold Council has achieved in the last two decades in liberalizing global gold markets.

Record prices for gold, however, may lead some investors to switch to silver. Certainly in India, which has a long history of silver demand, and is a large producer of the metal, high gold prices could encourage more buyers to turn to silver. In rural parts of the country, silver remains far more popular than gold.

Though there has been an increase in investor interest in silver in recent years—and the wide price differential could see some switching—it is probably true to say that investment demand for silver will never be as large a component of the silver market as it is for gold, nor would jewelry. But the growing industrial uses and demand for silver are unlikely to be matched by gold, whose industrial demand tend to be for highly specialized niche uses.

Overall, for the past decade, aggregate silver demand has increased about 1 percent a year. That may not sound like a lot until one considers that what was its primary demand component, photography, has declined by 40 percent. This has been offset by a 36 percent increase in industrial demand, as well as an increase in investor demand. The decline in photography use is slowing and will soon stabilize, whereas the increase from industrial users and investors is likely to continue. Mine supply can't keep up with ongoing demand.

Silver Supply: Most Comes from Mines

The supply picture for silver also has distinct features, differences from that for gold. Most important, most silver is consumed and not sitting in vaults available to come back to the market. Some 77 percent of silver supply comes from mine production, and another 20 percent from scrap, both far more than for gold, with only 3 percent from government stockpile sales. (See Figure 13.2.)

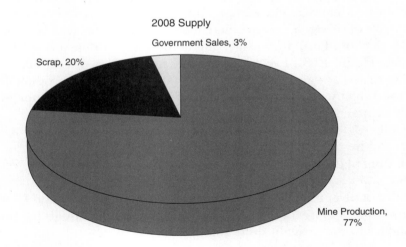

2008 Supply

Government Sales, 3%

Scrap, 20%

Mine Production, 77%

☐ Silver mine production is expected to fall slightly in 2009, with output expected to fall from all by-product sectors except gold

Figure 13.2   Most Supply Comes from Mines
Source: GFMS.

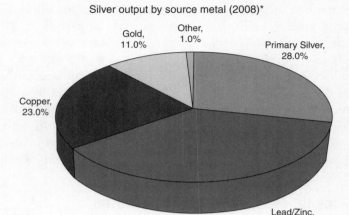

Silver output by source metal (2008)*

Gold, 11.0%

Other, 1.0%

Primary Silver, 28.0%

Copper, 23.0%

Lead/Zinc, 37.0%

☐ 70% of mined silver is produced as a by-product = significant growth potential in the silver stream space

Figure 13.3   Most Silver Comes from Other Mines
Source: GFMS, Silver Institute.

There is also a significant difference between the two as regards mine productions. There are relatively few primarily silver mines, in a couple of very well-known belts (in the Sierras, from Nevada, through Mexico and Peru, into Chile; and across eastern Russia and China). (See Figure 13.3.) Even for primarily silver mines, there is usually a significant amount of by-product metals. Most silver is produced as a by-product itself, either of gold or of base metals (usually zinc, lead, or copper).

Partly because of the strong demand for base metals in recent years, the production of silver has increased (as a by-product of the mining of these other metals) to a record 681 million ounces (2008). But silver is not nearly as widely distributed as is gold. Virtually one-third of silver mined comes from just two countries, Peru and Mexico; and over 50 percent from the top four producers, though the mines themselves are usually quite small.

Indeed, 70 percent of mined silver is produced as a by-product; one-third is from lead mines, one-quarter copper mines, and 10 percent gold mines. So even the "purest" silver mining companies, such as Pan American Silver and Coeur D'Alene, generate less than four-fifths of their revenue from silver, while for others, such as Silvercorp and Hecla, it is less than half.

Demand Exceeds Supply: Whence Comes the Rest?

New mine production typically accounts for only 75 percent of the fabrication demand. The gap is met by scrap and sales from stockpiles. It is unlikely in future years that new supply will keep up with demand, meaning there will be an ongoing supply-demand gap to be met from other sources, or by higher prices.

Scrap is an important ongoing component of the silver supply situation, but as we've seen, the amount of silver returned to the market as scrap is actually declining, despite higher prices and a greater sensitivity to recycling. This is largely the result of a decline in use by easily recycled photography, and a growing use in small amounts in electronic and high-tech devices. Most recycled silver is not discretionary, in the sense that it is ongoing recycling from industrial usage rather than consumer recycling prompted by price. Most still comes from photography, where about half the silver used is recycled.

A lot of old silver was turned in during the late 1970s, when the price of silver shot up in a relatively short period from $3 to $50 an ounce, providing a significant incentive to consumers to look for old pieces of silver. Scrap volumes jumped from 130 million ounces in 1979 to 165 million in 1980, and then fell back to 125 million in 1981. Clearly, the rapid increase in price provided an incentive to search attics for old pieces of silver. Sadly, to my mind, this included a lot of antique silver cutlery, tea sets and so on, which was melted down and gone forever.

From our perspective here, however, it meant that most silver likely to be melted down has already been done so. There is little incentive to search the attic with silver at $18 if one didn't at $50 three decades ago. Moreover, given the low unit price of silver, the fabrication cost in silver jewelry and cutlery is high relative to the silver value. Turning them into scrap may not generate much in the way of proceeds for the consumer. Of course it varies greatly, but the typical selling price of a piece of silver jewelry may be three to five times the silver value, compared with 10 times for gold jewelry (we are not discussing high-end designer jewelry, clearly).

So while scrap is likely to remain a significant component of overall silver supply, it is also likely to remain relatively stable and unlikely to grow much in the long-term or spike in the short.

Stockpiles Depleted

Again, unlike gold, only a few countries maintain large silver stockpiles, primarily Russia, China, India, and Mexico. These stockpiles have been consistently run down over the years—the United States used to have significant stockpiles—and are unlikely to be rebuilt. Unlike gold, there is no column titled "central banks" listed under "silver demand" in the analyst reports. For the last two decades, in fact, demand has exceeded supply each year, but until recently, the gap was met easily by sales from stockpiles (government and warehouse supplies). But those stockpiles have declined precipitously, and investors are no longer offloading silver. (See Figure 13.4.)

In the last few years, the gap has been smaller than earlier in the decade due to the increase in silver production, but each year total demand exceeds mine production. And in these same years, the amount of scrap coming on to the market has slowly declined. Thus,

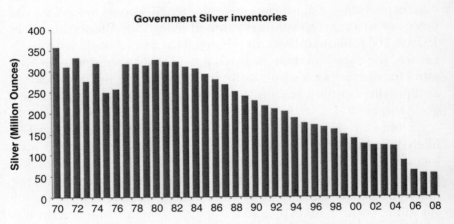

- Government inventories declining since 1980 to make up for supply deficits

Figure 13.4 Governments Have Little Left
Source: GFMS.

with the ongoing supply-demand gap, absent large stockpile sales, the price has been appreciating and is very much likely to continue to do so in the future. The difficulty is that, from time to time, a large new source of silver comes along, perhaps from a new copper or zinc mine, unrelated to the price of silver. But over time, the picture is clear: steady mine supply, slowly declining scrap, increasing industrial and investor demand, resulting in a supply gap while stockpile sales to meet the gap are declining.

There has also been relatively little silver hedging from companies, and, significantly, its character has changed in recent years. Certainly a silver company putting into production a new silver mine would usually be required by the lending banks to sell forward some of its silver production. But a company putting into production a large copper mine may not care too much about its expected silver by-product, but equally selling it forward for $20 million or so would not go a long way towards the $1 billion capital cost of the mine. The silver markets were never as deep as the gold markets for hedging.

A new form of hedging for companies, however, is very attractive both for the companies and for investors on the other side. This is the so-called "silver stream," whereby a zinc company, for example, will sell its future silver production for a fixed price, but that silver is not borrowed elsewhere and dumped on the market (as it all-too-often was with forward gold sales). A silver-stream company will buy that silver production, which will then be sold onto the market each year as it's produced. We'll discuss silver stream companies as investments later in this chapter, but for now the beneficial impact on the overall silver market compared with traditional hedging is our concern. The Silver Institute is an excellent source for data on the silver industry (www.silverinstitute.com).

Investing in Silver

Some of the attributes of silver in mine production and hedging, for example, point up some of the difficulties and opportunities for investors. Just as there are relatively few pure silver mines, so too are there few pure silver companies. Many of the world's largest producers of silver are mining companies whose primary business is mining copper or zinc or other metals. For these, silver may be a small component of overall revenues and certainly do not represent good

Table 13.1   Few Pure Silver Miners

TOP 20 Silver Producing Companies in 2008 (*millions of ounces*)

Company	Country	Output
1. BHP Billiton	Australia	42.3
2. KGHM Polska Miedz	Poland	38.4
3. Fresnillo Plc	Mexico	34.8
4. Cia. Minera Volcan	Peru	23.0
5. Pan American Silver	Canada	18.7
6. Cia. de Minas Buenaventura	Peru	17.5
7. Polymetal	Russia	17.2
8. Hochschild Mining	Peru	16.9
9. Kazakhmys	Kazakhstan	15.6
10. Southern Copper Corp.	USA	12.3
11. Coeur d'Alene Mines	USA	12.0
12. Teck Resources	Canada	11.6
13. Industrias Penoles	Mexico	11.2
14. OZ Minerals	Australia	10.4
15. Kinross Gold	Canada	10.1
16. Yamana Gold	Canada	9.8
17. Goldcorp	Canada	9.6
18. Codelco	Chile	9.3
19. Xstrata Zinc	Switzerland	9.0
20. Hecla Mining	USA	8.7

Source: Silver Institute.

silver investors. The largest producer of silver is BHP, yet silver doesn't even rank in their top 10 products. (See Table 13.1.) Even the silver companies, as we have seen, generate much of their revenue from other metals, and this can have a significant effect on the companies' profitability. Pan American Silver, for example, suffered considerably in the late 1990s from the low price of zinc, which eventually caused it to close one of its main mines. The prices of the by-products can make or break a mine's profitability.

Moreover, silver being a much smaller market than gold, our investment choices are more limited. Whereas there are dozens of significant gold producers and thousands of explorers, there are only a handful of producers or explorers that could be seen as silver investments. We've noted that the main silver miners generated at most 78 percent of their revenues from silver and in some notable cases less than 50 percent. New producer Silver Standard has more silver resources in the ground than any other pure silver company; nonetheless, silver accounts for only two-thirds of its resource value.

Silver Mining Companies

Such companies, nonetheless, do tend to respond very generously to higher silver prices, sometimes more than they should based purely on the changes in company revenues or value, simply because there are so few options available to silver investors. Of the silver producers, however, Pan American (PAAS, Nasdaq), which is the fifth-largest silver producer in the world, is our preferred pure play. Silver is volatile, though, and swings of 25 or 30 percent in the share price are quite common. Among the major silver companies, my next favorite would be Silver Standard (SSRI, Nasdaq), which put its first mine into production at the end of 2009 but has very significant silver resources.

Another miner I favor is Fortuna Silver (FVI, Toronto), a smaller but growing silver producer with one producing mine in Peru and a second in Mexico under construction. The company has a very strong balance sheet and top management.

In addition to the producers, there are of course numerous companies exploring for silver, some of whom have actually found it! But again, given the size of the market and the paucity of pure silver deposits, there are few options available to investors. The same issue affects the exploration companies as well. One of my favorites juniors is Esperanza Silver (EPZ, Toronto). As always, that circumstances and prices may be different when you read this book. I can, however, say that at current prices think it's a great investment. Esperanza Silver was looking for silver deposits and discovered the San Luis deposit in Peru; though it has a lot of silver, after full exploration it appears that the gold value is more than twice that of the silver. A second discovery in Mexico similarly has more gold than silver. Again, however, despite this, an exploration company like Esperanza Silver will respond to changes in the silver price.

A good source for investment information and analysis on silver is David Morgan, who can be found at www.silver-investor.com.

There are two other ways the equity investor can invest in silver. There is a silver ETF (SLV, New York), which, like the gold ETFs, provides a direct play in the price of silver. There is no operational leverage or exploration upside, but equally no mining risk; the share price directly reflects the price of silver. Unlike for the gold ETFs, the silver holdings of the silver ETF do not fluctuate much and barely budged when the price of silver collapsed in the second half of 2008, falling by more than 50 percent to under $10 an ounce from over $20. I suspect that a similar decline in the price of gold, to under $500, would see investor selling off the gold ETFs. The steady growth in holdings of the silver ETF is such that it now holds nearly 300 million ounces; annual demand is equivalent to about one-fifth of annual mine output, double stockpiles sales, and not much less than photography demand.

Moreover, silver is extremely undervalued relative to gold right now. I have expressed my caution generally with ratios of one asset to another. Often there is very little logical connection. There is no immutable law that gold should sell for between 10 and 20 times the price of oil (though that even that uncertain range is rather broad) any more than that palladium should sell at seven times the price of pork bellies. There are certain connections between various commodities—hogs eat corn, gas is substituted for oil, and so on—but many more individual factors.

Nonetheless, there are some logical connections between the gold and silver market. When gold becomes expensive relative to its historical pattern with silver, then some buying turns from gold to silver (as we suggested above with regard to Indian jewelry buying), and certainly investors frequently look at the ratio to decide whether to overweight one or the other. In the last decade, the ratio has ranged from 50 times (in 2006 and early 2008) to 80 times (in 2003). In the time since the two metals were freed from government price controls in the 1960s, the range has been even wider, a high of 16:1 to a low of 100:1. That's quite a range on which to base an investment decision! Today, at approximately 70 times, silver can be said to be undervalued relative to gold.

Attractive Low-Risk Investment

A relatively new and very attractive company is one that buys the silver production ("silver stream") from other mining companies. The silver stream company buys future silver production usually for a fixed up-front price, and a small ongoing per-ounce price, that, depending on the deal, may be subject to adjustment if the price of silver goes up or down significantly. The arrangement is attractive for all parties. The miner receives a fixed price, or at least a minimum price, and generates cash up front for a metal that is not its main product. This is less expensive than borrowing funds and less dilutive than issuing new equity. It also avoids the restrictions that banks would likely demand for product financing. The silver stream company pays a fixed price for silver into the future, gaining the upside for itself. And the investor has a pure silver play with upside. It is also a positive for the silver market in that, unlike typical forward sales, the silver is not borrowed and dumped onto the market.

It is not without risks, of course. Even if the silver stream company is not doing the mining, like the royalty company, it would suffer in lost revenue from mishaps at the companies from which it acquired the silver stream. Contracts normally have in place a minimum silver production each year, which, in the event of a shortfall, is paid in cash. But of course, if metals prices decline or for any other reason, the mine closes, there may not be any cash to distribute.

Nonetheless, the benefits are significant. Unlike a mining company, the silver stream company has an essentially fixed cost and has all the upside to the silver price, and no ongoing capital costs, closure costs, or political and environmental issues. Unlike an ETF, while retaining full upside to the silver price, it has production and exploration upside, as well as operational leverage from additional acquisitions. In the case of the leading silver stream company, Silver Wheaton (SLW, NY), its contracts typically are negotiated so that it does not pay more than the spot price should the price of silver drop. Its contracts also provide for minimum production each year. Silver Wheaton generates 94 percent of its revenue from silver (with most of the rest from interest income), making it the purest silver company around.

We can look at one of Silver Wheaton's largest transactions in detail to see how it works. In a deal with Barrick Gold, SLW agreed to pay $625 million over three years. In return, it obtained all of the silver production from three of Barrick's existing mines for the next four years. It received one-quarter of the silver production from a large new mine, Pascua-Lama, for the life of the mine. Barrick guaranteed that Pascua-Lama would be up to at least 75 percent of design capacity by the end of 2015 or it would be required to top up with silver production from three other mines. Wheaton had no capital or exploration expenditure obligations, nothing beyond the up-front payments (in four installments) and the ongoing per-ounce payment. That per-ounce payment is the lower of $3.90 or spot. So Wheaton is protected in the event of a precipitous drop in the price of silver, but keeps all the upside in the silver price. In this single transaction, Silver Wheaton obtained at least part of the silver production from three of the top five silver mines in the world.

Again, though I don't know what the price of Silver Wheaton will be when you read this book, I can be fairly confident that if, at that time, you want to invest in a silver company, Silver Wheaton will likely be as good as any and better than most.

In sum, the outlook for the silver price is very positive, and while silver is likely to follow gold, it has the potential for relatively short spurts that will see it move much faster than gold, providing opportunities for the investor. Similarly, though there are far few silver companies from which investors can choose, this paucity of options again means greater leverage when silver is in vogue. Though gold has a greater insurance component and a better profile in whatever economic scenario the world may throw at us in the years ahead, silver has the potential for much greater profits.

Platinum and Platinum Group Metals

P latinum has a foot in the camp of each different metal type: It is a precious metal, industrial metal, and strategic metal. On the face of it, that should make it perhaps one of the most attractive. Unfortunately, there are attributes of both supply and demand that make it sometimes difficult to analyze and very volatile, making it neither the most attractive precious metal, nor the most attractive industrial, nor yet the best strategic metal. It is a small market—just 6 million ounces traded last year—and in a delicate supply-demand balance. Indeed, these factors help account for the extreme volatility in price; from May 2008 to the end of the year, platinum fell from over $2,000 an ounce to less than $800. Nonetheless, platinum is attractive and we think particularly attractive at this time.

Precious as Well as Industrial

Platinum is not as widely recognized as a precious metal, nor has it been for as long. Indeed, the Spanish who found the metal in the rivers of Ecuador in the sixteenth century called it "platina" or "little silver" and threw it back in the rivers thinking it was silver that had not yet ripened. It later became popular, and during much of the nineteenth century it was used for most fashionable jewelry. Many of the famous Crown Jewels from Britain's Empire were mounted in platinum, including the Hope Diamond and Star of Africa. Today, platinum is particularly popular for jewelry in Asia. Japan was a large

Table 14.1 China a Growing Jewelry Market

	Platinum Demand Jewellery '000 oz					
	Gross[1]		Recycling[2]		Net[3]	
	2007	2008	2007	2008	2007	2008
Europe	200	200	0	(5)	200	195
Japan	540	535	(360)	(480)	180	55
North America	225	200	(5)	(5)	220	195
China	1,070	1,060	(290)	(210)	780	850
Rest of the World	75	70	0	0	75	70
Total	**2,110**	**2,065**	**(655)**	**(700)**	**1,455**	**1,365**

JM⊗

Notes:
[1] Gross demand is equivalent to the sum of platinum jewelry manufacturing volumes and changes in unfabricated metal stocks within the industry.
[2] Recycling represents the amount of old stock and old jewelry recycled whether the metal is re-used within the jewelry industry or sold back to the market.
[3] Net demand (our headline figure) is the sum of these figures and therefore represents the industry net requirement for new metal.
Source: Johnson Matthey. Platinum: Interim Review 2009.

consumer until recession cut into sales. But today, the heavyweight is China, where the Platinum Guild, the industry association, has made a concerted effort to promote the metal. (See Table 14.1.) This push has been extremely successful; to date it has focused on the wealthiest in only a few main cities, but will expand both geographically as well as into the middle class. With the beachhead established, platinum demand could grow considerably in years to come.

However, its uses as a modern industrial metal are key to platinum, and prime among these is its use in auto catalytic converters, which uses about 60 percent of all platinum produced. It is thus extremely exposed to the auto market, and the platinum price has tracked global auto sales very closely. (See Figure 14.1.) Though the U.S. and Western auto markets may recover, it is to the East that we look for the truly spectacular long-term growth. We've already discussed that China last year sold more cars than the United States. Regardless of any U.S. recovery, China is expected to sell as many as 15 million cars this year, up from 13.6 million in 2009, and that alone will require more platinum. Within 20 years, it is estimated, some 1.3 billion autos will be sold worldwide, up 40 percent from today.

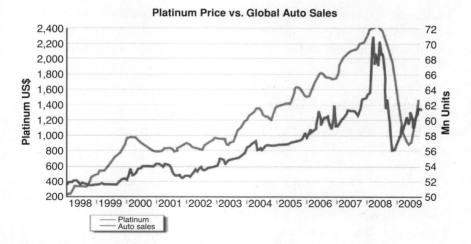

Figure 14.1   Platinum Tracks Global Auto Sales

Source: Johnson Matthey. Platinum: Interim Review 2009; Data taken from J.D.
Power & Associates.

The platinum demand for these catalytic converters would rise to
around 5.8 million ounces per year, just shy of the metal's entire annual production. Says London metals analyst David Hargreaves, "The
potential for demand escalation is scary . . . little short of daunting."
Of course, there is some substitution, but imperfect. Palladium works
well and is only one-quarter the price, but more is required for the
same efficiency. Besides, most palladium comes from the same unstable regions, often the same mines, as platinum, so it would not be
the cure to a sudden supply shortage. Other platinum group metals
(PGMs), such as rhodium, can also be used, but they are even rarer
and far more expensive than platinum.

We discussed work being undertaken on using silver, but that is at
an early stage. Nickel was tried, successfully, but the additional weight
for it to work would negate all benefits from the converter. Over time,
no doubt, other ways of reducing the carbon emissions will be found,
but a widespread substitute for platinum is a long way off. Hybrids
do not require catalytic converters but they do use platinum to make
both the batteries and fuel cells so that, ironically, more platinum
is used in the production of a hybrid than in a car with a catalytic
converter. Perhaps more important is the trend toward smaller cars
that still require a catalytic converter, but smaller ones using less

platinum. It is perhaps for its critical importance to the auto industry as well as its numerous high-tech uses—it was essential to the space shuttle program—that the U.S. government has classified platinum as "strategic."

Growing "Green" Uses

Platinum has a growing list of other industrial uses derived from its properties as a strong catalytic agent: its high corrosion resistance, excellence as a conductor, and high melting point (3,216 degrees Fahrenheit). These properties make it essential in many modern productions, including in LCDs, lasers, video equipment, and many medical devices, such as pacemakers. Platinum is used to produce high-octane gasoline for aircraft as well as automobiles. According to Michael Checkan of Asset Strategies International, one in five of all the products purchased by modern consumers either contains platinum or employs the metal in its production process. Fuel cell technology could become one of the largest areas of industrial demand. Indeed, many of platinum's new uses make it a very "green" metal.

In addition to its auto and other industrial demand, and growing demand for jewelry, is the relatively new demand for platinum as an investment. Though still a small market, and a smaller factor for platinum than for either silver or gold, it is gaining attention, and I would expect demand to grow significantly with the introduction of two PGM funds in the United States, one each in fact for platinum and palladium, following small funds in London and Zurich. The U.S. funds started trading in January 2010, and each held 100,000 ounces of metal by the end of its first month trading. In a 6-million-ounce market, that alone is enough to turn a precarious surplus into a deficit. I'll discuss how to invest in platinum later.

Expensive to Mine and Falling Supply

Platinum is scarce and expensive to mine. It takes 10 tons of ore to produce a single ounce of platinum. Unlike gold or even silver, platinum production is highly concentrated, with about 80 percent of the world's reserves in South Africa's Bushveld, and 70 percent in just the western Bush (as it is commonly called). Indeed, virtually all of the world's known platinum is in South Africa, Russia, and Zimbabwe, with small additional amounts in Australia and Canada. Much the same also holds for palladium, though there is also a significant palladium mine in Montana, except that the roles of South Africa and Russia are reversed, with Russia being the dominant palladium producer. To compound the problem, nearly all of the world's platinum is produced by three South African companies.

These large South African mines are getting deeper and more expensive. In addition, the country has growing problems: reliability of power supply (and platinum mining is very power-intensive), growing wage demands from a labor-intensive industry, increased calls for greater black or state ownership, and general political concerns. Together, these cause delays in committing to the vast amounts of capital required to expand or initiate new projects. In addition, the South African platinum industry, because of its near-monopoly position and easy profits in the past, has never been a very efficient industry, and one with a terrible safety record. Improving efficiency and safety will initially make costs even higher. Yet today, half of the industry is operating mines at negative cash flows. (See Figure 14.2.)

At the beginning of 2010, 10 of 19 producing mines had costs above the spot price of platinum. In fact, the average breakeven price across the industry was just a few dollars shy of $1,500, while platinum was trading at $1,543, having moved up from the $1,200 level. So platinum mining is marginal for most miners at best, despite

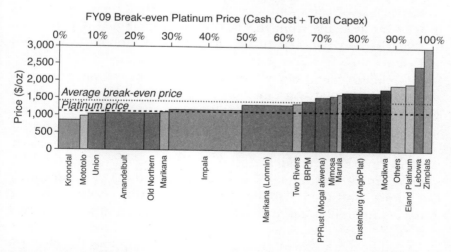

Figure 14.2 Most Mines Are Losing Money

Source: Platinum Group Metals; Data taken from JPMorgan.

the higher prices. This suggests that mines may start to close or the price will move up. The best source of information on supply and demand is from Johnson Matthey, which publishes an annual review of the market, with a semiannual update.

In sum, nearly 90 percent of the world's supply comes from South Africa and Russia, and growth is problematic. Although global supply was down in 2008 over 2007, in the six years up to then, mined supply has generally been modestly up, a total of 15 percent for the entire period, or less than 2.5 percent a year. During the same period, auto catalyst use was up by almost 50 percent. New mine production is unlikely to grow much more than it has in the past, with the potential for further disruptions. There is a growing gap and scrap, mostly from old catalysts, has increased to meet the gap; it becomes more valuable as the price goes up. But so much of the growing demand from Asia is *new* demand; people are buying a first car so there is no scrap to sell.

How to Invest

Platinum is available in the form of bars and coins, though these attract higher premiums than gold and silver because of the manufacturing and distribution process. The same popular coins available in gold and silver, such as the U.S. Eagle, Canadian Maple Leaf, and Australian Koala, are available in platinum. In addition, before these countries started minting platinum coins, a legal tender coin, the Noble, was available from the Isle of Man, the small dependency in the Irish Sea between Britain and Ireland. For bars, available in 1 ounce and 10 ounce format, the reputable hallmarks include Johnson Matthey and Engelhard. If you buy physical platinum, you want to ensure that you buy it in a form that will not require reassaying when the time comes to sell.

The popular Perth Mint Certificate Program, whereby the investor buys a warehouse receipt for metal stored and insured in Western Australia, includes platinum as well as gold and silver. The modest extra costs are more than compensated for by the security, the storage, and the reliability. For the Perth Mint program as well as for platinum bars and coins, I recommend Asset Strategies International.

Another way to invest in the metal itself is through exchange-traded funds (ETFs), now readily available to investors in the United

States, one each in fact for platinum (PPLT, New York) and palladium (PALL, New York). The price of the funds follows the price of the underlying metal and makes investing in these rather exotic metals easy.

Some investors prefer to look at the mining shares for leverage. The share prices of the big South African producers are often high, with the shares overvalued, partly because of the scarcity. Personally, I am a little skittish paying up for companies in an inefficient, often loss-making industry, located in a country with potentially significant problems looming. Nor am I keen on the Russian producers or on Stillwater, which has had its own mining issues in the past. You can gain exposure by buying Franco-Nevada (FNV, Toronto), my favorite royalty company, which holds a royalty on Stillwater's mine in Montana.

Another option is to buy carefully selected promising juniors that might become takeover targets. With the major mines going deeper and mining becoming increasingly expensive, I expect the big boys will start to acquire junior producers and development projects. Though small, they can reduce overall costs while adding incremental ounces. As I write, one clear candidate is Platinum Group Metals (PLG, New York).

Platinum's Outlook

Certainly, platinum looks attractive with enormous potential. Notwithstanding the problem of few producers and few major consumers, the demand for platinum is likely to increase in coming years, with the growth of the auto market in China and with growing investor interest. At the same time, the major mines are unable to increase their production significantly, with the potential for supply disruptions, whether from strike action or power outages, remaining very real. That is an explosive mix both in the near term and over the longer term.

Gold, silver, and platinum react to the same broad economic trends, including a weaker dollar and higher inflation. Gold and silver react more positively to monetary instability, while silver and platinum react more to economic growth. Right now, platinum, despite doubling in price during 2009, remains inexpensive, on its own fundamentals and in relation to gold. Platinum tends to sell at a higher price than gold because of its scarcity; it peaked in 2001 at 2.43 times. At the beginning of 2010, platinum was selling for 1.4 times the gold price; that's 23 percent below the 10-year average. At minimum, I expect it to move back to that average, but in a strong market, or if there are supply disruptions, it can move sharply higher.

Platinum tends to outperform in a strong market. I'm not betting on an economic rebound in the United States to make this investment work. The demand dynamics from China and other newly developing countries as well as the tight supply situation suggests higher prices.

CHAPTER 15

The Base Metals: Copper

Jimmy Wu in Shanghai proudly drives around town in his new automobile, the first in his family. In Phnom Penh, Kesor Sambath throws some fish into her new copper pot as she heats a stew. In Chiangrai, Northern Thailand, Parnpree Leekprai settles into a couch to watch his favorite TV program, while Roberta Gomide calls her friend in Brasilia on her cell phone. All are doing everyday things we do many times every day in the developed world, without giving it a second thought. But more and more people in the developing world are wanting and acquiring those same basic comforts. And each requires metal, lots of it.

Meanwhile, in the United States, high prices have led to the hoarding of copper pennies since the copper content is worth more than one cent. In fact, the humble copper penny is no longer made of copper but rather is a zinc token coated with layer copper. Now plans are afoot to remove nickel altogether from the 5-cent coin, which already contains more copper than it does nickel. And of course it's been over 30 years since any coin contained silver. It also led to a rash of thefts of metal from unusual places, including stealing of the brass bolts on fire hydrants, which led to tragic results in at least one instance in California when firefighters arrived quickly but found four hydrants not working.

The World of Metals

The story for the base metals is basically the same as that which I have discussed many times: growing demand from emerging economies, and particularly from China, which is at the economic take-off point when per-capita demand increases dramatically; a shortage of large viable deposits; and the potential for supply disruptions, all pointing to higher prices for years to come.

Uses for base metals are not as specialized as for platinum group metals or the rare earths, for example, and in some uses there is some substitution. But there is no substitute for metal. Virtually everything we use in our daily lives requires some metal. (I used to give talks at schools and asked the eager, impressionable—and brainwashed—environmentalists to take out a pen and paper, make a phone call, and listen to a song on their iPod . . . and then tell me how much they were willing to give up to stop mining and logging. For most, it was a sharp jolt to the total disconnect in their thinking.)

Each metal has its own attributes, its own uses, and its own supply and demand characteristics. Reams can be written, and are, each month of the near-term outlook for this or that metal. But the fundamental, long-term situation is much the same: more demand, inadequate supply, and higher prices. The same applies to investing in these metals: in some, there are numerous companies, in others, a few dominate; for some metals, essentially all is produced as a by-product, while there are near pure plays in others.

Base metals are typically found in mixed deposits, with one or several by-products that can be significant. This is unlike, say, gold or uranium—or oil for that matter—where there are many more or less pure deposits. Sometimes one metal is overwhelmingly dominant while other deposits are polymetallic. This has important implications for a company's decision whether to go ahead with a particular deposit, as well as the profitability of the deposit year by year. It also has clear implications for investors wanting to invest in one or other metal, rather than the entire complex.

Base metal mines also tend to be very large and long-life, meaning that much of the supply comes from old mines that can be expensive and subject to disruptions. This is unlike, again, gold, where a lot of production comes from relatively small and short-lived mines that can nonetheless be profitable. Typically, the capital costs of a copper mine are significantly more than that for a gold mine, other than the giant ones, and so they tend to take longer to put into production.

Even more so than with many other resources, base metal prices are extremely volatile, not only in the long term because of the long cycles we have discussed. Given the large scale of most projects, and given the significant amounts of metals often produced as by-products, supply of one metal does not always respond to changes in demand very quickly. There can also be a significant difference in a particular metal produced year by year, sometimes as a result of mine sequencing which sees ore with different compositions mined. Despite an absolutely static amount of copper produced by Freeport-McMoRan in 2008 and 2009, for example (4.1 billion pounds), the volume of molybdenum plunged from 71 million pounds to 58 million pounds. There can also be disruptions in supply, more often than in many other resources, because so many mines are old.

Some of this volatility is mitigated by the traditional method of sales that involves contract pricing, set each year in a series of negotiations between the largest producers and consumers. Once a price is set, other producers tend to follow. Although it varies for each resource, much is sold at this contract price, while marginal volumes are sold on the spot markets. This arrangement has benefits for both producers and consumers, who on the one hand want to ensure their mine output is sold and a fixed price helps mining operations plan for the ensuing period, while consumers are concerned with ensuring their needs are met. For both, the system prevents huge spikes or wide swings in prices, while marginal supply is always available, for a price, on the spot market.

More and more, however, consumers—particularly China—are feeling that the contract pricing system puts them at a disadvantage to the handful of big suppliers, while an increasing number of medium-sized producers are willing to undercut the large miners or sell at spot. Miners also feel disadvantaged when disruptions cause them to have to buy resources on the open market—usually at higher spot prices—in order to meet their commitments. Cameco had strife enough by the flooding of its huge Cigar Lake uranium mine as it was being built, but for the world's largest uranium producer to have to buy uranium on the spot market at record high prices caused by its very own supply problems must have been galling. The whole system is unraveling for many metals though it remains for others, such as platinum and uranium.

Dr. Copper Essential to Economic Growth

Copper is the central base metal—indeed in many ways, the central resource. It lays claim to being the first metal mined and fashioned by man, as far back as 13,000 B.C. It is used more widely than any other metal in a range of basic products, from car parts to phone lines, from refrigerators to pipes. It is crucial to both the housing and automobile industry, and thus central to the overall economy. (See Figure 15.1.) The chart shows consumption in the United States. Worldwide, a higher percentage is used in housing and construction, including infrastructure, and less for electrical and transportation equipment. No wonder it is dubbed "the metal with the PhD in economics"; the price of copper tells us a lot about the state of the economy.

Copper prices can be very volatile, since the metal is so linked to economic health. After prices plunged 70 percent in the last six months of 2008, they then jumped 160 percent in 2009. Though these were extraordinary moves up and down in such a short period, nonetheless copper prices are traditionally volatile.

Though the United States and Europe still account for about 70 percent of world demand, China is now the world's largest single buyer, and has been since 2003; it is from China where all the recent growth in demand has emanated. China, more than the United States, sets the price for copper. So although the economic weakness in the United States and Europe has cut into demand from those

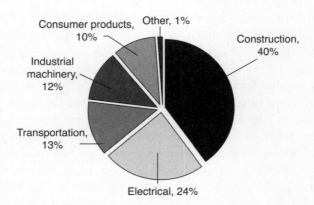

Figure 15.1   Copper: Broad Uses in Basic Economy
Source: Arizona Mining Association.

areas, increased demand from China and India has more than offset that decline.

The credit crisis of late 2008 caused a decline in demand for copper of 4 percent, the result of the collapse in the housing and auto industries, particularly in the United States. When copper prices collapsed in 2008, "Dr. Copper" foresaw the economic collapse ahead. There have been declines of such magnitude only six times since 1900, so it was not surprising that demand recovered the following year. There is little substitution for copper in most uses and demand tends to be resilient. With the rapid growth from China and global infrastructure projects, demand should continue to grow, offsetting any weakness in the developed countries' basic demand. At the same time, any recovery, however modest, in housing and automobile manufacturing in Europe and the United States, will be a positive given the low levels from which that recovery would start.

Less Scrap Increases Demand

Further, economic weakness in the developed world has reduced the volume of copper scrap, since in the current environment few old washing machines and refrigerators are being tossed out. Most of the demand from China and India, however, is "new" demand, meaning it is not replacing old equipment that is being scrapped. But given the shortage of scrap, China was forced to buy more copper concentrate than had been anticipated. In that environment, the price of copper futures in Shanghai shot up to a premium of almost 20 percent above London prices. There is always some premium to allow for transportation costs, usually just a few percent. Contrary to some analysts (and politicians), the high price in Shanghai was not (completely) the result of speculation but rather lack of scrap.

China's demand can be put in context by noting that in the month of March 2009, it imported 300,000 tonnes of copper, the equivalent of the total annual surplus forecast when the credit crisis hit. If we see periods of low prices, and therefore anticipated surpluses, again, they will likely rapidly evaporate by a surge in Chinese buying and stockpiling.

The optimum environment for copper is a period of overall global stability accompanied by rapid economic development in a large economy. We saw this prior to World War I with the rise of the United States and Germany, and again in the 1960s with the industrialization of Japan. China's growth will provide another example and will cause prices to rise, though economic stabilization in the United States and Europe would be icing on the cake.

China's Problem

Copper exhibits the basic characteristics of resources I have discussed, perhaps as much as any, and clearly illustrates China's problem as it develops in the years ahead. Given its wide use in basic products, essential to economic growth and development, it is not a surprise that copper demand in China and emerging economies has increased significantly in recent years.

Nor is it a surprise that the per capita use increases as economies grow. (We saw this in Chapter 2.) As per-capita income grows, so too does the per-capita use of copper, until the economy matures. Once an economy matures, however, there is noticeable decline in per-capita use of copper, unlike most other resources; the most developed also tend to be the most environmentally sensitive and service-oriented economies. This is clear in the recent case of Japan, for example. But the pattern during economic take-off is clear and has been remarkably similar whether for Germany, Japan, or Korea, at different periods in history. Already, the pattern for China, and behind it India, is similar. China's per-capita usage can more than double before it approaches the lower reaches of industrialized usage levels. (See Figure 15.2.)

In the post–World War II period, Japan consumed less than 1 kg (2.2 pounds) per person of copper. As late as 1960, it was less than 2 kg per person. As the economy industrialized, per-capita consumption increased steadily, climbing to a peak over 13 kg at the beginning of the 1990s. Then, as I described earlier, per-capita usage actually declined, partly because of Japan's economy but partly because it was a mature economy. Today, Japan, with a weak economy, consumes over 9 kg of copper per person. China consumes 4 kg. Behind China stands India, currently using less than half a kilogram per person per year, but slowly increasing. As I have mentioned, there's an awful lot of "capitas" in those countries, so the absolute increase in demand will be mind-boggling.

China is also a major copper producer, the fourth largest in the world. (Chile is far and away the leading country, producing as much as the next six together.) But many of its mines are small, and it does

Economic Development and Mineral Consumption

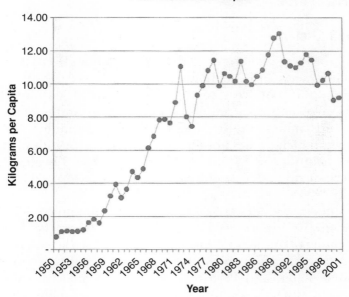

Copper Consumption per Capita
Post–World War II Japan

Figure 15.2   Copper Use Grows as Economy Develops
Source: USGS.

not have large reserves. Critically, because of China's top position as consumer, but despite being a major producer, it produces barely a fifth of its own annual requirements. It is a major buyer of world scrap as well, of course, of new mine output. This is important since it can't control the price, as it can to some extent where it has a large production internally. This is why the Oyu Togloi in Mongolia is so critical to China, and one reason that insightful entrepreneur Robert Friedland was so keen and determined to stick with the project.

So critical is copper to China's development that the country has a strategic stockpile. Just how much of the imports into China in 2009, after the credit crisis as prices collapsed, was buying by the State Reserve Bureau is not clear, given the lack of transparency in China's statistics. Certainly there was some, particularly in early 2009, but we don't know the extent to which imports ran ahead of end usage, and thus the sustainability of the improvement in 2009. Demand, and therefore prices, is likely to moderate but not collapse for the rest of 2010 and next year, absent a sharp contraction in China's economy. That is always possible, but beyond that, the long-term outlook is more certain in any event.

Big and Old

At the same time, mining is challenged. Although copper's total worldwide reserves of 1.8 billion tonnes are spread among 953 distinct deposits, both reserves and production are dominated by a few large deposits. Copper mines tend to be huge and have very long life. Five of 10 mines with the largest reserves (only nine of which are currently producing) are more than 50 years old, the oldest, Andina, starting operations in 1865. Similarly, five of the 10 biggest annual producers are over 50 years old, four of them over 100 years old! (See Figure 15.3.)

As mines age, grades mined tend to decrease and costs increase. Ore grades have experienced a dramatic slide, from 0.98 percent at the beginning of the century to 0.85 percent today. (See Figure 15.4.) As important has been the shift from stable countries like Chile, the United States, and Peru to less stable ones such as the DRC and Kazakhstan. This is a trend we have seen for many resources, including, for example, oil.

Problems, leading to supply interruptions, also occur more frequently. The average grade of copper mined is declining, partly

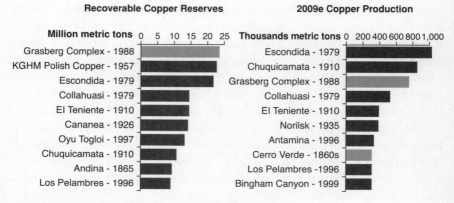

Figure 15.3   Most Copper Is in Old Mines
Source: Freeport-McMoRan, Data: Brook Hunt.

Supply: Growth Constraints Will Re-emerge

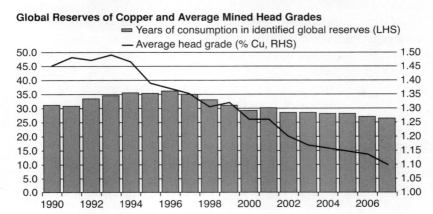

Global Reserves of Copper and Average Mined Head Grades

Figure 15.4   Declining Grades as Mines Age
Source: U.S. Bureau of Mines, U.S. Geologic Survey, CRU International.

because higher prices enable lower-grade deposits to be mined, but also because older mines are experiencing declining grades. Interruptions can be inherent in the age of the mine—rock falls become more frequent, for example—but they can also result from the growing technical and cost challenges. Old mines struggle to pay miners as much as at brand-new high-grade mines, and less capital may be available for necessary infrastructure improvements.

We saw this in 2008 with power interruptions and labor strikes at Chuquicamata, in Chile's arid Atacama desert; Chuqui, as it is commonly called, the second-largest producer, started operations in 1910. With grades declining and technical challenges increasing as the reserves deplete, the willingness to commit huge amounts of capital also declines. (I am not suggesting that Chuqui, like many of the old mines, is on its last legs, but that production interruptions will likely continue.) It is not unfair to say that many of the largest and older mines—like Chuqui, or Escondida, the world's largest producer and a relative spring chicken at just over 30 years old—have poor operating performance, though not always due to operator error, but rather due to inherent factors. When mining at Escondida went deeper, operator BHP found a sharp decline in grade, leading to a 30 percent lower output than had been planned.

However, we should emphasize that the marginal cost of world copper—that is, the cost of the most expensive producers—is around $2,700 per tonne (using LME format for copper prices), or $1.22. This is at a time when the spot price is $7,430 per tonne (or $3.37 per pound). That makes even the most expensive production profitable, while most producers can produce copper at only half the world price. So the lack of increased production is not a result of the current price. The price is right and the demand is there.

Where Is It Coming From?

In addition to the difficulties at existing mines, there is a deficit of large new mines on the horizon. The largest—Oyu Togloi in Mongolia and Olympic Dam in Australia (also the world's biggest uranium deposit)—have challenges, the former political and the latter technical and environmental, compounded by the new tax proposal. There are no other world-class assets likely to come on in the next 10 years or more. Equally important, there seems to be a lack of brownfields developmental projects.

Brownfields projects are expansions of existing deposits rather than brand-new projects, and these have traditionally been a major contributor to increasing production for the copper industry. They tend to be less expensive to bring on since much of the infrastructure has already been built for the original mine. Sometimes, brownfield deposits can be trucked and processed at existing facilities, further reducing the capital costs. The best copper mines, large and long life, also often have other large deposits nearby, such as the Freeport's Grasberg mine that "took over" from the Ertsberg mine in Indonesia. When, in 1960, Freeport geologists discovered Ertsberg in the extremely rugged terrain of what was then a Dutch colony on the island of Papua, it was the largest aboveground copper mine ever. But it was dwarfed by the subsequent discovery of adjacent Grasberg. There seem to be fewer of these likely to come on stream in the next decade.

The world copper industry is not replacing pounds mined with new reserves, either in conversion of resources to mineable reserves, nor in new ounces discovered. In addition, there is at some mines a focus on high-grade ore to enable the mines to generate extra profit while the price is high. But high-grading is a self-defeating long-term strategy.

Moreover, many of the most recent large mines, such as Tenke Fungurume in the Democratic Republic of the Congo (DRC), could be problematic as the DRC continually revises the rules of the game for mining companies. Indeed, given the long life of copper mines, political change is the norm. Think of 50 or 100 years in the life of Chile or Indonesia or the DRC; fundamental political upheaval, coups, and civil wars, are to be expected, let alone repeated changes in the law or tax rates for mining companies. This is something big miners deal with all the time; production interruptions in the Congo are definitely a potential.

Politics and Technology the Problem

Certainly, there is still potential for new copper discoveries. This could be in frontier countries, such as Mongolia; that country and northwest China could host more mines and have potential for future discoveries. Similarly, Papua (formerly Irian Jaya), the Indonesian half of the island of which Papua New Guinea is the other, almost certainly has more copper than the enormously rich Grasberg Mine. Due to both the size and challenges of developing that known deposit and then to the difficulties and dangers of exploring in the virgin territory around the mine, exploration has been limited; for a period, due to separatist activity, Freeport suspended all activities outside its major mine site. But it would be surprising if more copper were not found, though when and whether it would be economically viable at today's prices is another question. Similarly, there is a lot of undeveloped copper in the DRC, but mining companies want more stability before committing the millions and billions of dollars necessary to explore, develop, and mine.

Lastly, it appears that Bingham Canyon in Utah, which commenced operations at the end of the nineteenth century, could continue to depth, but the technical challenges and low grades (and therefore high cost) could prevent serious exploration and development for years. Indeed, there is likely potential for deep underground copper mines at mine sites around the world; most copper today is produced from large open pits, but again the cost is likely to be high.

No doubt, over time, technological innovations in development and processing will help make other deposits viable. The world's first open-pit porphyry copper mine started producing in 1906 (at Bingham Canyon a few years after traditional operations), but such mines now dominate world production. Similarly, in the 1980s, the advent of SX-EW processing made many erstwhile uneconomic mines profitable. Though they tend to be small operations, they nonetheless add incrementally to supply. Going forward, the price of copper may largely depend on both the success of brownfields exploration, and any as-yet unknown technological innovation reducing costs and enabling other deposits to be brought onstream. What is less uncertain is the continuing growth in demand for many years, and the struggle to replace production with new reserves, as well as the decline in production from major existing producers. Absent success from brownfields or technology, there will be a massive supply gap by around 2020 and with it significantly higher prices for that most basic of all metals, copper.

This is why copper is near the top of our list for potential in the coming decade or more. Copper exhibits, more than most, all the characteristics of increasing demand and challenged supply affecting all the resources. But in addition, copper is essential to economic development, and yet China hardly produces any relative to its demand. This is a combustible combination that has the potential for dramatically higher prices than we have already experienced.

Price Volatile

As I have discussed, the copper price can be particularly volatile, so investors need to be wary of chasing prices higher unless there are fundamental reasons for the price spurt that are likely to be sustained. In addition, there is a seasonal pattern of which investors should be aware; typically the summer is weak as factories in the northern hemisphere close for worker holidays and maintenance work. But the underlying outlook is of higher prices over the long term. So copper is one of my top choices, and even more so if the developed world starts to exhibit signs of economic recovery.

There is a U.S.-traded copper exchange-traded note, the iPath DJ UBS Copper ETN (symbol JJC on the New York Stock Exchange). It gives exposure to copper but has the problems associated with commodity-based ETNs that I discussed earlier. There are also London-based exchange-traded commodities (ETCs), which are difficult to buy for Americans, thanks to "investor-protection" regulations. Copper is also actively traded on the commodities markets, for those comfortable with commodity trading.

I prefer the ease and operating leverage that comes with operating companies. The difficulty for equity investors is the lack of pure copper plays. Of the 10 largest copper producers in the world, only three can be called pure copper investments: Freeport (#2), Southern Copper (#7), and First Quantum (#10). Of these, First Quantum is in the Congo's vice-grip, while Southern Copper's output comes from a single country—Peru—which adds risk.

Of the rest of the top 10, two are state-owned enterprises, and the other publicly traded companies are large diversified mining companies. Of the three largest, BHP, Xstrata, and Rio, although combined they account for 3 million tonnes of annual copper production, being the third-, fourth-, and five-largest copper producers, for each, copper accounts for only a minority of its total revenue. Thus, for BHP, all base metals combined contribute less than one-quarter of its revenue. Xstrata, a major coal and lead producer, receives less than half its revenue from copper, while Rio, which for some reason lumps copper and diamonds together, sees less than 10 percent of corporate revenue from this division. So these are hardly copper investments. Similarly, Norilsk, if you can overcome the risks of owning Russian shares, is more a nickel company than a copper one.

A Great Company and a Pure Play

That leaves Freeport-McMoRan (FCX, NY), my preferred copper investment. But even after its merger with Phelps Dodge copper, which catapulted it to the number two position after Chile's state-owned Codelco, Freeport generates a significant part of its revenues from other metals, primarily gold, molybdenum, and silver. Still, about three-quarters of its revenues typically come from copper. Its legacy Grasberg operation in Indonesia, the world's third-largest producer, has the world's largest reserves. The same mine is also the world's largest single gold mine! As we have seen, however, those by-product revenues can jump around; gold production doubled to 2.6 million ounces in 2009, before dropping to 1.8 million in 2010, for example.

Freeport has many great attributes, in addition to being the world's largest and near-pure publicly traded copper company. It is a great company, with a strong balance sheet and fiscal discipline; management that is both entrepreneurial and conservative; multiple world-class assets diversified in several countries. It is also committed to increasing (again) its modest dividend over time. The negative, however, is that so many of their mines are in problematic countries. Indonesia is relatively calm now, though there remain safety issues at the mine site. The DRC is a difficult country with lack of infrastructure, and lack of experienced personnel. Yet the DRC continues to make unreasonable demands of the companies operating in the country, as well as repeated renegotiations of contracts. The situation is unlikely to improve much, and even if the risk of expropriation or mine stoppage is low, companies may be less prepared to commit the vast amounts of capital required to build and expand operations.

When all is said and done though, Freeport is the best producing company to offer relatively pure exposure to copper, and we are fortunate that it also happens to be a fine company.

The world changes, however. A list of the top 20 copper producers from 20 years ago includes eight companies that no longer exist and others that are no longer significant copper producers. As for juniors, there are fewer smaller producers or exploration companies looking for copper than other resources, though there have been some successes.

Most notable of these in recent years has been Lumina Copper, founded by mining entrepreneur Ross Beaty, who built two gold companies, then what has become the world's largest pure silver mining company, before moving on to copper. Beaty saw the same lack of future supply and lack of exploration success by major companies as he saw in the gold business, but far fewer juniors looking. He reasoned that, with the price low at the time he started his copper company, any success would meet eager buying from resource-hungry majors when the market recovered. And so it was. He split his company into four separate units, and three of the four have now been sold to senior companies, and the last, Lumina Copper (LCC, Toronto) may not last much longer. Each of the three companies sold went for a multiple of prior trading prices, and investors in the original combined company saw their investment multiply by several thousand percent. Beaty's latest venture in the resource world is in geothermal, which I will discuss later (in Chapter 21).

So, whether for major producers or small exploration companies, the world changes, making it difficult to discuss specifics for investors that will stand the test of time. I can say with certainty, however, that copper is at the top of my list for resource investments, and that, at the right price, Freeport is a top investment choice.

Copper is key for economic development and, without any unusual uses or supply attributes, it nonetheless exemplifies the basic commodity thesis. As such, it is central to our story and should be central to our resource investments.

CHAPTER 16

Base Metals and Rare Earths

Though the fundamental argument for all the base metals is essentially the same, each specific metal has its own characteristics, different supply and demand factors affecting both the long-term and short-term outlook. And there are numerous factors affecting the outlook for near and long term, changing all the time. It would be unrealistic to discuss all this in a book that is not intended as a short-term forecasting analysis. We can say, however, that the essential fundamentals are broadly similar for each individual metal as they are for copper. Broadly similar, but not quite as compelling in many cases. Deposits of nickel, zinc, and lead are more plentiful than those of copper, so higher prices could more readily be met with increased production. I went into some detail on copper in Chapter 15 because of the metal's critical importance to economic development and because it is my favorite base metal for which pure plays are available. But others are attractive, too, in varying degrees at different times. A good place to start is with China: What does China need? And what does it not produce? These are not the only factors to consider of course, but it is a starting point, particularly for base metals.

China produces gold, oil, coal, and rare earths, but that does not mean I do not like those resources. China's demand for gold is not the critical component in the demand equation, but is likely to increase, and there are other reasons to like gold anyway. China does not produce sufficient quantities of either oil or coal for its own needs. And China's domination of global rare earth supply is one of the main reasons to like those resources. So clearly China's lack of production is not the only reason to like a particular resource. China is also rich in iron ore, bauxite, zinc, and nickel, but it can sustain high domestic production of most of these only with high prices. If prices decline, China's output will also decline, as we saw in late 2008 and early 2009. So we don't need to be concerned with China flooding the market in weak times. But China has a huge appetite for several resources it does not produce in sufficient quantities, including copper, uranium, and iron ore.

The Hungry Steel Mills of China

Critical to China's economic development is its need for steel, and the country dominates global steel production, with virtually half of the total. Number 2, Japan, produces just one-sixth of China's output. This dominance is likely to continue; steel demand is increasing as the country continues to urbanize and build infrastructure across the country. Most of China's steel production is consumed locally, a reason that China's steel production continued to increase throughout 2009 even as global output declined. China is a significant producer of pig iron, more than 60 percent of world output last year, though that was partly because of declines in production from other countries. Nonetheless, it cannot produce enough for its own needs and has become a large importer for its hungry steel mills. Steel exports to other countries have dropped between 10 and 50 percent, as China's internal needs grow. Construction takes about half of China's steel output. Urban land is at a premium, so buildings get higher, and that means more steel consumption. Similarly, bridges and railways require large amounts of steel, as do consumer durable goods such as refrigerators.

This huge demand for (and local production of) steel equates to more demand for the prime ingredient in steel production, iron ore, as well as for the coal to fuel the furnaces. Iron ore used to be almost entirely subject to annual price negotiation. One of the major mining companies would come to an agreement after lengthy negotiations on the year's price with a major consumer, and that would be the reference price for the rest of the industry. The so-called benchmark system has now broken down and is unlikely to return. After China demanded a significant discount to the price negotiated with Japan, Australia's BHP baulked and decided to offer some iron ore based on spot prices. Shortly thereafter, in March 2010, two of the three leading producers, BHP and Brazil's Vale, agreed with major Chinese and Japanese steel mills to new quarterly pricing based on prevailing spot prices. The third producer, Britain's Rio Tinto, which sells more iron ore to China than any other company, quickly joined the others. Initially, this new spot-based pricing system could mean a jump in finished steel prices by as much as a third, but over time should mean a more efficient and transparent pricing of iron ore. China had long wanted to move away from the annual benchmark system, but it had been difficult for its fragmented steel industry to present a unified front in price negotiations. It is also, as I have discussed, attempting to acquire some resources of its own, both to ensure some reliability of supply as well as to have another bargaining chip in price discussions.

Nickel and zinc also play key roles in steel production. Some 70 percent of nickel worldwide is used for stainless-steel production, with 55 percent of zinc used for galvanized steel. Thus, the demand outlook for these two metals will be largely determined by China's on-going urbanization and economic growth. As with iron ore, though China is richly endowed with both nickel and zinc, it has not nearly enough to meet their domestic needs and it has turned from net exporters to heavy importers. A recent Goldman Sachs report included zinc as one of the four commodities with the greatest leverage to China's economic growth, the others being copper, cotton, and soybeans. In each, it consumes about one-quarter of the world's output and is a "structural" importer.

In the range of metals, I am less keen on lead, given the increasing restrictions and prohibitions on its use; and on aluminum, given that one-third of all production today is losing money. Of course, the latter will change; buying the low-cost producer, the last-man standing, in such an environment can be a good investment.

The World's Mining Giants

Most of the world's production of base metals (other than copper) comes from major diversified miners. There are very few worthwhile pure plays in most of the metals, a completely different situation from a decade ago, before Canada and Australia's large independent miners were gobbled up. Iconic names like Falconbridge and Inco were pure plays on nickel. Alcan was a stand-alone aluminum company.

Today, the big five—BHP Billiton, Rio Tinto, Vale, Xstrata, and Anglo American—account for most production of most of the metals.

They are all diversified, both in resources produced and in countries in which they operate, though the emphasis and mix is different. In some cases, it's a matter of choice, such as Anglo divesting its holdings in AngloGold to get out of the gold business. Rio too has tended to avoid gold. In some cases, the emphasis results from the company's roots, such as Vale's exposure to iron ore and Brazil. But each is diversified and each offers investors broad exposure to the resource complex.

This has obvious benefits and drawbacks for investors. To some extent, one can obtain adequate long-term exposure to the entire resource complex by buying one or two of these companies and then relaxing. On the other hand, of course, it is more difficult to get pure exposure to a specific metal, and one is always buying some things one doesn't necessarily want along with things one does.

Comparing the Big Five

Comparing the companies, clearly BHP, Vale, and Rio are significantly larger than the other two, more than twice as large in terms of market cap and much larger in revenues. (See Table 16.1.)

Rio, Vale, and Xstrata are less diversified than the other two, with each company earning more than 40 percent of its revenues last year from a single resource: aluminum (Rio), iron ore (Vale), and copper (Xstrata). BHP is the most diversified, with its top revenue earner, iron ore, generating only 20 percent of the group's revenues, and with at least some production of a broad range of resources. Xstrata also, despite copper's dominance, is otherwise broadly diversified.

As to where they sell, both Vale and Rio generate a little under 20 percent of their revenues from sales to China, with BHP, somewhat surprisingly given its proximity, only 10 percent. Anglo and Xstrata do not break down their China sales, with each earning about one-third of revenues from the Asia region. Vale and Anglo are least diversified in terms of geographic source of revenues; BHP the most.

In term of political risk, BHP and Rio again could be rated as lower risk, though none is highly concentrated in high-risk countries. BHP, Vale, and Xstrata are generally rated higher with respect to their balance sheet and fiscal discipline, with Rio and Anglo less, though it was not always so. (Rio floundered and took on debt to fight off BHP's unwelcome interest. The two companies subsequently did, however, agree to combine their iron ore operations in Western

Table 16.1   Major Products of the Big Five

	Market Cap
Rio Tinto	$115 Billion
Aluminum	43%
Iron Ore	30%
Energy & Minerals	19%
Also Copper & Diamonds	
Vale	$146 Billion
Iron Ore	46%
Nickel	15%
Briquets	14%
Also Copper, Aluminum, Alumina, Coal	
BHP Billiton	$185 Billion
Iron Ore	20%
Metallurgical Coal	16%
Oil	14%
Base Metals	14%
Also Chemical Coal, Aluminum, Manganese, Diamonds	
Anglo American	$50 Billion
Platinum	24%
Base Metals	22%
Coal	20%
Also Ferrous Metals, Industrial Minerals	
Xstrata	$50 Billion
Copper	41%
Coal	28%
Zinc Lead	11%
Nickel	11%
Also Vanadium, Platinum, Chrome	

Source: Company reports, Bloomberg.

Australia, in the world's richest iron ore belt. These combined operations produce about 40 percent of the world's sea-borne trade. Though the companies say the combination is for operational efficiency, it has raised hackles in China and sparked a probe by the ever-vigilant bureaucrats in Brussels.)

BHP has an advantage in having many of its mines closer to the main market for so many resources, reducing shipping costs and thereby giving it a cost advantage. Vale has an advantage in being based in Brazil, a country China is actively courting for resources. The management of these two, BHP, Vale, as well as of Xstrata, is generally more highly regarded than the last two, though again this changes. BHP went through a weak stretch around the turn of the century, when they seemed to be floundering, changing strategic direction frequently. Rio's management used to be more highly regarded. So things change, and these can only be regarded as broad assessments as of now. It is quite likely, in fact, that within just a few years, one or more of these companies will no longer exist, but most certainly they will look somewhat different than they do today. So there will be times to buy and times to avoid, times to favor one or the other, but over time all provide broad exposure to the commodity super cycle.

A Diversified Junior

In addition to these major diversified resource companies, there is one company on the junior side that offers reasonably broad exposure to many base metals as well as other resources, and that is Altius Minerals (ALS, Toronto). I discussed this company earlier (Chapter 12). Altius has built the company in a low-risk manner. Based in and focused on Newfoundland and Labrador, one of the most resource-friendly jurisdictions around, Altius has generated projects through grassroots exploration and then developed the projects in a variety of low-risk, innovative techniques, either bringing in a joint-venture partner or spinning off the project as a stand-alone venture with its own management. Thus, Altius today has a royalty interest in Vale's Voisey's Bay Nickel Mine; it has equity and royalty interests in gold, uranium, rare earths, and iron ore companies (in various stages of development); several joint-venture deals, mainly in gold and uranium, with exploration in oil and gas, and several base metals. Altius's recently spun off its iron ore project into a new company, Alderon (ADV, Toronto), retaining 48 percent ownership, valued at $35 million, plus a royalty on any further production. Alderson itself is an attractive investment in a growing deposit in a known iron ore district. Altius also has a strong balance sheet. I don't know what the price of the stock will be six months from now, but you probably won't go wrong buying Altius for low-risk exposure to a broad range of commodities.

The supply and demand of different metals changes over time, and those changes affect relative prices and attractiveness of the different metals. For most investors, it makes sense to stick with one or more of the diversified companies, with the major miners or a low-risk junior like Altius that will ensure you have not hitched your wagon to one particular metal that might be a laggard in the period ahead.

Minor Metals

Of course, there are dozens of metals and I have only touched on a few. They are generally divided into base metals and minor metals, with the base metals being either ferrous or nonferrous metals. There are more than 30 of these so-called *minor metals*, each with its own supply and demand characteristics. Uses are both high-tech and low-tech, but usually quite specialized. Cobalt and titanium are used in the manufacture of jet engines and ruthenium in high-capacity computer memory storage discs, while cobalt is used in paints and bismuth to make bullets and treat ulcers (someone has a good sense of irony). Several are also used in steel making; molybdenum (often called moly) and vanadium are used in alloys with steel to prevent corrosion, while manganese is increasingly being used as a less expensive alternative to nickel, the main nonferrous metal used in stainless-steel making.

Supply tends to come from only a handful of mines, often as a by-product (moly of copper, or bismuth of lead), so supplies can be erratic and subject to disruption unconnected with the fundamentals of the particular market. At the same time, end consumption is often for only one or two primary purposes and sometimes there are just a few buyers; frequently, the particular minor metal is essential to the end product but its price is only a small part of the overall price of the product. Thus, supply can be volatile while demand is price inelastic, and given that these markets are usually very small, this leads to volatile prices. In recent years, many of the minor metals have shot up to new highs; ruthenium jumped tenfold in just the two years to mid-2007. Few are accessible to investors.

Titanium Critical for Aircraft

Titanium is one of the largest markets among the minor metals, with a key and growing role in aircraft. It has the highest strength-to-weight ratio of any metal, and it is highly resistant to corrosion. Thus, we can see why it is increasingly attractive to manufacturers of the new breed of aircraft, as well as military aircraft. Today, both Boeing and Airbus want to make planes that can carry large numbers of passengers over long distances, and that means making planes lighter and more fuel-efficient. Most advanced planes are using more and more titanium, for this purpose. It has other uses as well, particularly in new water systems, for which its corrosion-resilience makes it attractive.

Unlike many of the minor metals, there is a solid pure-play company, Titanium Metals (TIE, NY), which controls about 20 percent of the world's smelting operations, and just a little less of global mill operations. Of course, since it doesn't mine the metals, a rising price hurts it on the input side, but it can still add its margins to the processing, and even widen the margins in periods of high demand.

Molybdenum: Ups and Downs

For many of the metals, most supply is from larger companies whose primary production is of other metals. Molybdenum is a good example. Much of it is mined as a by-product of copper production, although there are primary mines. The world's leading producer is Freeport, and Freeport will have some moly production regardless of the price. Of course, a by-product like moly can add tremendously to the company's bottom line. In fact, in Freeport's latest quarter, despite the price of moly at $13.45 per pound being barely half the price of a year ago, it still contributed over 20 percent of the company's revenues. Freeport does not offer pure moly exposure, but if you want some moly in your portfolio, Freeport is the place to go.

There is also a large company offering pure moly exposure, Thompson Creek (TC, NY), which has mines in both Canada and the United States. It has a very strong balance sheet, with hardly any debt, and moves more-or-less in line with the metal price.

Most molybdenum is used in making stainless steel (with much of the rest in the chemical industry) and lower demand from those sectors saw prices down sharply last year. The price will probably move back up, if not to the levels of 2008 and prior, where for most of the previous five years it traded between $27 and $36, the demand should continue to be strong.

One indication of the growing importance of these minor metals is the introduction in February 2010 of exchange trading in cobalt and molybdenum on the London Metals Exchange (LME). Such trading will bring more transparency to prices of these metals, which heretofore had been traded directly between producer and consumer. There is some concern, however, that investor activity in such thinly traded metals could lead to increased volatility in prices.

Lithium: From Batteries to Depression

Lithium is another minor metal with disparate uses: It is used in advanced batteries, for computers and electric cars, as well as for the treatment of depression. It is also used in the manufacture of glass and ceramics. But the growth potential is in batteries, whether long-life batteries for laptops and other electronics or the rechargeable batteries for hybrids and electric cars. In most batteries, large and small, lithium represents about 5 percent of the cost, although it is essential.

Currently, most hybrid cars use nickel-cadmium batteries; plug-in hybrids and electric cars use lithium-ion batteries, but increasingly hybrids are using lithium batteries as well, and they are expected to dominate the market in the next year or two. Lithium has the highest energy-to-weight ratio, so it becomes more attractive for hybrids. Its use in batteries for electric and hybrid cars makes lithium a "green" resource, likely to be increasingly attractive in years to come. Currently, about a quarter of lithium's demand is for batteries, but research firm Fuji-Keizai forecasts the global market for lithium batteries for automobiles will grow ninety-fold in the next five years. As with many of these resources, reliability of long-term supply is critical to end users, more critical than price. Toyota recently gained a 25 percent stake in a lithium project in Argentina, controlled by an Australian company, by paying for the feasibility study. The project is expected to commence production in 2012. Japanese electronics makers control the majority of the lithium-battery market, supplying various product manufacturers around the world.

Lithium is found in many places around the world, but only in a few places does it lie below salt flats making it most economical to extract. Chile is at present the largest producer, from vast salt flats in the harsh Atacama Desert, reputedly the driest spot on earth. I traveled for miles across this desert, without once seeing a living thing, not a bird above or an insect or lizard below. Certainly, the output from Chile could be increased, but too-rapid extraction can harm the reservoirs, not unlike the oil industry. Along with Australia, it is responsible for over two-thirds of the world's production, while just four companies control 85 percent of the total world production. Chile perhaps has a quarter of the world's reserves, with neighboring Bolivia hosting up to half of the world's reserves, in the Uyuni desert, though as yet largely untapped. Japanese, French, and Korean firms are currently negotiating with the government to commence production.

Lithium prices have shot up, more than doubling from 2005 to 2008, with the prices of producing companies and any company with the word "lithium" in its name, some of which have shot up five- or tenfold. As lithium prices move above marginal costs, it is possible that some smaller but high-grade deposits could become viable. Lithium from brines (under salt flats) cannot be used directly in ceramics and some other uses, making these high-grade deposits more valuable.

Very Rare Indeed

Even rarer than these minor metals are the rare earth metals, sometimes called rare earth elements, or simply rare earths. These are the 30 elements that occur at the bottom of the periodic table, are very rare, and yet they have often unique attributes and are critical to so many uses, from hybrid cars to iPods. Together, the minor metals and rare earths were popularly called *strategic metals* in the 1980s, due to their specialized uses often in defense and other strategic areas.

If you have at least heard of some of the minor metals, it is likely that many have never even heard of the rare earths, minerals like ytterbium and dysprosium, protactinium or medelevium. The rare earths are garnering increased attention in specialized press, however. "Remember the oil crisis?" asks *The Truth about Cars*. "Get ready for the Chinese dysprosium crisis." And *Business Insider* says "Investors are crazy for rare earth metals."

No wonder. Up to 25 percent of new technologies rely on rare earths. Lanthanum and praseodymium are essential in the manufacture of carbon arc lamps; cerium in laser crystals; neodymium and samarium in powerful magnets; gadolinium in MRIs; erbium in surgical lasers, and so on. Like lithium, they are also often used in "green" technologies, ensuring continued demand. Because typically only a small amount of the rare earth is used in any item and because there are only imperfect substitutes available, the *cost* of the rare earth is far less important than the *reliability* of supply.

Unbelievably, China currently supplies about 95 percent of the world's rare earths, and in some specific ones, it is the only supplier. Indeed, a single mine, Bayan Obo, supplies half of the world's total production of rare earths. Bayan Obo is an iron ore mine, with rare earths as a by-product. Although many rare earths are found in other places around the world, they are often not mined for various technical reasons that make them uneconomic. In actuality, rare earths are not rare at all as chemical compounds in the earth's crust, but they are rare in minable concentrations. But of all known deposits, viable or not, China still controls over 50 percent, making it far and away the dominant player now and into the future.

China Controls the Market

China also is the dominant consumer of rare earths, nearly 60 percent of the world total. Much of this is for use in products that are then exported, but if China's economy is to continue to grow, its manufacturer of re-export goods will continue to be important. Processing plants and factories are built close to the source of the earths for economic reasons, so China's demand is a reflection of global demand. Given its dominant position in production and the importance of the supply to the country's economy, there is concern about possible manipulation. Deng Xiaoping, the former Chinese leader, once noted that while the Middle East had oil, China had rare earths.

And indeed, the country has successively tightened export quotas over three years, limiting exports to just 35,000 tonnes per year. Some, particularly *heavy rare earths*, such as terbium (used as a stabilizer of fuel cells, as well as an activator of green phosphors in color televisions) and yttrium (strengthening agent in steel, and use in portable X-ray machines), are prohibited from export all together. There are reports that the country may increase the number of rare earths to which such bans pertain, focusing on rare earths where its own domestic demand might outstrip supply in the near future, though China has denied this. Rather, it points out that the free export of these earths has led to over exploitation and environmental damage; it is possible to damage the long-term productivity by extracting too rapidly. China also wants to build a strategic supply of the earths, particularly since the government has projected a shortage for its own domestic needs for many of the earths within just a few years.

No doubt, these changes will accelerate moves to look for and develop rare earth deposits elsewhere; according to the U.S. Geological Survey, about 43 percent of all rare earth reserves are outside of China—still an overwhelming dominance to a single country—though few of these are being mined. And, though typically more than one rare earth is found in a deposit, the distribution of the different minerals varies considerably; for some, it is thought that China may have the world's only deposits.

How to Invest in Rare Earths

It would be very difficult indeed for an investor to hold any of the rare earths, though a new fund was launched in early 2010 intended to build a stockpile of rare earths. It is too soon to say whether Dacha Capital (DAC, Toronto), just launched by industry veteran Stan Barti, will prove a valid investment—storage as well as trading complexities could be a hindrance—but it is certainly worth looking at.

If one is going to buy companies, there are many approaches. Certainly most of the production outside of China is lost inside huge diversified companies. But there are other approaches.

Given the unique characteristics of each rare earth, they have different uses, but uses change rapidly given new technologies. Many investors like to buy stock in companies developing new technologies, but all too often the investment riches do not materialize. There may be a larger competitor who comes to market first, or perhaps the millions of dollars raised to continue nonrevenue-generating research dilutes shareholders, or perhaps the technology is not as promised as originally thought. Rather than buy the companies developing the new technologies, one could buy shares in the companies mining the rare earths, and though not without its own risks, at least you would have a winner regardless of which technology horse won the race.

The main difficulty to this approach is finding companies that actually produce the resource and for whom it is a meaningful part of overall company revenues; or else an exploration company with a real prospect. Again, this is not a question of whether the company owns land on which some rare earth or another can be found, but whether it is likely to ever be produced. Otherwise, you are dealing in "trading sardines," to use Doug Casey's memorable phrase, and need to make sure you trade it on before it gets stale. Such trading is not the concern of this book.

If, however, you can find a company that you like anyway, and rare earth exposure is simply icing on the cake, then so much the better. One that fits the bill is Midland Exploration (MD, Toronto), one of my favorite exploration companies and one that follows the prospect generator model (see Chapter 12). Although most of Midland's projects are in gold and base metals, it does have a prospective rare earth project in Northern Quebec that is in joint venture with the Japan Oil, Gas and Metals National Corporation (JOGMEC). Japan is the single largest buyer of rare earths, purchasing over half of China's exports. JOGMEC can earn 50 percent of the project by spending $2.7 million over the next two years in what could potentially be an emerging rare earths mining camp.

The more exotic the metal and the more obtuse its uses, the easier it is to be lured into the dream of vast profits. Better to stick with a solid diversified company, with a BHP or a Midland, and hope you may get a boost from rare earths rather than better the farm on what is at best a long-odds speculation.

CHAPTER 17

Energy

The 800-lb gorilla of the resource industry is energy. In all its forms, energy represents over 80 percent of the value of all commodities together. It covers a broad spectrum. For major sectors like oil, coal, and uranium, the very broad themes I have discussed previously for different resources apply equally: growing demand from China and other developing countries, with Chinese per-capita consumption set to rise dramatically; reserve replacement below current production; and increasing political and environmental risk internationally. For these broad reasons, the prices of oil, coal, and uranium are likely to continue to rise over the next several years.

Separate Markets

For other forms of energy, these influences are more indirect. Clearly, higher oil prices will have an impact on gas prices and spur development of alternative energy, but the impact of Chinese demand and production challenges is less direct. Natural gas is a regional market because of the expense of getting from a field to market; we don't (yet) have pipelines from Alberta to Shanghai. The same applies for hydro, geothermal, solar, and other forms of alternative energy. At the same time, there are other critical factors affecting these markets, most important, the environmental pressures.

This is not going to be a thesis on the oil market (or any other energy sector), but we will look at the broad themes affecting each sector, particularly as they pertain to investors. The conclusion, however, is that the world is desperately in need of more energy. We are unlikely to have sufficient oil to meet the needs of the next couple of decades at anything like the current price, so oil prices will rise as will demand for, and prices of, other forms of energy. This would all be true without any environmental pressures.

But these other forms of energy have problems associated with them, just as oil does. Few people are seriously willing to reduce their energy consumption significantly; they don't realize what it would mean for their standard of living. All forms of energy have a cost of some type associated with the production or consumption.

Oil and Coal Dominate Global Energy Supplies

Look at the major energy sources by current consumption. This consumption is largely to generate electricity, for transportation, or to generate power for industry. The traditional forms, most unloved by environmentalists, are most important, with oil and coal accounting for around 70 percent of world consumption. In fact, the world generates almost as much of its energy from coal as from oil. (See Figure 17.1.) Hydrocarbons have the side benefit that they also produce feedstocks for plastics, whereas most other sources of energy have no beneficial by-products.

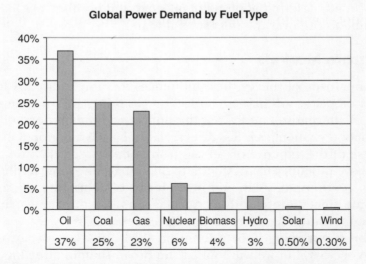

Global Power Demand by Fuel Type

	Oil	Coal	Gas	Nuclear	Biomass	Hydro	Solar	Wind
	37%	25%	23%	6%	4%	3%	0.50%	0.30%

Figure 17.1   Oil and Coal Are Most Important Power Sources
Source: International Energy Association.

The United States, with 5 percent of the world's population, is the major consumer, just over 20 percent of the world's energy. China, with 25 percent of the population, consumes just 18 percent of the energy; Japan, the third-largest consumer of energy, with 2 percent of the world's population, consumes 4.5 percent of the world's energy. The United States and Japan, of course, have gross domestic products (GDPs) well above their population-weight, and much of the energy consumption goes into production.

The patterns of the world's major energy consumers are different. The United States generates 22 percent of its total energy from oil and 17 percent from coal. China, whose energy consumption is rising rapidly, generates over 40 percent of its energy from coal and just under 10 percent from oil. The United States gets 22 percent from natural gas, whereas China gets hardly any of its energy from this source; China gets over 18 percent of its energy from hydro, while is the least important of major energy sources for the United States.

Most of the green energy sources don't register into the overall equation today and are likely to remain relatively insignificant in the total energy scheme for some time. Given the dynamics of nuclear and the minor contributions from various alternative and green sources, including hydro, the world will continue to need oil and coal for some time to come. Indeed, half of the U.S. electricity comes from coal-fired plants, and absent a massive nuclear program, that's not going to change significantly soon. For the rapidly developing countries of China and India, coal too is likely to remain dominant for the next decade and more. This is even more true if we look at a subset of overall energy requirements, that is the source for electricity. As the table shows, coal remains the most important power source of the generation of electricity in all major areas. (See Table 17.1.)

Table 17.1   Electricity Generation Power Source

	Coal	Gas	Nuclear	Alternative	Oil
U.S.	49%	18%	20%	10%	x
Europe	29%	22%	28%	15%	5%
China	79%	x	x	16%	x

x = Minor Contribution.
Source: CERA, IEA, McKinsey & Co data, April 2010.

Dirty or Expensive

All these sources have drawbacks. Oil causes pollution and is too expensive for electricity generation. Gas can't be economically transported around the world; though it is clean energy, new lifting technologies (fracking in particular) are causing environmental concern. Coal is perhaps the dirtiest energy source and also unhealthy for miners. Hydro, like gas, needs to be sourced relatively near to a market. Nuclear has huge capital costs, only generates electricity, and is politically controversial.

Hydro is the cleanest source, though uranium is also clean, since absent an accident it generates only steam to produce electricity. Gas is also relatively clean and it is delivered direct to the consumer in pipes.

As for most green energy sources, such as solar, wind, and biowaste, they have one major disadvantage and that is that they are uneconomic. The cost per kilowatt hour of energy produced by wind is 6 cents and for solar is 8 cents, compared with 3 cents for coal and 2 cents for uranium. These green sources are viable only because of government subsidies of one type or another. They also generate insignificant amounts of energy, in aggregate, and their potential is equally modest, certainly compared with oil or coal.

Each also has its own drawbacks: For solar, it is the night! Solar plants must be built greatly in excess of capacity to allow them to capture sun for the times when it is at its brightest. One green idea is to generate energy from poultry waste. Unfortunately, it is estimated we would need 2 trillion birds to generate enough droppings for this to be at all meaningful, and there is not enough food for that number of poultry birds to survive. (Only a dedicated greenie could come up with such an idea!) Many green sources are not without their own environmental impact. Ignoring two trillion birds, solar cells are good for only 25 years and they retain some unfriendly materials that will fill up landfills. Geothermal can be economic, though the amounts of energy produced in the grand scheme of things are also modest.

None of this means that there may not be investment opportunities in these energy sources. I will examine these opportunities separately. But from the point of view of meeting the world's growing energy demands, we will need to use all conventional energy sources, including nuclear, as well as developing alternate energy and new technologies, while also looking to improve efficiencies in use. So for us investors, there may be opportunities in all types of energy, including in service and technology companies.

Peak Oil?

We will start by looking at oil, since it is the world's largest source of energy and is critical to transportation. As with all the other resources we've looked at, there are both a growing demand and supply constraints that combine to indicate higher prices ahead. There has been a lot more general media discussion of future shortages of oil than for other commodities, partly no doubt because the price of oil largely determines the price of gasoline at the pump. Though the inflation-adjusted price of gasoline is no higher today than it was in the 1950s, the rising (nominal) price of gas prompts newspaper headlines and congressional hearings. Whereas the starting point for our discussion of most resources has been demand, for oil it is appropriate to start with supply.

The amount of oil in the earth's crust is clearly finite, though this does not mean that we are about to run out of the stuff any time in the immediate future. However, some things are clear:

- The world is discovering less oil each year than it consumes, and has for the past 30 years.
- The peak years for discovery of new oil were in the early and mid-1960s, and since then, the amount of oil in new discoveries has been trending downward.
- Much of the newly discovered oil is problematic, because of either political or technological challenges.
- Production in many countries has clearly peaked.

This all adds up to an alarming picture wherein global production will be hard-pressed to meet growing demand. The world may yet have years' worth of oil contained in its crust, but we can say that there is not enough in politically safe jurisdictions with today's technologies to meet demand for many years without higher prices.

We can see clearly the decline in new discoveries since the major discoveries of the Alaska North Slopes and North Sea oil in the early 1960s. Since then, new discoveries have declined fairly consistently and at an alarming rate. Both of these two major discoveries have long since peaked and are on their inevitable downward slope. Just

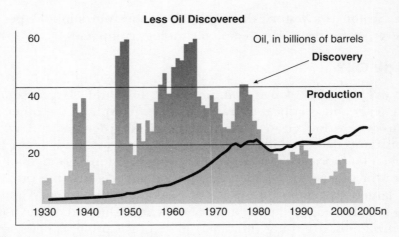

Less Oil Discovered

Figure 17.2   Major Oil Discoveries a Thing of the Past?
Source: ASPO International.

as dramatically, the long-term increase in global oil demand, comfortably under the rate of new discoveries for the first seven decades of the twentieth century, finally crossed over discoveries in the early 1980s and has remained above it since. In other words, each year we are discovering less than is used. (See Figure 17.2.)

Put another way, between 1960 and 1989, the world discovered more than twice the oil it produced and consumed. But since 1990, oil discoveries have equaled only half production. The reserves from earlier discoveries are being run down.

Few New Big Discoveries

For the past 20 years, there has hardly been a year with 10 billion barrels of new oil discovered. And the world consumes 1 billion barrels every 12 days. All oil fields mature and decline, though for some, there can be long decline tails. Right now, about 20 percent of daily production comes from 14 giant fields with an average age of 60 years. That is old, and most of the world's big fields are declining, including the Alaska North Slope and the North Sea, which peaked respectively in 1970 and 1999; Mexico's more recent Cantarell (discovered in 1976), once thought to hold promise of major production for multiple decades; and Ras Budari, in Kuwait, the second-largest field in the world, declining by 20 percent a year.

The North Sea produced 2.5 million barrels from nine fields in 1985. Almost a quarter of a century later, it is producing 1.7 million barrels but from 100 fields. North Sea's output may decline to just 500,000 barrels within a decade as the big fields decline precipitously and run out of extractable oil.

Cantarell, which started production in 1979, had the third-largest ever initial reserves of any offshore field. From a billion barrels a day, production increased in the late 1990s and early part of the last decade to a peak of over 2 billion barrels a day in 2003, the second-highest production from a single field ever. It was thought by many that Cantarell would be a major producer for decades to come, but from that peak production, it has declined rapidly, now producing barely more than half a billion barrels a day, and it is not clear yet when production will stabilize. The decline of Cantarell has been perhaps the most rapid of any giant field ever.

Russia is the second-largest oil producer, only marginally behind Saudi Arabia, but its production slipped in 2008 and 2009. It may be too early to say with certainty that Russian production has peaked; one leading oil executive, Leonid Fedun, Vice President of Lukoil, the country's largest independent oil company, said he believed Russia's 10 million bpd production was the highest he would see "in his lifetime."

Within a year or two, over half of non-OPEC oil will have demonstrably peaked, and non-OPEC accounts for about 60 percent of the total output. Of large non-OPEC countries, only Canada has clearly not peaked, with the jury still out on Russia. As for OPEC, particularly the Middle East, one must ask how reliable are their numbers. Significantly, when OPEC moved in the 1970s to base quotas of allowed production on reserves, every single country in the Middle East doubled its reserves. Were the old numbers inaccurate? It is noteworthy that since then reserves have remained more or less flat for every country. Both facts cast doubt on official figures.

How Much Does Saudi Have?

The world's largest field, Ghawar in Saudi Arabia, with 13 percent of annual production and 23 percent of global reserves, officially holds 50 years or more of reserves at today's production rate. The Saudis claim that undiscovered reserves could be around 125 billion barrels, equivalent to about half of proven reserves. The Saudis also claim, alone among major producers, to have excess capacity, saying they could increase output if the need arose.

But there is much controversy about the official figures. Interestingly, the reserves tend to be flat; they never change, whereas more typically, allowing for annual production, reserves would fluctuate year by year with new discoveries and changes in the oil price. The controversy over Saudi reserves was sparked by Houston's iconoclast Matt Simmons, who, in his acclaimed *Twilight in the Desert*, argued that Saudi reserves are smaller than claimed and that production could start to decline in coming years. Simmons notes that the Saudis do not allow independent audit of national reserves, but on a visit a few years back noticed various signs of aging, including the water that had to be stripped out of the crude as it was pumped out of the ground. In most oil fields, oil sits on top of water, and the amount of water increases toward the bottom of the reservoir. (See Table 17.2.)

The Saudis also claim to have significant excess capacity, so that they could increase production should world demand require; in this, they are alone of all major fields. Tellingly, the Saudis did not—or could not—boost their output when prices rose to $147 in 2007, despite proclaiming they wanted lower prices. Even for those not

Table 17.2   Saudi Arabia Crucial for Oil Supply

	Reserves Billion Barrels	Shares of World
Saudi Arabia	267	22%
Canada	178	14%
Iran	138	11%
Iraq	115	9.3%
Kuwait	102	8.1%
Venezuela	99	8.0%
United Arab Emirates	98	7.9%
Russia	79	6.4%
Libya	44	3.7%
Nigeria	36	2.9%
Kazakhstan	30	2.4%
United States	21	1.7%
China	16	1.3%

Estimates for January 2009.
Source: CIA, *The World Factbook*, April 2010.

convinced by Simmons's argument, his analysis raised questions that have not been satisfactorily answered yet.

This is crucial, for about 10 percent of the world's supply comes from seven fields, all in Saudi Arabia. If Saudi is pushing the envelope on production and it starts to decline, then the world would be in greater trouble than is now apparent.

How Many Years to Go?

But even if the Saudi's numbers are, in fact, correct, that would only stave off the coming oil crisis for a few years. Other fields have indisputably peaked and are in decline; many major oil producing countries similarly are in decline; and global oil is likely to peak in the next decade. That's controversial, of course, but it's no longer just wild-eyed Houston oilmen, end-of-world environmentalists, and gold-bug bears who believe in peak oil. Indeed, Dr. King Hubbert, who was Chief Consulting Geologist for Shell Development, first discussed the concept of "peak oil" as far back as 1956. Hubbert astonished the oil world with his first prediction that U.S. oil production would peak by 1970 and decline thereafter; that proved right on the money. His subsequent prediction was that world oil would peak in the early years of the twenty-first century; subsequent work by "peakers" has pushed that back a few years.

We are not here arguing whether Hubbert was essentially right or not, though for a prediction made more than half a century ahead of the event, with multiple moving parts involved, it has been quite astonishingly accurate. But whether global oil has already peaked, is peaking, or peaks a decade or two from now is irrelevant. It is clearly late in the day for an economy—a civilization, perhaps—built on oil consumption.

But now the International Energy Agency (IEA), a respected independent source of energy data, has proclaimed that, absent major new discoveries, "the output of conventional oil will peak in 2020." This forecast is predicated on oil demand growing on a "business-as-usual" basis, but without even taking into account a possible acceleration in demand from China and other emerging economies.

This is the first time the IEA has publicly come down on the side of the concept of peak oil, even though it has been steadily reducing its estimates for 2030 oil supply. Part of the reason for the IEA's new caution is the faster-than-expected decline rates in many major fields that have peaked; it estimates that the annual decline rate for all fields, large and small, is over 9 percent, and it does not expect the figure to slow much over the next two decades. The rapid decline of many big fields is astonishing; the United Kingdom's production from the North Sea, currently 1.7 million barrels a day, will drop to half a million by 2030.

IEA Chief Economist Fatih Birol notes that "even if oil demand were to remain flat [*a huge assumption—AD*] the world would need to find more than 40 million barrels per day of gross new capacity—equal to four new Saudi Arabias—just to offset this decline." Put in those terms, the very idea—four new Saudi Arabias over the next 20 years—seems preposterous to the point of impossibility.

Indeed, within just five years, nearly half of global demand will have to come from new fields, not yet producing, and beyond that, from the end of the decade onward, an increasing amount from fields yet to be discovered. Not that there have not been significant finds in recent years, most notably the series of discoveries deep offshore Brazil, in the Santos and Campos basins. There have been eight major finds in the last four years, including the proclaimed Tupi and Carioca fields. Tupi has been named the largest discovery in the western hemisphere in the past 30 years, and commenced production in mid-2009 at a modest 15,000 barrels per day. Petrobras plans to produce 500,000 barrels per day by 2020, with eventual output of one million barrels a day from 300 wells. That's an ambitious target; if met, it would be the first million barrel-per-day discovery since Cantarell in 1975.

New Finds Are Not So Easy

There is no question that these underwater reservoirs hold significant amounts of oil—estimates range upward of 100 billion barrels, but the technological challenges are very real. The deposits are up to six miles below the ocean surface, almost twice as deep as the world's deepest producing well. The explosion of the Deepwater Horizon drilling rig in the Gulf of Mexico in early 2010 is a reminder of the difficulties and risks of drilling in deep water. But depth is the least of it. The oil lies under a layer of salt that's more than one mile thick (so old it's called *pre-salt*), and that's under thick rock and sand. The oil is under greater pressure, and hotter, than any currently producing field. It will require equipment to bring up the oil that can withstand 18,000 pounds per square inch of pressure, and pipes that carry oil over 500 degrees (Fahrenheit). So not all of the reserve is recoverable, perhaps 10 billion barrels, truly significant, but still only about 12 percent of the world's annual consumption.

Then there are the political challenges; once it became clear how significant these oilfields were—enough to leapfrog Brazil into the world's top seven oil producers—President Lula put on his populist hat and called Tupi the "second independence for Brazil." Amid talk of "Brazil's resources for the people," Lula mandated that the government retain ownership, and that the country's state-operated Petrobras take a 30 percent interest in all the oil offshore, as well as be the sole operator.

The companies that took all the risk and spent all the money discovering the fields (exploratory wells cost upward of $60 million) will keep a share in the production. Those costs plus the increasing number of dry holes make laughable the comment of Lula's chief of staff and heir apparent as next president, Dilma Rousseff, that because of the "low level of exploratory risk and high levels of returns," the government should keep more of the revenues. Notwithstanding all the geological and technical challenges, it is clearly not beyond the whit of government to diminish the potential of this huge source of wealth.

But the oil is there, and with a high-enough price, the technological, political, and economic challenges will be overcome. And that is the key: *with a high enough price.* Again, I am not suggesting that the world is about to run out of oil (though the Peak theory is valid), but that to repeat what I said about resources in general: there is not enough oil in politically friendly jurisdictions that can be extracted with today's technology to meet growing demand at today's price.

Big, But Not Big Enough

The offshore Brazilian discoveries are the most dramatic new finds in recent years. There have been others, including some deep discoveries in the Gulf of Mexico. One much heralded discovery, called the Tiber Prospect, lies 250 miles offshore, below 4,000 feet of water, with another 35,000 feet below surface (a total of over six miles). These are tremendously challenging fields, but they can be tackled, though at a price. Oil needs to be at a high, sustainable price to encourage and justify the exploitation of such fields. At the dawn of the mass oil age, in the early twentieth century, producers could extract 100 barrels of oil using the energy equivalent of one barrel input; this was true whether the field was in Texas or in Arabia. Today, for the same energy input, just 15 barrels can be extracted, and it is getting more expensive as time passes.

Tiber is initially thought to hold as much as 4 to 5 billion barrels; that's the size of the North Sea Forties Field, the first major find in Britain's North Sea. It would add about 15 percent to U.S. reserves, which is clearly significant. But now consider that with today's technology, perhaps only half a billion barrels of the 4 to 5 billion in the reservoir, can be produced. And now consider that the United States produces nearly 7 billion barrels and consumes almost 20 billion barrels each year, and this massive, much-proclaimed find is put into context, and the difficulty of the problem clearly seen.

Beyond the pure geological problems are the technological, political, and environmental ones, all clear in the case of Brazil that I have discussed. A BP chief executive recently noted that "the challenges the world faces . . . are not below ground, they are above ground. They are human, not geological." Clearly, there are both geological and human challenges, though the former can be more easily overcome.

One of the human challenges is the growing control of oil fields taken by governments. The Mid-East fields have long been in the hands of governments, and that adds to the disclosure difficulties I discussed regarding Saudi's true reserves. Today, four-fifths of the world's oil reserves are under the control of state-run companies. Indeed, the largest 10 oil reserves are in the hands of national oil companies, and the next six largest are owned by mixed state-private companies (such as Petrobras or PetroChina). Exxon, at number 17, has the largest oil reserves of a purely nongovernment oil company. Most of the state oil companies are inefficient, and subject to political objectives at one end and corruption at the other. (See Figure 17.3.)

At best, the oil company is seen as a golden goose to fund the government's social programs with the result that the oil company does not have enough capital, and technology is often outdated. To what extent Mexico's declining production is geological and to what extent human cannot be determined, but it is likely some of each. Hugo Chavez's dictatorial direction of Venezuela's oil industry has seen production drop by 30 percent. There is little doubt that Iran has huge reserves, the second largest in the world, but its output has

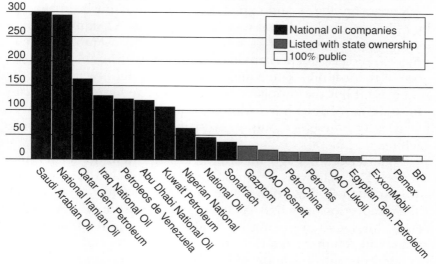

Figure 17.3   Most Oil Is Controlled by Governments
Source: PetroStrategies, Inc., www.petrostrategies.org.

been dropping precipitously. These are only the most extreme and obvious examples. Political interference in other countries, rather than control, has deleterious effects on production though not as extreme.

Even where there is no or little government control, increasingly oil is found in unstable places. Whereas the big fields of the 1960s and 1970s were found in the United States, Britain and Norway, and Mexico, increasingly oil is found in Nigeria, or Côte d'Ivoire, or the Stans, clearly less stable areas. In Nigeria, for example, the antigovernment rebel group, MEND, frequently attacks oil facilities in their ongoing rebellion, adding to cost, and causing frequent interruptions in activities.

New Technologies and New Frontiers Will Help

There are those who deride the concept of Peak Oil. Theoretically, it is true that most forecasting is simple straight-line extrapolation and there are always many people working on current conditions to make them change. We must appreciate that new discoveries have reserves that last for years. The world is still consuming oil from the North Sea discoveries of the mid-1960s for example.

New technologies and exploration constantly push further out the estimates of global reserves, despite the lack of significant new discoveries. Only a part of known reservoirs is recoverable with current technologies, but perhaps in the future, we will be able to recover more of the lost oil. (The issue, as one oil insider put it, is not the supply of oil but the supply of production.) We have seen in many different commodities how technological advances have improved efficiencies and increased output, everything from pesticides to heap leaching.

A quarter century ago, oil drilling in water went no deeper than 600 feet. The platforms were not stable enough and the pipes not strong enough. Today, drilling takes place in 6,000 feet of water, such as the discoveries made by Anadarko recently, offshore Côte d'Ivoire. New technologies are being used all the time, in exploration, recovery, and refining, to add to the output. Horizontal drilling has increased output (and more significantly for natural gas, as I shall discuss). Chevron has started adding hydrogen to its oil output to squeeze more oil out of known reservoirs. And so on.

The IEA believes that oil companies will need to invest about $360 billion a year until 2030; that's a 25 percent increase over current expenditures in order to boost production to meet demand. This is a combination of increased exploration and new technologies. Certainly exploration and development is becoming increasingly expensive. Chevron, drilling through nearly five miles of rock, in the middle of the Gulf of Mexico, is paying half-a-million dollars a day to lease its drilling vessel. Chevron's nearby floating platform cost $650 million to build. In all, this 10-year exploration project an hour's helicopter ride south of New Orleans, has cost Chevron $2.7 billion with no assurance they would ever get their money back. Exxon, the world's largest privately owned oil company never known as a wildcatter, spent $2.7 billion on exploration in 2009, most of it in high-risk areas. This is where one must go to find new oil.

In addition, there are known sources of oil and high-potential targets that are currently off-limits to exploration and development. ANWAR is thought to contain 10 billion barrels; that's 1 million barrels per day for the next 30 years. Fields offshore Florida are very prospective. The entire Arctic could be explored and most assuredly contains large deposits of oil, even though it would be costly to explore and recover the oil. And lastly, of course, there are the other sources of energy.

The Arctic region is highly prospective. Already, there have been significant finds on the heavily explored onshore area, representing about 10 percent of the world's known petroleum resources. But there's more untapped potential, including the shallow waters of the continental shelves. The U.S. Geological Survey (USGS) suggests these shelves may be "the largest unexplored prospective area for petroleum remaining on Earth." The USGS estimates the undiscovered resources to be about 1,669 trillion cubic feet of natural gas and 90 billion barrels of oil, as well as significant gas liquids. Those numbers represent about 30 percent of the world's undiscovered gas and 13 percent of the undiscovered oil. No wonder the states surrounding the Arctic—Russia, the United States (via Alaska), Canada, Norway, and Denmark (via Greenland)—have been jockeying for positions on the unclaimed territory and waters.

Easy Days Are Over

The IEA's discussion is about conventional oil. There is little doubt that as demand for oil continues to overtake supply, and existing reserves decline, the price of oil will rise to the point that more unconventional sources will become economic. These unconventional sources include Canada's hard-to-extract, expensive, and dirty tar sands, as well as manufacturing it from coal or gas. The Cambridge Energy Research Associates are considered optimists on the question of oil supply, arguing that there is more to be extracted from challenging geological conditions, from coal and gas, and increased recoveries from known fields, but their arguments depend at least partly on higher price. And they argue that all this would allow us to meet demand for only a couple more decades, after which "supply may well struggle to meet demand." And they are the optimists.

The days of relatively easy and inexpensive oil—the days of big, light oil discoveries—are a thing of the past. In mid-2008, Shorki Ghanem, chairman of the Libyan National Oil Corporation, connected the dots. "The easy, cheap oil is over," he said. "Peak oil is looming."

For Canada, to take an extreme example, 97 percent of its reserves are now heavy oil and oil sands. Certainly, these will boost reserves and production for years to come. Canada's oil-sands deposits are about the same size as Saudi Arabia's reserves, but they are expensive, both capital intensive and requiring large amounts of energy input. Oil-sands projects have required capex of $3.8 billion to $8.6 billion to get going. New pipelines are required to bring the oil to market, specifically to the U.S. hubs. Refineries need to be retrofit, since most U.S. refineries are designed for lighter, sweet crude.

In all, it is estimated that the cost for tar sands will be more than $15 billion a year. The ongoing cost of production has declined significantly as the projects have started and economies of scale have kicked in. From $35 a barrel at the onset, in 1991, it costs around $10 a barrel to produce from oil sands today. (That is just the cash cost and excludes capital, overhead, and so on.) There are also other constraints, however. Oil sands require a significant amount of energy in order to produce the oil from the sands projects (part of my thesis for favoring small Canadian gas producers), and there are also pipeline constraints at present, though that will be overcome. Nonetheless, notwithstanding all this, Canada's oil sands represent the most substantive solution to the world's pending oil shortage, one that is real if costly.

Demand Increases

The demand story for oil is broadly the same as for other commodities, namely huge potential increases from China as it reaches the economic take-off point and per-capita consumption moves up. (We discussed this in Chapter 2.) With developed countries having reached a plateau in their per-capita usage, but none declining in any appreciable way, it is clear that even if total supply of oil can increase, the consumption will continue and the crisis only postponed. High prices will eventually cut into demand, though the rise to $147 in 2007 did little to reduce U.S. or global demand. Eventually, however, high prices would slow the rise in demand and spur increased substitution. (See Figure 17.4.)

The problem is that for much of oil use, specifically transportation, there is no meaningful substitution currently available. Everything else, from electric cars to nuclear submarines, is marginal. The only meaningful way to cut oil consumption in transportation in the near future is to stop using automobiles, and there are millions of Chinese who will not willingly give up their aspirations in this regard.

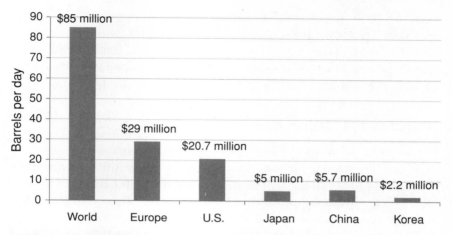

Figure 17.4 Emerging Economies Match Developed
Source: CIA World Factbook, December 2008.

Nor, any time soon, are Americans going to take to gas-fueled public buses. Today, just over half of world use of oil is for transportation, so this is the critical area. A little over one-quarter is used for industry and power, and around one-tenth each for raw materials and home heating. Certainly, there are substitutes for home heating and power, but transportation remains the largest and most intractable use. China, however, uses only one-third of its oil for transportation, but that is precisely the area where China's demand is likely to experience the strongest growth.

Global demand for oil has been growing consistently for decades, but in recent years even more dramatically as China's use has picked up, overtaking its own supply. As the rest of the world slowed in 2009, China's economy surged ahead, and with it, its oil consumption, up nearly 8 percent year on year. The IEA forecasts another increase this year, up to 8.9 million barrels per day. Although just a 2 percent increase from 2009—and it may prove conservative as previous IEA forecasts in this regard have been upwardly revised more than once—that consumption is still up almost 30 percent from 2007.

More significant, however, is the per-capita consumption. Most newly industrialized nations have followed a similar path in per-capita consumption. Japan's consumption was about 2 barrels per person until the economy took off in the late 1960s and per-capita consumption shot up within five years to 15 to 16 barrels, where it remains today. A decade later, South Korea's consumption, from under 1 barrel per person started to move up and then, in the late 1980s, shot up within five years to that same 15 to 16 barrels per person.

China Plays Catch Up

For the last 40 years, China's per-capita oil consumption was less than one barrel per person, slowly moving up at the beginning of this century to about 2.2 barrels per person today. If China's economy follows a traditional development pattern, and oil consumption follows Japan and Korea, we can expect that number soon to shoot up. Perhaps it won't reach that 15 barrels per person any time soon, but it will increase meaningfully from the current 2.2 barrels, which, given the country's huge population base, will have a significant impact on overall consumption.

Here's the scary part: If China's per-capita oil consumption were to move up to the level of Korea, China would consume all the oil produced in the world.

Behind China is India. That country's oil consumption is still less than one barrel per person, though it has been slowly increasing in recent years. India's take off point will be a few years hence. But if China and India were to consume just 5 barrels per person, that's one-third of Korea and Japan, and substantially less than countries like Mexico, then the world's supply of oil would have to increase by 40 percent. *That* is unlikely (and *that's* a British understatement).

Now, China sources a greater amount of its energy from coal and hydro than do many other countries. But cut and dice the numbers how you will; make conservative assumptions on demand and aggressive ones on supply: The simple fact is that oil supply cannot keep up with increased demand over the next decade or two without significantly higher prices. The immensity of the potential gap points to growing shortages and higher prices.

I have not argued that there are not large volumes of oil still to be found and produced, but that it will require significantly higher prices to extract them. The spurt to $147 per barrel in mid-2008, though admittedly short-lived, did not increase production, nor did it cause significantly lower demand. Certainly, higher prices than today's $70 to $80 trading range will be required on a sustained basis before we start to see increased supply. More likely, however, the long-term answer to the dilemma will come from changing demand patterns; so what price is necessary to limit demand while spurring new production?

Investment Opportunities and Pitfalls

Investing in the oil and gas patch offers lots of opportunities but many risks. Overall, it is not an industry with high returns on capital. In a study by Philippe Petit, presented at a Goldman Sachs conference in 2005, it was shown that 40-year returns on invested capital for each sector of the industry—integrated oil and gas, refining and transportation, exploration, and drilling—were below the returns for all U.S. industry. Given the risks involved in these sectors as well as the inherent volatility, one would have expected higher returns.

The major integrated oil companies, such as Shell and BP, are problematic as investments. First, they tend to have fairly low rates of return, particularly given the high risks involved. As with the major producers in all the commodities, they have the burden of replacing their depleting reserves and that is not an easy, or inexpensive, matter. They have little growth. And for low-growth entities, their multiples are not always so low, nor their yields so attractive.

Most important of all, as integrated companies, they are involved in the entire chain, from exploration and production to refining and retail. Higher prices affect them in different ways along the chain and can be a detriment in downstream activities. At times, they can be commodity-price neutral, which while not making them necessarily a poor investment does negate a major reason we wish to be involved in the sector. Of course, I am painting with a very broad brush here, and at different times, and at different prices, specific companies can be very good investments. Exxon is perhaps my favorite as a company; it has a strong balance sheet, is involved in both oil and gas, and has exploration exposure around the world.

I also tend to shy away from the national oil companies, which are subject to political pressures and whose stocks tend to be hit harder by downturns. PFC Energy, a consulting firm, notes that national oil companies often face a shortfall of investment capital; profits are often diverted to the government. Majors with more dependable cash flow tend to invest more strategically, especially in a downturn. Whereas the global majors' shares dropped from 20 to 45 percent in the year following the oil highs over $100, the public shares of national companies dropped from 47 to 75 percent, a significant gap.

My preferred sectors in which to fish are the major independent Exploration and Production (E&P) companies, both oil and gas, particularly those that are potential take-over candidates. I will look at some of these after I discuss the natural gas market and the fundamental changes taking place therein.

CHAPTER

18

Gas

There has been a revolution in the natural gas market in the last few years. Another hydrocarbon like oil but cleaner, gas was thought to be in desperately short supply just a few years ago. Conventional gas peaked in the lower 48 as far back as the late 1960s, followed by Gulf of Mexico gas in 2001. Existing fields were maturing quickly, and, increasingly, despite more rigs exploring, less was being found. What was being found was increasingly small with high decline rates.

Then Along Came Shale

Then gas got a second lease on life as new technologies were adapted to free significant amounts of gas previously locked away in tight rock formations. It has been a revolution in the U.S. gas industry. It had long been known that there was gas in tight-rock formations, but it had long been thought small and difficult to extract. In 1990, so-called unconventional gas, primarily gas from shales and coal-bed methane, accounted for around 10 percent of U.S. gas production. Then innovators and early movers, including Mitchell Energy, EOG, and Devon, started trying to extract more gas from these formations. Using two technologies together, they have succeeded beyond their wildest dreams and given natural gas a second lease on life, and perhaps changed the face of energy in the United States for years to come.

Horizontal drilling allows wells to go sideways once they reach a deposit, which opens up a much greater expanse of a deposit. This is essential for deposits that may be large but disseminated instead of a concentrated pool of gas. Hydraulic fracturing, known in the industry as *fracking*, injects a mixture of water and sand at high pressure, breaking up ("fracturing") the rock and freeing the trapped gas These two techniques had been known and used for some time, but when companies were able to combine them, the potential for these formations broke wide open.

The breakthrough came in 2002 when Devon acquired small producer Mitchell Energy and with it large acreage in the Barnett Shale, around Fort Worth, Texas. Mitchell had been a pioneer in shale extraction in Texas, and Devon's president Larry Nichols saw the potential. The company made a large gamble on Barnett, increasing its debt above its traditional levels to make the acquisition, and then stepping up exploration and expanding a processing plant it owns. But Barnett became, for many years, Devon's largest and fastest-growing gas project. The shale concept was little known and understood at the time, so much so that Devon had to hold a "Shale School" for financial analysts soon after the acquisition.

Barnett was the first large shale operation and it has continued to expand, while other large shale plays are underway in Arkansas, Pennsylvania, and New York. Unconventional gas, particularly shale, became an increasing topic for gas companies, but its importance crept up on people—both companies and analysts—slowly. There were many doubters even after Devon's Barnett coup. Today, unconventional gas represents 40 percent of U.S. gas production, with shale by far the largest and the fastest-growing portion. That has helped boost overall gas production, up 15 percent in recent years, and put the U.S. market into an oversupplied condition again, with full storage facilities, and diversion of other gas (such as Liquefied Natural Gas, or LNG). U.S. gas reserves have jumped 58 percent in the past four years (35 percent in the past year alone), thanks to shale, and some predict the country now has 100 years' supply.

Shale got the imprimatur of big oil when Exxon agreed to pay $41 billion to acquire XTO Energy, an active shale player. Exxon has also leased acreage in the Horne River Basin, in British Colombia, Canada's largest shale play. The company estimates there is one quadrillion cubic feet of shale gas worldwide, and outside of the United States, exploration is only just starting.

Going Global

For sure, shale is not just a North American phenomenon. There are also known to be large shale resources around the world, some suggest larger than all current proven natural gas reserves. In other countries it will be slower to get underway, owing to greater regulations and a less entrepreneurial oil industry. Already, though, some U.S. companies are trying to export the technology. Exxon has drilled exploratory wells in Germany. Devon has teamed up with Total and wants to drill in France, while Conoco has an agreement to drill in Poland. EOG, one of the early movers in the Barnett and all significant North American shale plays, is drilling in one spot in China and has also bought up land in Europe, though it won't say where for competitive reasons. In China, the initial program is a test to see if the technology might work on the local geology. If successful, however, EOG has other potential projects in that vast country.

One of the largest global joint ventures is between Chesapeake and Statoil. Cash-strapped Chesapeake sold the Norwegian company a large stake in its Marcellus shale holdings, in Pennsylvania, for $3.9 billion, but the two companies are now looking at shale fields in China, India, Australia, and other countries. At the beginning of this year, Chesapeake sold a 25 percent stake in its Barnett Shale fields to France's Total. Clearly, European companies want to get involved in shale, as much for the expertise it brings for them to develop their domestic shale as for the interest in U.S. fields. For that reason, we are likely to see more partnerships than all-out takeovers, such as Exxon's buy-out of XTO Energy. If companies can obtain the necessary permits, shale could take off internationally as it has in the United States.

However, the environmental issues could prove more considerable in some areas, particularly in Europe where not only is there perhaps a heightened environmental awareness generally, but population density is higher. It is one thing to have rigs, pipelines, and heavy trucks in Texas and Louisiana where residents are used to drilling and the economies are more dependent on oil and gas. It is altogether another thing in densely populated Belgium or pristine Switzerland. However, many European nations would welcome a new source of gas to lessen the dependence on Russia's volatile Gazprom. Nine nations obtain more than 60 percent of their gas from Gazprom; three over 90 percent. The new Russian-friendly government in the Ukraine, through which the gas flows on its way to Europe, makes the issue even more critical.

Problems with Shale

Though shale has given the industry a second chance in North America and turned around production, there are differences of opinion in the industry as to its longer-term impact, particularly overseas. While there are some analysts who assert that shale will provide the United States with 100 years of gas reserves, the potential overseas is less known and the impact could be less than in the United States for geological as well as environmental reasons. Certainly, output from a typical shale well drops very sharply in the first year, around 45 percent for a new well, but the question is how long production at lower rates might flow, and how much expansion potential is there at the shale plays. Chesapeake estimate production could last 65 years. Others think that, other than Barnett, most producing shale deposits are likely to peak soon, over the next three to four years. Compounding the difficulty is that the U.S. Department of Energy's Energy Information Administration (EIA) may have been overstating production from shale through faulty statistical extrapolation, as it now itself admits. Some in the industry, such as EOG's CEO Mark Papa, have long been skeptical of the EIA's numbers.

Although natural gas is a fossil fuel, it is much cleaner than others, giving off about half as much CO_2 as coal and about 30 percent less than oil. For that reason, environmentalists have had an ambivalent attitude toward it. At first, the promise of shale gained support of environmentalists, including the somewhat extreme Sierra Club and Environmental Defense Fund. A large, reliable, supply of clean gas held promise for U.S. energy needs.

However, more recently, many grassroots environmentalists have charged that the gas and chemicals used in fracking are seeping into the water supply. Fracking has been specifically exempted from the Safe Drinking Water Act, which does not help the industry defend the practice. Now Congress has got in on the act and wants hearings. With industry bogeyman Exxon now involved in shale, there will no doubt be much grandstanding. The Environmental Protection Agency has launched a study on the practise. It is difficult to see that Congress would prohibit the technique seen as a clean solution to

America's "foreign energy" crisis (but one should never say never where Congress is concerned).

Other than LNG, gas is a much more regional market than oil, which is transported around the globe to reach markets. There are huge known supplies of natural gas in other countries, but they don't directly affect the U.S. gas market. Russia, Iran, and Qatar have known reserves of gas four to eight times those of the United States. So does Saudi Arabia, though much of that is in oil wells not available for use. The Saudi oil company Aramco claims to have other large gas reserves and recently—and unusually—opened up exploration in its "Empty Quarter," the arid southern desert, to foreign companies. But so far, the results have been extremely disappointing; Total backed out of its consortium in 2008 after several dry holes. This has led to skepticism about Aramco's claims—if it had the gas, why didn't it keep it to itself?—which has not helped Saudi's claims for its oil reserves. This could have important implications for the region, as well as the global energy market, since if the gas reserves are not as plentiful as hoped, Saudi Arabia may have to divert some of its oil production to domestic needs in order to continue to fuel its rapid development and avoid internal strife. That would mean less oil for the world market however.

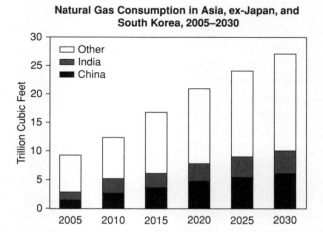

Asia's Appetite for LNG on the Rise

Figure 18.1   China and India Buy More Gas

Source: AgoraFinancial.com.

Supply of LNG itself has increased in recent years, but much of this has gone to China and other Asian countries that have locked up supply. (See Figure 18.1.) With expensive tankers and terminals, securing long-term supply is essential. Liquid gas is transported to a facility that then turns it back into gas for local use. Asia is the largest and the fastest growing market for LNG, with Japan and South Korea—an early mover in LNG—together accounting for over half of the world's regasification capacity. But China is catching up, as is India. Although LNG can be tanked around the world, the growing facilities throughout Asia are a boon for Australia, whose huge $50 billion Gorgon project (a joint venture of Exxon, Chevron, and Shell) has just received the go ahead.

Increase Demand Ahead

Ironically, the new source of gas from shale may improve the prospects for the gas market. In the short term, there is still too much supply for current demand. But indications of a long-term reliable supply will encourage gas demand and encourage switching from coal-fired plants to gas-fired plants, and encourage the building of gas-fueled transportation, including buses and even trucks. Gas remains very inexpensive as an energy source compared with oil, coal and uranium; the EIA projects gas prices below $7 through 2025. Reliable long-term supplies and a stable price will see demand increase.

Gas prices have traditionally been very volatile. Not only do they fluctuate with the season, they can move dramatically with the weather, including cold winters or warm summer, or incidents such as hurricanes which can knock out rigs in the Gulf and reduce supply suddenly. Gas prices almost quadrupled in 2000 from $2.50 million BTU to nearly $10 at the end of the year, before falling back under $3. After hurricanes Katrina and Rita, they peaked briefly at $15 before falling under $7. They then spiked at $13 in mid-2008, before collapsing under $5 again. That's a wild ride for any consumer, all the more so when the consumer is looking at alternate sources of energy at the same time.

Now more production, more reserves, a more stable price environment, a new network of pipelines (nearly 4,000 miles added in 2008), and the presence of major oil companies make gas more attractive again.

Not only are gas-fired power plants cleaner than coal, but they can be built more quickly. With existing coal-fired plants running at full capacity, the aging nuclear plants experiencing increasing maintenance shut downs, as are oil refineries, there has already been significant switching. Gas could move up from 20 percent of U.S. electricity supply much closer to coal (currently almost half supply) over coming years.

With the new demand, however, as well as the large amounts of gas required for Canada's oil-sands projects, and the potential for decline rates in shale to be faster than currently anticipated, gas could see higher prices after the current storage supplies are drawn down. Prices could move back to $6 mcf and above—they are currently, June 2010, less than $5—which would still make gas relatively inexpensive to oil considering long-term ratios between the two. But at those prices, gas companies would be very profitable.

Investment Opportunities

Where do we look for opportunities in oil and gas? There are three main areas I favor. These are areas in which to fish, not for across-the-board buying:

- The major independent Exploration and Production companies, commonly called E&P companies, both oil and gas, particularly those that are potential takeover candidates.
- The stronger Canadian royalty companies, which, despite their loss of tax benefits, can still sport high yields.
- Key players in the Canadian oil sands, which has long-term potential.

The large independent E&Ps, like Devon, Chesapeake, and Apache, are possible targets for a global major needing to add to reserves. They have assets that can be attractive to the majors to plug gaps in their portfolios, and the prices can be reasonable. I have discussed how many European companies have sought joint ventures with U.S. companies to gain a foothold in the shale play and to gain expertise and partners to take back home. But such acquisitions do not involve only new plays, but are rather ongoing. Chesapeake sold its U.S. gas assets last year to BP and Statoil, which were in need of such assets and paid a good price for them. Devon has agreed to sell its international assets, including offshore Brazil, as well as its Gulf of Mexico interests to BP, in a strategic shift toward more aggressive development of its nonconventional onshore assets. Buying an established asset from a company like Devon can be less expensive in the long run than starting from scratch, and certainly quicker. Beyond that, the large E&P companies must be on the radar of the global integrated companies, which have had difficulty replacing reserves. Buying a large independent, though not inexpensive, could prove cheaper than starting from scratch in the many frontier areas the companies are now forced to go.

Companies like Devon Energy, EOG Resources, and Encana Corp. are all solid companies apart from any possible merger and acquisitions (M&A) activity. As companies, they are my favorites, though price is always critical when deciding whether and when to buy a stock. Of these, Devon (DVN, NY) is the biggest, the largest of the U.S. independents. The company has grown largely through acquisition over the years, but it has also been nimble and quick to move into emerging plays. It has generally maintained a strong balance sheet (with a current net debt to cap of around 27 percent). President and CEO Larry Nichols, who helped his father found the company in 1970, is one of the most approachable big-company executives around. His own children are not involved in the business, so Devon's name always comes up as possible acquisition. The company is involved in both oil and gas, primarily in onshore North America, following its strategic decision to exit many high-potential but high-capital foreign operations.

Canada's Encana (ECA, NY) is somewhat smaller than Devon. It has a higher debt level than Devon, but with more consistent cash flow due to an ongoing hedging program, it is certainly manageable. Following a split in the company that saw most oil assets go into a new company, Cenovus, Encana is a pure gas company, focused especially on unconventional resources. It is active in the Horn River Basin shale play mentioned earlier, as well as other unconventional plays throughout North America. Cenovus (CVE,NY) is also attractive, with steady cash flow from conventional oil and gas production as well as an interest in Canada's oil sands.

EOG Resources (EOG, NY) was part of Enron, but Chairman and CEO Mark Papa always seemed like a fish out of water in that environment. Only slightly smaller than Encana, EOG has traditionally been focused on gas, including LNG, though more recently it increased oil exposure, and is expecting to move to 50-50 gas and liquids. EOG has consistently been on the cutting edge of new technologies and new plays, and Papa has built the company through organic growth and the maintenance of a clean balance sheet. With a current net debt to cap ratio of 17 percent, it is one of the strongest in the industry. EOG has consistently increased reserves, without acquisitions, "through the drill bit," even when prices have been depressed. The company has always focused on return on capital, looking to be profitable rather than bigger.

Its technological edge, which evidenced itself in its early success in the Barnett Shale, continues to serve the company. EOG is now at the leading edge using shale gas techniques on areas of oil saturation, and after much trial and error, it has successfully produced oil in the Barnett, as well as in a very small Manitoba discovery. Though small, it proves the concept of getting oil out of tight rock formations with horizontal drilling, and EOG is the leader with several other potential deposits in the pipeline. Importantly, it is exporting this technology internationally, with the first effort underway in China. EOG, through a conservative balance sheet and cutting-edge technology, has put itself at the top among U.S. independents on return on investment, on costs, and on internal growth; and has been consistent on these measures over the years. Like Devon, though taking a different approach, EOG is a fine company and one that belongs in any resource portfolio.

Unconventional Opportunities

The Canadian oil sands are a long-term opportunity, given the enormous size of the reserves and the U.S. demand for oil. Many of the major integrated companies have bought into the area, though oil sands are only part of their overall company. I favor more pure exposure, such as Canadian Oil Sands Trust (COS-U, Toronto), which has a 37 percent working interest in the large Syncrude Joint Venture.

Although established as a trust, Canadian Oil Sands is quite different from most of the Canadian oil and gas royalty trusts. Canadian trusts themselves are different from most U.S. oil and gas royalty trusts, which usually own a stream of cash flow from a particular deposit (such as the San Juan Royalty Trust with its ownership of cash flow from the San Juan Basin). The trust pays out virtually all of its income to shareholders as dividends, but as the underlying asset matures and depletes, the dividends decline. Canadian oil and gas royalties are essentially operating E&P companies, but simply organized as trusts.

However, since the favorable Canadian tax treatment is set to be abolished next year, the Canadian trusts have been reorganizing themselves. The abolition of special tax treatment was a highly controversial decision since many investors bought these companies for the high dividends. However, many of these are attractive companies in their own right and stand up to comparison with other independent E&P companies. The weakness in the shares as we approach the abolition of the preferential tax treatment, however, means investors can buy good companies cheaply.

True, not all trusts were created equal; some have slashed dividends and will have to do so again. Others can continue paying relatively high dividends since they were generating strong cash flows. Some have "tax pools" that allow Canadian companies to offset current income from taxation. My favorites—again, always dependent on developments and current stock prices—include Arc Energy AET-U, Toronto), one of the largest and oldest of the Canadian royalty trusts, which has always operated with a strong balance sheet and steady growth. Despite cutting its dividend steadily since the tax proposals were introduced, it still yields almost 6 percent. For a solid company with growth prospects in the resource area, that's a pretty good yield.

Finally, we should be aware that there is a strong season pattern for oil and gas. Oil generally increases from December through August, declining until the onset of winter. May and June usually see flat prices during the long uptrend. (See Figure 18.2.) The reasons for this are obvious; both autumn and spring tend to see more moderate temperatures, between the winter heating needs and summer cooling, while the autumn especially sees a reduction in driving after summer. Gas follows the same broad pattern but has been much more dependent on weather. The energy stocks tend to anticipate these patterns, rising in December through to May. So looking to buy in the autumn lull is not a bad idea, and if you want to take profits, waiting until April or May is usually a good idea. (See Figure 18.3.)

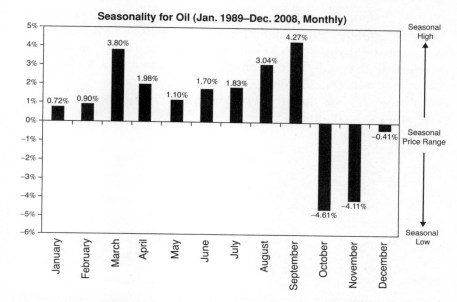

Figure 18.2   Seasonal Pattern to Oil Prices (Jan. 1989 to Dec. 2008, monthly)

Source: US Global Investors.

Spring Fling

The Average Monthly Percent Change of the S&P 500 Energy Index during the Last Twenty Years

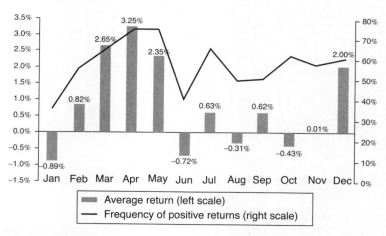

Figure 18.3   Oil and Gas Stocks Strong in Spring

Source: US Global Investors.

But we should not get carried away with short-term consideration, and remember the long-term super cycle that applies as much to oil and gas as to other resources. The demand for energy will increase dramatically in coming years as China and other Asian countries continue to develop and industrialize, and we can position ourselves with good quality North American and global oil and gas companies.

CHAPTER

19

Coal

Coal is dirty and dangerous, but there's lots of it, it's cheap, and it's in demand. Right now, 42 percent of the world's power generation comes from coal, but given that it dominates in China, India, and other emerging countries, that demand is likely to only increase. Many countries, including China, are dependent on coal for their electricity and for their economic development. China derives 80 percent of its power from coal, and India 70 percent. Coal is not going anywhere soon, but up. Mining analyst David Hargreaves calls coal his favorite investment sector because of the need to supply the exponential demand for energy.

Less in United States, More in China

The United States also consumes a lot, with fully half its electricity generated by coal-fired plants, which are not only low cost but long life. However, it is increasingly controversial in developed countries, since it is the prime source of CO_2. New technologies can clean particles (sulphur, nitrogen, and so on), and state-of-the-art plants are much cleaner than older plants. But however much one scrubs emissions, there is still CO_2 emitted into the atmosphere, and moves have been afoot in the United States for years to reduce the reliance of coal. (See Figure 19.1.)

Such moves may finally begin to have an inroad, now that gas supplies seem reasonably plentiful for the foreseeable future and, perhaps more important, nuclear has been largely rehabilitated. There are also moves to tax pollutants in some way or another, and if that

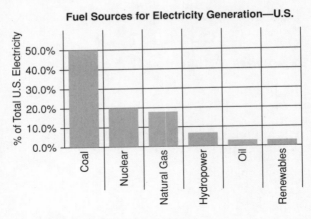

Figure 19.1 **Coal Is Important for Electricity**
Source: U.S. Department of Energy.

came to pass, coal would likely move from the lowest-cost fuel to one of the most expensive. So coal's use in the United States is likely to decline in years ahead, or at least grow only slowly.

But this will be more than offset by the growth from China and other emerging economies. China already consumes 41 percent of the world's coal, both thermal coal, used for power generation, and coking coal, used in steel making. Coal's use in steel making was a critical factor in the 30 percent jump in prices during 2009. Self-sufficient not so long ago, China's imports have shot up from the 4 to 6 metric ton level throughout the early 2000s, to over 16 metric tonnes last year. How much of this has been consumed and how much stockpiled is not known for sure. We do know, however, that China has taken steps to build a strategic coal reserve; China Shenghua Energy, a state-owned corporation, is building 10 coal storage sites across China.

As for supply, the United States has about a quarter of total world supplies, with Russia, India, and China also housing large supplies. China remains the world's largest producer and used to be self-sufficient. But its demand has shot up dramatically. Its coal is of a lesser quality, and the mines' safety and environmental record is very poor. In addition, most of its mines are in the north, far from major users, and it is cheaper to import coal from overseas than ship across land. The same applies to India.

Biggest Exporters, Close to China

Australia and Indonesia are the two major coal exporters, even though their supplies are not among the largest. Australia is by far the largest exporter of coking coal, with two-thirds of total exports, most of which go to China, the world's leading steel producer (and consumer of that type of coal). Australia is the second-largest exporter of thermal coal, beaten by Indonesia, with nearly one-third of total exports. Like Australia, Indonesia is close to market via sea lanes, but Australia is investing heavily in port and other facilities that should further boost its coal exports.

Again, as with other resources, China has been making efforts to tie up supplies, most notably with a $1.9 billion loan from the government to Indonesia's largest coal miner, Bumi Resources. And at the end of last year, the Yanzhou Coal Mining Co. acquired Australia's Felix Resources in a A$3.5 billion deal.

Much of the world's coal is produced by the major diversified miners, and as I have discussed, how owning some of these provides investors with broad exposure across the resource spectrum. BHP (BHP, NY) generates more revenue from coal (thermal and metallurgical, or coking) than from any other division, about 30 percent of total revenues. (Of course, the numbers fluctuate a lot depending on relative prices of the various resources, but this is mitigated by owning a large diversified company.)

A much smaller diversified miner, Teck Resources (TCK, NY), also generates more than one-third of its revenue from coal, with the balance from copper and zinc (and a little from gold). The largest pure play is Peabody Energy (BTU, NY), which has been acquiring Australian assets aggressively, so now Australia accounts for over a third of its revenues and nearly half of its earnings. Peabody's focus is on the high-margin metallurgical coal. At the other end of the spectrum are many smaller coal companies particularly in emerging countries.

So however much we may not like it, coal is here to stay. The simple fact is that China's energy needs as well as those of other developing economies require coal for many years to come.

CHAPTER 20

Uranium

Many energy analysts believe that the only practical solution to the world's energy needs is in nuclear power. Nuclear is clean and, once built, low cost. It could also be abundantly available. The same supply and demand issues we have discussed for all the commodities apply to uranium, the ingredient that produces nuclear power: increased global demand, particularly from China; and a shortage of large-scale supplies in the years ahead.

Bad PR for Nuclear

But nuclear power, not withstanding its advantages, has three main drawbacks: its reputation, waste disposal, and supply of uranium. Say "nuclear" power to most people and they immediately think of Hiroshima and Nagasaki. Nuclear power first came to the public's attention with weaponry, and that image has stuck. But a nuclear power plant is not a bomb waiting to go off. Uranium must be enriched to 90 percent to create a weapon; for a reactor, it is enriched only to 3 percent. So the uranium, let alone the power plant, is not explosive. Then, there are concerns about possible terrorist activity. First, stealing the uranium would do little good absent enrichment facilities. Dropping a bomb on a plant would not cause a nuclear explosion. Modern power plants themselves are safe; a test has been conducted of flying a F-4 jet straight into a concrete wall the same thickness as that on a nuclear power plant; the plane was destroyed but no hole was created in the wall. As for Chernobyl and Three Mile Island, they don't build plants like that anymore.

Nuclear waste is largely a problem of our own making. More than 95 percent of the material in a spent fuel rod can be recycled for energy and medical isotopes, but presidents Ford and Carter banned the recycling of nuclear waste. Thus, we have a lot of waste and have to import medical isotopes from countries that do recycle. France has a long history of generating most of its electricity from nuclear power, and has long recycled its spent fuel rods. The small amount left that cannot be recycled fits into a space beneath the floor of one room at La Hague.

Even without recycling, nuclear waste could be stored safely inside salt domes, where radioactivity cannot escape. Nuclear waste could have been safely stored inside Yucca Mountain, but the plan was recently scuttled by President Obama as a "thank you" to Nevada's Senator Harry Reid. "Nimby" dynamics operate overtime when nuclear is concerned. The sight of Osthammar and Oskarshamn, two Swedish municipalities that each host reactors, competing over the right to be the site of a new nuclear waste facility is rare indeed.

The third problem concerns the supply of uranium, a necessary ingredient to generate nuclear power. A nuclear plant cannot be retrofitted to enable it to use coal or gas to generate electricity; it must have uranium. Is there enough uranium to fulfill the needs of all the nuclear plants currently on the world's drawing boards? The answer is no, not at today's price. But the good news is that the cost of the uranium in the overall operation of the power plant is relatively small. To generate electricity at a nuclear plant costs less than 3 cents per kilowatt hour, of which the cost of uranium is only 0.45 cents; the price of uranium could double or triple, and nuclear power would still be competitive. Interestingly, the cost of generation from nuclear has been relatively flat for 20 years, while costs for oil and gas are up dramatically in recent years, to 17 cents and 8 cents, respectively. There are many uranium mines that could be brought on if the price doubled, and assuming the political will to permit the mines. So availability of uranium itself is not an issue.

Besides these drawbacks, nuclear energy is used to generate power and electricity but not, for the most part, for transportation, where oil remains far and away the dominant power source. So, at best, increased use of nuclear power solves only part of the overall energy problem.

Despite these real and perceived problems, even many environmental activists have reluctantly recognized nuclear as a relatively clean fuel source, some have even embraced it. Stewart Brand edited the great 1960s hippie handbook *Whole Earth Catalog.* They don't come much greener than he. In Brand's latest book, *Whole Earth Discipline: An Ecopragmatist Manifesto,* he supports nuclear energy, noting the strong safety record, commenting, "I've learned to disbelieve much of what I've been told by my fellow environmentalists."

The Energy of the Future

Unlike some of the resources we've looked at, the demand for uranium (for power plants) is very widespread while the supply is not. Currently, nuclear plants operate in 30 countries, and they are planned for another 13. Some countries have long generated much of the power from nuclear: 33 percent for Japan, 75 percent for France. Others have only recently starting generating nuclear power.

There has been a rebirth in interest in nuclear in recent years, following a long hiatus, provoked by the growing concern about availability and price of oil as well as about CO_2 emissions. A plant in Finland is the first nuclear power plant built in Europe since 1986. Everywhere around the world, in major and developing countries, the revival of nuclear is underway. Britain, whose last plant was built in 1995, is planning four plants to add to its existing 19, but the plants are bigger, so the four alone would generate more than half as much power as the existing ones. The United States generates more than 20 percent of its electrical power from its 104 nuclear reactors, but has not built one since the 1970s. The political will to expand is widespread, with even the current administration willing to support new nuclear facilities. Several plants are underway. Even in Germany, a long-standing plan to phase out all existing plants is under attack by Chancellor Angela Merkel. In all, the EIA is forecasting the construction of 1,000 new reactors by 2050; there are 445 reactors operational around the world today.

In truth, the building of new reactors in the developed West has been much slower, partly due to government, environmental, and permitting delays. But the tide is turning, and it seems that each week some positive announcement is made somewhere. One potentially intriguing advance is the development of refrigerator-sized nuclear reactors, developed by Hyperion Power Generation of New Mexico, and Japan's Toshiba, which could power a small factory or town distant from the utility grid. The small reactors might also prove more politically palatable.

China's Ambitious Growth Plans

Over the next 20 years, there are planned or proposed 376 new reactors worldwide, up from 318 in August 2008, and we expect the number to increase further in coming years. The big plans are emanating from the East, with China leading the world in planned reactor builds. Its plans are astonishing for a country that only built its first reactor in 1994. Today, 11 are operating, with another 20 under construction (to be housed in six new plants). Beyond that, 33 more are in the planning stage, and another 90 have been proposed for the next quarter century, with as many as 250 at some stage of planning. (See Figure 20.1.)

They may not all get built; this is true of proposed reactors and plants in many other countries as well. But it is an astonishing and ambitious growth profile. As recently as 2005, China upped its long-term plans from 30 reactors to 40. The rapidity with which the plans

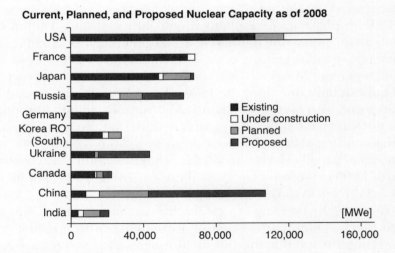

Current, Planned, and Proposed Nuclear Capacity as of 2008

Legend:
- ■ Existing
- □ Under construction
- ▨ Planned
- ■ Proposed

Figure 20.1   Nuclear: The Power of the Future

Source: Agorafinancial.com. Data taken from CLSA Asia-Pacific, International Energy Association, WNA, IAEA.

are being raised, as well as plants being planned, is amazing. In all, China is planning on increasing its nuclear capacity sixfold, to at least 60 gigawatts of energy by 2020, with a further increase to 160 GWe by 2030.

But it is one that is necessary. If the Chinese were to consume the same levels of electricity per person as South Korea or Japan, they would need the equivalent of 1,000 1-gigawatt nuclear plants. (Its current plants are a little less than 1-megawatt on average, while its new ones will be a little more. One megawatt is equal to 1 million watts; a gigawatt is 1 billion.) This isn't going to happen—the per-capita consumption will be lower than for South Korea, other forms of power generation will take some of the load, plants will become more efficient—but the numbers give us a glimpse of the size of the problem. China's planned build will increase the share of its power-generating capacity from less than 2 percent today to close to 5 percent by 2020.

China has increased its nuclear projections a few times recently. Like most of the reactors being planned, China's new reactors have more capacity than its existing ones. China only recently upped its nuclear capacity to 60,000 megawatts by 2020 and now is considering increasing it to 70,000 megawatts; currently, it produces about 8,500. That again provides insight into the increased demand we can anticipate in coming years.

The increased demand will clearly have an impact on the price of uranium, though there will be other bottlenecks as well. The companies that build power plants will have full order books for years to come. There is only one shell fabricator in the world, in Japan; China has the entire capacity back-ordered for eight years. Only five shipping companies transport uranium, through very few shipping lanes, so they too can anticipate increased business. In fact, given extra time requirements to load and unload uranium, in tight shipping markets, some companies don't want to ship uranium.

So we have had the experience in 2007 where some producers were unable to deliver what they had committed to, even though they were producing. One U.S. utility had three instances of *force majeur* imposed in a 12-month period. In addition, there are services that, if unexpectedly closed, can cause bottlenecks. Port Hope, in Ontario, the main conversion facility for Cameco, the world's leading uranium miner, was closed for 12 months from mid-2007 after soil contamination was discovered beneath the facility. Port Hope processes a quarter of the world's uranium and Cameco was forced to sell from inventory. Then again, it suspended production of a form of uranium (UF6) for six months at the beginning of 2009 when the company was unable to purchase an adequate supply of hydrofluoric acid, a primary feed material.

Demand for Uranium

But the most important impact for us will be on uranium. We have noted that once a nuclear power plant has been built, it needs uranium feedstock. There is no alternative and the plant cannot be retrofitted for another fuel source. Moreover, given the very large capital costs, plants are likely to continue operating even at reduced margins. As we've seen, once built, generating costs compare very favorably with alternatives. And lastly, uranium itself is a relatively small part of the cost of producing power at a nuclear plant. Thus, once the plants are built, they will demand uranium at almost any price. Given the breadth of demand worldwide, but the small number of significant producers, and given that demand is likely to be relatively inelastic, the potential for price spikes on the back of supply interruptions is very real, apart from the ongoing squeeze in prices as more plants get built.

For the next few years, demand could grow by a little less than 5 percent a year, but more from the mid-teens on. At the same time, supply should grow—absent interruptions—by around 5 percent for the next few years; though production growth matches demand growth, there is an annual deficit each year met from stockpiles. But supply will decline after around 2015 as reserves are depleted. That is when it gets interesting. The current uranium price (around $50 per pound) is too low to stimulate much new production, and certainly too low to generate production to meet anticipated demand in the 2015–2025 period.

The simple conclusion is that there is not enough uranium production, including all planned production, to satisfy reactor needs, including initial core requirements, for the next 20 years. A higher price is inevitable to ration supply and stimulate new production. Right now, the spot market is oversupplied because of new supplies from largely small mines in Africa and Kazakhstan, which hit the market ahead of the increased demand from new reactors. But this is very much a temporary phase.

The World Nuclear Association pegs global uranium consumption at 65,000 tons a year (130 million pounds). Almost 60 percent of that goes to three countries, the United States (with 29 percent), France (16 percent), and Japan (13 percent); 80 percent goes to the top eight consumers. After the big three, demand is spread around many countries taking 3 to 5 percent each. China right now consumes 3 percent of the world's annual uranium supply.

But even at that low level, China cannot meet its own demand. Its five operational uranium mines together produce around 840 tons; China does not publish uranium production numbers, so these are WNA estimates. At that, it produces less than half its current needs. China aims to increase that, with the country's main producer, China National Nuclear Corp., forecasting domestic output of 2,000 tons by 2020. By that time, China's needs will dwarf that production. It is more than likely that China, and perhaps other countries, will start stockpiling uranium again for strategic reserves. After all, if a significant amount of a country's electricity is generated by nuclear power, then uranium is as strategic as oil.

Uranium Producers

So where does all the world's uranium come from? As with most resources, there is primary supply (from mines) and secondary (in this case mostly recycled and processed military-grade). Primary supply accounts for about 60 percent of current supply, but is likely to increase in coming years. Just as three countries account for about 60 percent of uranium demand, so too do three countries produce 60 percent of the world's uranium, Canada, Kazakhstan and Australia, each with about 20 percent. After that, there are five other producing countries of any significance, including the United States, which currently produces about 3 percent of the world's uranium. These eight countries account for 93 percent of the total production. China does not even figure on the table. As for companies, the 10 largest account for almost 90 percent of supply (though not all of them are publicly traded companies). (See Figure 20.2.)

All of Canada's production comes from the Athabasca Basin in Saskatchewan, the richest land in the world. Mines in Athabasca are 18 and 20 percent uranium; Areva is mining in Namibia at 0.1 percent! Most of Canada's output comes from two mines owned or partly owned by a single company, Cameco, the world's largest

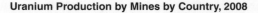

Uranium Production by Mines by Country, 2008

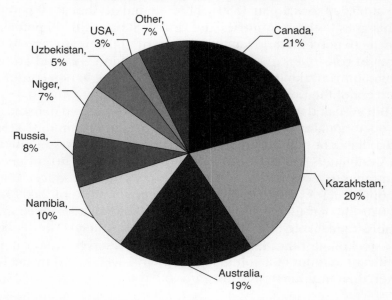

Figure 20.2   Three Countries Supply over Half the Uranium
Source: World Nuclear Association, February 2010.

nongovernment producer. The next-door province of British Colombia has a moratorium on uranium mining, though active exploration is taking place elsewhere, notably in Newfoundland.

Cameco is also 50 percent owner of the troubled Cigar Lake mine. The world's richest known uranium deposit, Cigar Lake was originally scheduled to commence production in 2007 with 18 million pounds a year, or 15 percent of the world's production. But twice, in 2006 and 2008, the mine was flooded during development, and the start date for the mine has been continually pushed back. Some analysts do not expect it to start production until 2013. Part of Cigar Lake's production will take up the slack from Cameco's two big mines that are beginning to see production declines.

Problems at Major Mines

But if it can start production before these two start to deplete meaningfully, and before a significant pickup in demand from new reactors, that will keep a lid on the uranium price for a few years. This is why my forecasts point to the possibility of a relatively flat uranium price for the next couple of years with significant price increases in the second half of the decade.

But as Cigar Lake has demonstrated, these are not easy mines. The world's largest producing mine, BHP's Olympic Dam in Australia, with about 10 percent of the world's production, has experienced technical difficulties that forced a sharp reduction in output. There is the ever-present risk of supply disruptions that should they come a few years from now when demand is picking up, could drive the price up, if only temporarily.

There is certainly potential for more uranium mines in Canada, both in Saskatchewan and elsewhere. But given the concentration of uranium in small areas, exploring for uranium is a bit like looking for a needle in a haystack. Australia too has potential to increase production, arguably even more in the near term than Canada. But uranium mining has a troubled history in that country. Until 2007, it had a Three Mines Policy, limiting the number of uranium mines to three, while some states had outright bans on mining. In addition, Aboriginal groups have proved obstacles to development of uranium projects and they have increasing clout in the permitting process. Now there is another threat to Australia's uranium production. The country's proposed new "super profits" tax on mining may affect BHP's decision on expansion at Olympic Dam, the company has said. CEO Marius Kloppers said it would be "very difficult" to approve the Olympic Dam expansion, as well as another uranium project, Yeelirrie in Western Australia, because of the proposed tax. So though the geologic potential is certainly there, it may take some time to get new mines approved and into production.

The other of the big three producing countries, Kazakhstan, has far more smaller mines in production, partly because it can use in-situ leaching, which is much less expensive than conventional mining and allows smaller deposits to be profitable. When Paladin opened a mine in Namibia in 2006, it was the first new conventional mine in over a decade.

Kazakhstan also has much potential; its original, ambitious, 2010 target of 15,000 tons—it currently produces around 8,500—won't come to pass, but certainly the country has the potential to boost production. But its failure to meet its own target by such a margin, due to technical problems at many sites, again shows the fragility of the market. There is also potential for increased production from other countries, including Uzbekistan, where currently all production is state owned. The government wants to increase production, but its financial situation precludes this unless it cuts a deal with the Russians or others.

United States: Big Reserve, Little Production

There is also potential to step up production from the United States, which was in the 1960s a significant producer but despite having the fourth-largest reserves in the world, currently imports 95 percent of its uranium. Conventional mining is expensive in this country, requiring a price of $60 a pound just to be economic. Several of these mines have shut in recent months. But there is potential also for smaller in situ projects, particularly in Wyoming, Texas, and New Mexico, but the permitting process, both for exploration and then for development and eventual production, is tortuous.

Right now, much of U.S. "production" comes from an agreement with Russia on highly enriched uranium (HEU) under which Russia's weapons-grade uranium is being downgraded, generating a little less than 8,000 tonnes a year. The HEU agreement ends in 2013, however; it could be renewed, though perhaps on stiffer terms. It is also not clear just how much more weapons-grade uranium Russia may have available for conversion to power plant use.

The Supply and Demand Gap

Existing facilities worldwide are forecast to show a steady decline from around 35,000 tons to 28,000 tons by 2020. The problem is that that production is less than half what is known will be required, and only one-third of the higher estimates for demand requirements. Of course, there has been an ongoing annual mine deficit since 1985, the first year production was below reactor requirements. The gap has been met from inventories, including large government stockpiles from the Cold War era of the 1950s and 1960s as well as dismantling of warheads and recycling of the weapons-grade uranium. Currently, about 20 percent of global supply comes from the downgrading of nuclear weapons. (See Figure 20.3.)

So how is that gap going to be met? Planned mines should add another 10,000 tons by 2020, bringing us close to 40,000 tons. These numbers are likely conservative, given that WNA is perennially

Uranium: Supply/Demand Gap

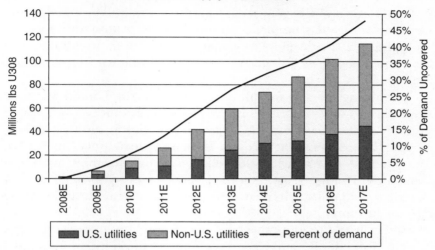

Figure 20.3   Growing Gap Ahead

Source: Goldsheetlink.com; Data from RBC Capital Markets.

high on its production estimates. Expected demand will be between 60,000 and 80,000 tons. There may be continued sales from stockpiles, but it is not clear just how depleted those stockpiles are. Clearly, though, the inventories won't last forever and there is a long lead time for new mines.

Let us go further out, into more speculative territory. Over the next 20 years, demand could be around 4.7 billion pounds, supply from existing mines around 1.8 billion pounds, and estimates of secondary supplies 0.8 billion. That leaves 2.2 billion pounds, not far from half, to be found. This is an enormous challenge.

It has been a quarter century since the last uranium cycle, which means there has been little capital spent on mines and projects and, as important, technical expertise is thin on the ground. A mining engineer might be able to work as well in nickel or in zinc, a geologist might be able to adapt his skills for gold or for copper. But uranium certainly requires a specialized skill set in all phases of exploration and mining, and there simply are not that many skilled, let alone experienced, personnel.

No doubt more known ore bodies will be developed, though old projects with defined resources outlined during the last cycle will need a lot of reworking on new economics, as well as new permitting. Perhaps some of the existing political restrictions will be eased. Some new discoveries may be made. Restrictions on uranium mining are everywhere in the developed countries. Some of the richest land in the United States, in Arizona, was recently withdrawn from uranium mining.

Permitting for a uranium mine anyway in the United States or Australia and other countries is likely to generate a lot of local opposition. And then power plants themselves meet opposition. Seabrook, in New Hampshire, went through 14 years of regulatory hurdles before opening in 1990, while Shoreham was shut down by protests in 1989, after 16 long years, before it had generated a single watt of electricity, and putting its owner, the Long Island Lighting Company into bankruptcy.

Today, with greater awareness of oil's decline, populist antagonism to "foreign oil," and the green lobby—many environmentalists support nuclear energy—nuclear power plants may have an easier time, though it still will not be quick and easy.

Fragile Supply

But however optimistic the assumptions on the supply side, it still appears as though we have deficits and therefore robust price markets by the end of the coming decade. Already there have been problems meeting supply. In mid-2008, India, for example, had 17 reactors operating at less than 50 percent capacity due to their lack of uranium. The mines, the infrastructure, and the logistics are all fragile, and we are likely to see much more of this going forward.

Because of this fragility, and its essential nature to the operation of plants, consumers have long sought large, long-term contracts, often for years in advance. Indeed, over 90 percent of uranium purchased by utilities is under such long-term contracts. These will typically have floor prices, with the producer receiving the spot price when delivery is made, if higher. There are fixed-price contracts as well. Of course, even with a long-term contract, the uranium still has to be produced and get to the consumer, and there have been many cases recently of *force majeur*, whereby the producer has declared itself unable to fulfill the contract due to circumstances outside its control.

There are numerous wildcards in the supply and demand equation for uranium over the next few years:

- New reactors could come on stream sooner than we expect
- Governments and private end users could start stockpiling sooner and in greater numbers than we anticipate
- There could be increased buying by hedge funds and other investors
- There is ever-present risk of production problems
- Secondary supplies may run down sooner than we expect

On the other hand, there are some unknowns that could have a negative impact on the uranium price:

- Those secondary supplies could be more plentiful than we expect
- Permitting for new mines could come much quicker than we expect through exercise of concerted political pressure
- New reactors could take longer to be built, either because of bottlenecks, financing, or permitting issues

All these factors would affect the supply or demand, either in an immediate- and short-term basis or on a multiyear basis.

Absent unexpected events, we are anticipating a relatively flat market for another year or two, followed by moderate surpluses in 2012–2014, followed by a steadily increasing shortfall and higher price. All along, any sudden supply curtailment could lead to a sharp spike in the price. Since markets usually anticipate developments, I expect to see the uranium price slowly increase from current levels in the low $40s for the next few years before accelerating upward thereafter. It cannot stay at these levels for long, once demand starts picking up. The current price is not sufficient to promote much new development, according to analysts at Canada's Cormark Securities. And we need that development pretty soon if mines are to be producing when demand picks up.

The uranium market is a small one, very small compared even with other metals. (See Figure 20.4.) Given the spot market is only 10 percent of the overall, that is tiny, and it can be very sensitive to any buying or selling; this was amply illustrated by the spike up to $150 when hedge funds started buying uranium and again when there was forced liquidation by funds, driving the price down.

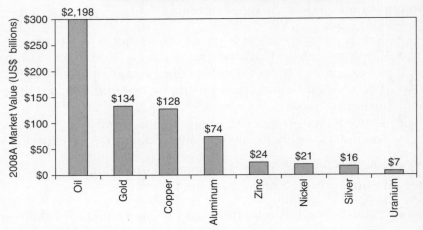

Figure 20.4   Uranium: Very Small Market
Source: World Nuclear Association, RBC Capital Markets.

In the first instance, it moved 50 to 60 percent above the average long-term contract price, and in the second, fell well below it. Movement in new, long-term contract pricing is more indicative of the true market. Because most uranium is sold on long-term contracts, short-term fluctuations in the spot price are less important.

Few Big Uranium Companies

There are only a handful of publicly listed, pure uranium producers, including Cameco (also owner of Canada's only processing facility), Energy Resources of Australia, Paladin, Uranium One, and Denison. ERA and Paladin are Australian companies, the rest Canadian. There are as many as 400 exploration companies, ranging from reasonably diversified and experienced ones to one-trick ponies often little more than mania chasers. Many of the exploration stocks, with or without the goods, rose many hundreds of percent in 2005 and 2006, but fell on average some 80 percent from the end-2007 peak to the lows after Lehman went belly up. There has been a good recovery from the lows, and many of the stocks remain overvalued relative to their real assets.

A straightforward investment for the long run is the Uranium Participation Certificate (U, Toronto) similar to a closed-end fund invested in uranium. The "fund" has traded at both a premium and a discount to its net asset value at different times, usually trading at significant premiums in a rising markets, at one point in late 2007, as much as a 60 percent premium to the spot price. The discount is rarely more than 10 percent. We would be wary of paying much of a premium, though the convenience of a direct play on uranium is certainly valuable.

Cameco (CCJ, New York) is the world's leading publicly traded producer and an obvious choice. Though the company has experienced various challenges and setbacks over the years, it is difficult to imagine the uranium price moving significantly higher on a sustained basis without Cameco doing reasonably well. We should not forget, however, that Cameco has in the past been forced to *buy* product on the market in order to fulfill its contracts, and the rise in Cameco shares may not match the rise in the uranium price.

An interesting uranium play is the French company Areva (CEI, Paris), which is involved in all aspects of the industry, from exploration and mining (37 percent of Cigar Lake among others) to recycling and waste disposal to power plant construction. Areva is one of the leading nuclear reactor construction companies in the world, often in joint venture with other firms, such as Siemens or GE. Delays and cost overruns on the Finnish plant, the first new one in Europe, dented its reputation somewhat. Areva is actually owned by the French government; rather than equity in the company, investors own participation certificates issued by various banks in anticipation of a long-awaited privatization. Another significant downside to the company is the continual political interference. Nonetheless, it is a well-run and respected company, and it offers investors broad exposure to the entire industry.

Of the smaller producers, Denison Mines (DML, Toronto), a company with a diversified asset base, and part of the entrepreneurial Lundin stable, is among the best. Whether the shares will be a buy at any particular time in the future, of course, is difficult to say.

Although there are a handful of exploration companies with competent managements and real assets, their stories can change dramatically. One way of investing in uranium exploration, however, is through a well-managed, well-financed diversified exploration company that happens to have some uranium exposure. Altius Minerals (ALS, Toronto), Virginia Mines (VGQ, Toronto), and Midland Exploration (MD, Toronto) are among my favorite prospect-generator companies, all with top management and well financed. All three have uranium exposure—Altius more than the others—but all three have been smart enough to joint-venture the uranium assets to people who know more about this sector than they do, while retaining an interest in any discovery. If the same names keep coming up for different resources, it's a good indication that you can obtain broad exposure to the entire resource sector through these well-managed and low-risk companies.

CHAPTER

21

Renewable Energy

W hich "green" energy has perhaps the lowest environmental impact of all; is low cost, widely available in the United States; is very profitable and keeps on giving permanently? No, not solar or wind, but geothermal. You may not have heard of geothermal energy. Certainly, it does not receive the attention of other renewable energy sources. Yet it has benefits its headline-grabbing cousins don't have: It can keep giving 24 hours a day and it can make money.

Renewable Is Low-Cost and Green

Most resources are depleting assets; they are no good once consumed. There may be some residual recycling value, but the mine depletes and eventually exhausts itself. The concept of a renewable resource, especially where the global supplies are limited, would clearly be a tremendous advantage. Well, there are sources of renewable energy, which have been all the rage because of the environment and global warming scares, as well as thoughts of impending oil shortages. I am not going to devote much space to discuss much renewable energy, whether derived from the sun or chicken poop; they are only within the scope of resources by the very loosest definition. And they don't make economic sense.

Renewable energy certainly has attractions, however. We can't avoid the political considerations:

- Many utilities around the world have mandates to provide a certain amount of their energy from "green" sources. In the

United States, 33 states have set renewable portfolio standards (for California, 30 percent of its energy) and federal legislation is in the works. In the European Union, the mandate is 20/20; that is, 20 percent of energy from green sources by 2020. Because of this, green energy has a premium demand.
- Green energy attracts various subsidies and preferential treatment from governments.
- Permitting is likely to be smoother; with backing of governments and little environmental opposition, the process should go much easier.

New Energy Finance, a research group, estimated that $155 billion was invested in clean energy companies and projects worldwide in 2008, and that excludes hydroelectric. The largest sums went to wind, $52 billion, and solar, $33.5 billion. This is a "hot" area and companies with solid assets are likely to be able to find the financing.

Geothermal and Hydro: Two *Profitable* Renewables

My preferred renewable energy sources, geothermal and hydro, have the added benefit that they are profitable; they make money even without government subsidies. In addition, they do not have the negative consequences of other renewable energy sources, including smaller environmental imprints. True, wind farms do not generate much CO_2, but it hardly beautifies the "green, green grass of home" to have thousands of giant turbines strewn across the hills. If we truly were to "think globally, act locally," then these eyesores would not get off the drawing board. Nor is it particularly environmentally responsible to kill thousands of migrating birds that get caught in the giant turbines; one wind farm in Altamont Pass, California, kills an average of 80 golden eagles each year out of the 10,000 birds destroyed by this single farm. Another controversy has arisen from the constant hum of the turbines that causes sleep deprivation to nearby inhabitants.

Beyond this, so much of the fashionable renewable energy simply does not make economic sense. Boone Pickens, the Texas oil man who garnered headlines and invitations to the White House with his "Pickens Plan for U.S. Energy," quietly abandoned his centerpiece for the largest U.S. wind farm in Texas. Half the turbines are being sold to other projects, with orders for the other half having been cancelled. The problem: no transmission lines to get the energy generated to where it was wanted.

Solar is often touted for the money it saves on monthly utility bills, but the upfront cost can be exorbitant. In Berkeley, California, of all places—no greener place exists—a small program to lend money to homeowners to convert to solar has proven a less-than-rousing success. Initially, 40 homeowners signed up, 27 of whom subsequently withdrew because the loans were too expensive; interest payments would negate the ongoing energy savings. Other homeowners found that they needed expensive roof strengthening to support the panels.

In Spain, when the cash-strapped government cut generous subsidies to the solar industry, it collapsed, leaving a glut on unwanted equipment and job losses. In a widely publicized story, one Pennsylvania couple spent $58,000 on a solar panel system for their house in an effort to push their utility bills toward zero. They sold a single carbon credit to a metal fabricating company, in return for $21.50. That's not $21.50 per month, but $21.50 for a lifetime carbon credit. If they actually do eliminate their electricity bill completely—a dubious assumption—then, assuming a pre-solar bill of $300 a month—it would take 16 years for them to recoup their initial investment. That doesn't take into account the time value of money, what they could have earned on that $58,000. By that time, they would have had to replace their solar panel batteries, and the whole system would be deteriorating, becoming less efficient. And it hardly needs adding that, in Pennsylvania, they would have to clear snow from the panels during the winter.

Another real-life story of comparative energy sources involves plans for a 620-megawatt-output nuclear plant proposed for Austria. The greenies didn't like nuclear and it was never allowed to be built. Instead, the government announced it was replacing this with a solar plant, but unfortunately only with an output of 20,500 watts. Because of Austria's less than equatorial climate, the solar plant has less than 10 percent average output of its capacity. That is, the plant had to be built to a capacity of 200,000 watts in order to generate 20,000 watts. The cost: $1.7 million, and the plant will last a maximum of 25 years with declining power output in the second half.

As for biofuel, not only does it not make economic sense for the most part—Brazil's sugar cane program is about the only viable program in the world—but that effort has had the cruel effect of diverting food from livestock and humans. The Food and Agriculture

Organization estimates that the world's biofuel program added 10 percent to the cost of food worldwide.

Green Energy That Can Generate Green

Geothermal and hydro avoid these drawbacks. They are truly environmental . . . and they are profitable. Geothermal, as a source of energy, has several advantages over most others, including other so-called *green energy sources*. It is not new technology. In fact, the Romans used it to heat homes and baths. The earth's core is as hot as the sun, about 9,900 degrees Fahrenheit. Deep underground reservoirs contain hot rocks saturated with water. The hot water is pumped up to a geothermal plant and drives electric generators. Once the water is cooled, it is piped back to the reservoir. Geothermal has numerous advantages over other so-called green energy sources as well as other forms of energy:

- It is arguably the greenest source of energy, with no carbon emissions or other emissions (other than steam). It has a small footprint, with a very small land use, smaller, as we've discussed, than those green darlings, solar and wind.
- It has very low operating costs, with no fuel input. Other energy sources require an input of energy to obtain the new energy, and that can sometimes be very high. We should point out that the capital costs are quite high, and I will discuss that. But right now, under the American Recovery and Reinvestment Act, companies can obtain a refund of 30 percent of the capital costs as a grant from the government, making the overall costs even lower. Personally, I don't like to count on ongoing grants, and the beauty of geothermal is that it is economically competitive even without these grants.
- Geothermal runs 24 hours a day, 365 days a year. It is what is known as *base-load*. Solar has a problem called nighttime. Clouds are not too friendly either. Wind does not always blow. So solar and wind systems need capacity to accommodate peak generating periods, meaning a lot of waste. Geothermal runs at about 90 percent capacity all the time, and it is permanent, constantly renewing itself.
- There is untapped potential. Today, about 9,000 megawatts are generated worldwide, about 3,500 in the western United States. But that could jump to 30,000 quite readily.

- It is a mature industry (over 2,000 years) with very low technology risk. The risk is in finding the reserve, not in operating it.

The most significant drawback to geothermal is the capital costs, among the highest for any form of energy. The major part of these costs is the exploration, given that drilling even known areas has a success rate of only about 25 to 30 percent. Success means finding a reservoir of adequate size. After that, confirmation drilling, to confirm the resource, has a success rate of about 60 percent. Obviously, skill and experienced management are critical in keeping these costs down but the plain fact is that the drilling costs are going to be high. In all, this drilling is nearly one-third of the total capital cost.

However, once one has confirmed an adequate reservoir and built a plant, geothermal becomes inexpensive, partly because the amount of electricity relative to its rated capacity is so high and because it is constant and permanent. In Iceland, it can be less than 1 cent per kilowatt, compared with 6 cents more typically, and, say, 10 cents for wind. Even hydro can operate as low as 35 percent of capacity, compared to 90 to 95 percent for geothermal. (See Figure 21.1.)

Putting capital and operating costs together, then, geothermal is one of the lowest-cost energy sources. With grants and loan guarantees available, resource entrepreneur Rick Rule estimates that rates

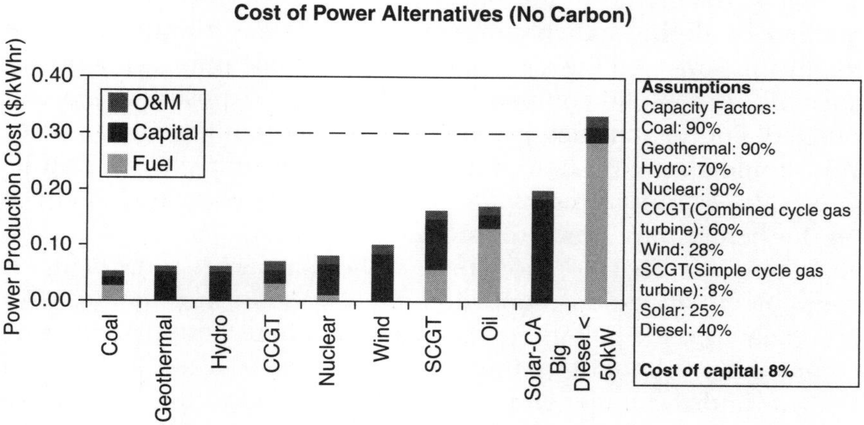

Figure 21.1   Geothermal Is the Lowest-Cost Energy

Source: National Bank Financial.

of return of 22 percent at 5 percent cost of capital are feasible. Coal is the only source of energy that is cheaper than geothermal but, of course, that is much dirtier. If "cap and trade" or similar were to pass, and the cost of CO_2 emissions added to the capital and operating costs, then coal would leapfrog over geothermal. Hydro is also competitive with geothermal but has its own drawbacks.

There is a high degree of risk associated with the exploration and development phase of a geothermal operation, all of which takes place before one can be certain one has an adequate resource. Once the resource is confirmed, however, companies can negotiate long-term offtake agreements to help with the remaining capital costs.

Companies Are Big or Very Small

For investors, the problem with geothermal is that the market is bifurcated between a few very large players and several tiny companies. The largest geothermal generator is Chevron, but one would not buy that company for its geothermal. The only pure play in the sector is Ormat, which is a fully integrated geothermal company, involved in building and operating power plants, and therefore does not quite have the leverage as a smaller operating company. Calpine, a wholesale power generation company, is also a large participant in the industry, but its gas operations overwhelm them.

Another major player is the Italian utility Enel. It is also involved in many forms of energy, including hydro, nuclear, and geothermal, as well as integrated in the business. Far from a pure play—in the manner of all fine Italian companies—it also has interests in some totally unconnected businesses, including mobile phones and insurance. But it is a solid company and offers good exposure to a broad range of energy activities, just not a pure play geothermal company. You should be aware, however, that Enel is planning to spin off its Green Power unit as a separate publicly traded company, so check on this before purchasing the stock.

There are a dozen or more tiny geothermal outfits, some of which have current operations, some domestic and some international. We are likely to see a roll-up in the industry, where better projects or companies are bought by the new entrepreneurial outfits between the tiny and the huge. However, these companies' tiny size makes access to essential capital difficult, and I would avoid these unless you can watch the companies on a constant basis.

A better investment might be one (or both) of the new mid-sized geothermals, Magma Energy (MXY, Toronto) and Ram Power (RPG, Toronto). These two companies were each formed in 2009 by successful mining entrepreneurs with the aim of building geothermal companies of scale. They both have good balance sheets and, more important, have the size to make additional capital raising feasible.

Magma is the more advanced of the two. Founded by serially successful mining entrepreneur Ross Beaty, it has large assets in the United States, Chile, and Iceland and aims to build the largest pure geothermal company. Ross has an astonishing track record, successfully building two gold companies, a silver company, a copper company, which was split in four (Lumina), and now Magma. The two gold companies and three of the four components of the copper company have been sold at huge profits to investors, while Pan American Silver is the largest pure silver company in the world. He is likely to do the same with Magma, and the plan here could be to build a large company and then at a certain stage, possibly start paying dividends to shareholders. Whatever the final end-game, I suspect investors who attach themselves to Ross's coattails will do exceedingly well.

Ross told me he was attracted to geothermal because he believes in protecting the environment, but it is a lot like mining, in which he has been eminently successful. It is similar to mining in that it involves subsurface discovery potential and above-surface development of operating assets, both with potential to be great wealth creators. "So I can join two passions while building what I hope will be a world-class company," he told me. "How cool is that!" He also emphasized that geothermal is a great business on its own, without the need for subsidies.

Of course, there are differences between geothermal and mineral mining. For a start, electricity is sold on domestic markets, rather than worldwide, so revenues can be more dependable. Ross points out that this allows you to leverage the business more. On the flip side, there is more politics involved in energy, and like most entrepreneurs, Ross admits to not liking playing politics. In short, Ross says he hopes he can succeed "using the same simple strategies: successful exploration; successful operations; smart acquisitions; simple focused, achievable business plan; global reach; diversified portfolio approach; mission to become a world leader in the space; and a great management team." In a grand understatement, he concludes: "It's not exactly rocket science, but it sure is easier to say than do." If anyone can do it, though, he can.

Ram Power was put together by equally dedicated Rick Rule, who hired Hezy Ram from Ormat to run the company. The team has been more prepared to buy existing companies to build Ram, which now has operations in several countries, though these are not people known to be loose with the wallet. More so than Magma, which started from scratch, Ram has an extensive portfolio of early-stage properties that offer the potential for multiple discoveries. One is likely to do very well attached to these coattails as well.

Wind and Water

Two other renewable companies are attractive with big-buck potential. Plutonic Power (PCC, Toronto) is involved in both hydro and wind farms in British Columbia, in joint venture with GE Capital for funding. Well financed and managed, with access to deep pockets, Plutonic is likely to grow steadily, acquiring various renewable projects in western Canada. The other is Reservoir Capital (REO, Toronto), which is developing hydro projects in Serbia and other countries in southeast Europe and has recently added geothermal projects there. The location is ideal, with numerous fast-flowing rivers and nearby to the European market that is hungry for renewable energy. Reservoir will likely eventually be sold to a larger company, but not before it has built a pipeline of projects that should reward early investors very well.

CHAPTER 22

Agriculture

Agriculture is the most critical resource of all, and perhaps the area with the most challenges ahead. In many ways, however, the fundamental story is much the same as that for the other resources we've looked at. Demand is growing, partly from the development of China and other economies, while there are significant constraints to increasing supply to meet the demand.

More and Better

The increase in demand for food comes about from three areas. First, the population is growing and there are and will be more mouths to feed. The United Nations estimates a world population of 9 billion by 2050; that is, 35 percent above the current number. Most of this growth will be in the developing nations; Asia will add approximately 1 billion people over that time frame.

But the demand for food, like the demand for other commodities, is leveraged to the simple increase in population. As emerging economies develop, and as people grow less poor, they want to eat more (more consistently as well as more). As they grow richer, they want to eat better. And as they move from rural areas to cities, they are producing less of their own requirements and they need to purchase more.

More people, each wanting more food, better food, and having to buy more: that's a recipe for a huge increase in food demand over the next decade and more. The UN estimates the demand for food will increase by 70 percent by midcentury. And therein lies the opportunities for us as investors. Standard Chartered Bank recently put out a report titled provocatively "The End of Cheap Food."

In addition to the increase in absolute demand, as people become a little wealthier, their diets change. They want to get protein from meat; they move up from pigs and goats to lamb and beef; they want more fruit and vegetables; and so forth. Food is the most recession resilient of all products. Of course, we in the West, when times are hard, might cut out the *foie gras*; we might move down a grade in restaurants; we might even substitute generic for brand-name cereals. But we still eat. And that is the standard experience in recessions throughout the world.

Less Farming Land

On the other side of this equation is the supply of food. We are already close to a crisis stage. For eight consecutive years now, the world consumed more food than farmers produced, according to the University of Technology in Sydney, Australia, running down storage supplies. There are increasing constraints in the ability to grow more, most notably the decline of arable land. As populations have increased and economies grown, development has taken over farmland. And this has not been just a Western phenomenon. The UN again estimated that in 1960, there were 1.1 acres of arable land per person in the world. (*Arable land* is land that is suitable for agriculture, not necessarily being used for agriculture.) By 2000, that number was down to 0.6 acres per person, and by 2030, they estimate, it will have dropped to half an acre.

So the amount of land available to produce food is declining dramatically at the same time that the demand is exploding. Food has always been a volatile commodity, subject to the whims of nature, whether typhoons or droughts. But systemic shortages and higher prices at the same time as demand is increasing has led to much discussion of food security. The issue is real: There has been an enormous surge in the number of undernourished people, up from a low of 840 million people in 1996 to well over 1 billion today, according to the Food and Agriculture Organization in a November 2009 report on *Food Security*. That year, prices of basic food commodities exploded: tea and orange juice were each up over 80 percent, sugar up 165 percent. And at the end of the year, the UN held its first food summit since 2002.

Winners and Losers

Now, of course, as with any price increase, there's a seller as well as a buyer, and higher prices for agricultural commodities have helped countries that are big producers and exporters.

The bigger winner is Brazil, with a total amount of arable land equal to that of the United States, but only a small part currently under cultivation. (See Figure 22.1.) The potential increase, therefore, is huge and the largest by far in the world. Some countries, such as India, despite a relatively large amount of arable land, have it all under cultivation; the potential for any increase is very minor indeed. Increases in supply will have to come from improved efficiencies.

We have already mentioned the competition for grain from biofuels; the U.S. target is to produce 15 billion gallons of ethanol by 2015. It probably won't reach that goal; when was the last time any government anywhere met any target? But perhaps there will also be increased political pressure to abandon the economically unviable, food-destructive program. But for now, it is another driver of higher agricultural prices.

Just as countries are locking in long-term supplies of metals and energy, so too are they beginning to look at establishing reliable food supplies. South Korea has invested $6 billion to lease half of the

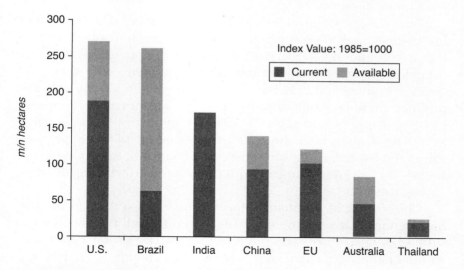

Figure 22.1   Brazil Has Most Land Potential
Source: AgoraFinancial.com.

arable land in Madagascar. China also is establishing relationships with food-producing countries around the world. It imports beef from Argentina and soybeans from Brazil. And it has a $5 billion plan to buy farms throughout Africa to provide for its food needs.

One can't help but think that the seeds of future armed struggles are being planted; will African governments like to see their countries' food production exported across the world when their own populations are starving? The food price spikes of 2008, and the relatively mild crises they produced, led to several major producing countries banning the export of crops. Thailand and Vietnam banned the export of rice among others, leading to riots in rice-importing Philippines and a plan there to grow more rice domestically. This is only the beginning, so we need to be careful where and how we invest in this sensitive sector.

Water, Water Everywhere

One of the biggest challenges for agriculture in the decades ahead is water. We know that a majority of the world's surface is covered by water, but 97 percent of that is saltwater. And of the remaining 3 percent, much is hidden in glaciers or under permanent snow cover. Only about 1 percent of the world's water is available for us, whether from rainwater or groundwater.

People need clean water to drink, but farmers also need water for livestock and to grow produce. What has been deemed an endless, free commodity is increasingly becoming restricted and expensive. Monsanto's CEO Hugh Grant thinks arguments over water "will dwarf the discussion that has taken place over food." As with any product, there is a wide disparity among countries as to those with plentiful supplies and those with very limited resources. Brazil is again the winner, with three times the amount of water per person as the United States and most other countries, while China and India—the two large countries with the greatest growth ahead—have among the least.

China's lack of adequate water is a reason its arable land supply has been in steady decline since 1988, even though the government subsidizes agriculture. This has had a critical affect on China's agricultural patterns; it is no longer able to grow enough to feed its own population. Soybeans are an essential source of protein in much of the developing world. Not so long ago, China not only produced a sufficient amount for its own population but was the world's largest exporter. In 1995, it became a net importer and has remained so since, becoming the world's largest importer. This is an amazing shift in such a relatively short period. Water has been key; soybeans require a lot of water, as much as 1,500 tonnes of water for one tonne of soybeans, and China simply does not have the water. Across the North China Plains, the aquifers are being sucked dry; at the current rate, these aquifers will be exhausted within 10 years. Even in Beijing, the water table is declining by 3 feet a year.

Similarly for India, where extremes of hydrology are exacerbated by mismanagement and corruption. There are conflicts between states over who gets water from rivers that divide them. There are riots between farmers and factories. And there is corruption. But India's aquifers in the northwest are being depleted at a rapid rate; they fell by over a foot a year between 2002 and 2008, a loss of water three times the volume of America's largest reservoir. (This is according to satellite photos released by NASA, as reported August 2009 by ScienceBlog and numerous other news media.)

China and India do not have water, but Brazil does. (See Figure 22.2.) So that country has become a huge grower and exporter of soybeans (second-largest exporter behind the United States). Brazil has among the largest amounts of arable land in the world, the largest uncultivated arable land, and the largest water supply.

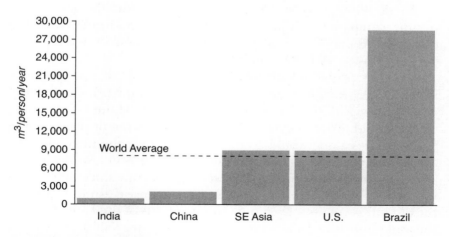

Figure 22.2   Brazil Has the Water

Source: PotashCorp © 1997 to 2010. Data from Food and Agriculture Organization.

In combination, that makes Brazil the agricultural giant of the next 50 years or more. Canada is the world's most water-rich country. In all, less than 10 countries possess 60 percent of the world's freshwater supply. In many cases, countries with the largest populations and most demand have the least water (including China and Africa).

Water Usage Will Increase

One fundamental problem with water is that it is not priced appropriately. Whether in India and China or in California, water is underpriced and is diverted to politically popular constituencies by governments.

Water is not just used by farmers, of course. Industry consumes a lot of water, as does housing development, and all compete for supplies. It takes 1,000 gallons of water to make one cotton shirt. It takes 100,000 gallons to make an automobile. As China and India industrialize, their water usage will increase dramatically, and right now both countries have per-capita water usages well below global average. This increasing per-capita use comes from two sources: food and industry. As people become richer, they move from dry grains to wet, and eventually to beef. In that transition, water usage goes 1,000 to one. The same applies to industry; the water used in the manufacture of a car is a multiple of what it takes to make a bicycle. And so on.

In all, water usage in North America is around 850 gallons per person, compared with just 13 gallons per person in the emerging countries. As people's diets change and the economies develop, that per-capita usage will move sharply higher.

Another problem with increasing the supply of potable water is the creaky infrastructure. In most of the world, including the developed world, the water infrastructure is aged, much of it over 100 years old. Just to replace old pipes and treatment plants in the United States alone would cost $250 billion over the next 30 years, according to a 2001 report from the American Water Works Association. The costs have surely increased significantly since that report was issued. That's expensive, but not as expensive as not replacing the old infrastructure. Even now, in some parts of the United States, the water lost through leakage of old pipes is over half the water put into the pipes. As time goes on, the losses and breakages will only increase. Increasing usable water supply, whether by desalination or drilling deeper for water, requires energy, so it is not inexpensive.

Agricultural Commodities Are Volatile

Agricultural commodities are always susceptible to weather patterns. We saw how in 2009 sugar and cocoa prices exploded upward, while wheat and corn were depressed. A poor monsoon in India and unseasonal rainfall in Brazil hurt sugar crops in both countries, the world's two largest producers. But the weather patterns in the United States and Europe were ideal for bumper grain crops. These are temporary factors and difficult to predict, but they should be seen as overlays on the fundamental long-term bullish outlook.

Despite price rises in the last couple of years, agriculture commodities look very attractive now for investing. Real (inflation-adjusted) prices for many are close to multidecade lows, while inventories are the lowest in decades. For 30 years there has been very little capital put into this sector, though that is now changing with the heightened focus on the growing food crisis. It is no wonder that famed investor Jim Rogers, who cofounded the Quantum Fund with George Soros, is a bull on agriculture. He likes all resources, but he seems most strongly attracted to the agricultural commodities—"all of them," he says.

There are many ways for the investor to gain exposure to agricultural commodities. First, one can buy the commodities themselves, either on futures exchanges or through an exchange-traded fund (ETF) or exchange-traded note (ETN). We discussed many of the ETFs earlier (see Chapter 9), so I don't want to repeat all the caveats about buying commodities through ETFs. There are costs, but for many this will be the simplest way to gain long-term exposure to commodities.

Second, we discussed the shortage of arable land, and the conversion of available land to farms. The largest untapped amount of arable land is in Brazil, which, though it receives lots of sun and rain, has soil that is often nutrient poor. So that means adding fertilizers. Since one of Brazil's key crops and exports is soybeans, that means phosphate and potash, the key nutrients for soybeans. As an investment, potash is more desirable than phosphate; high-quality mines are rare and there is less competition. Global capacity for potash is about 54 million tonnes, but Passport Capital estimates that the potential demand from just the BRIC countries (Brazil, Russia, India, and China) is an additional 30 million tonnes, so potash prices are likely to appreciate in coming years.

In the fertilizer area, Potash (POT, NY) is the world's leading supplier of potash, with a strong balance sheet and high margins. Mosaic (MOS, NY) is the leading phosphate fertilizer producer, as well as one of the lowest-cost producers. Although earnings are split evenly between phosphate and potash, Mosaic plans to boost its potash over the next decade to a 60/40 split. A third key company is Germany's K+S (SDF, Germany), which makes various fertilizers, including potash. K+S also manufactures salt products, but the various fertilizers account for 85 percent of revenues. It has a solid balance sheet, though like the others, the stock price fluctuates depending on market prices.

The third way to invest is in various agribusiness companies, as well as specialty support businesses. Top companies here include Bunge (BG, NY), a diversified agri-business company, integrated from farmer to consumer. Its businesses include processing soybeans and milling corn and wheat and other products. Most of its operations are in the Americas, particularly Brazil, where the company had its origins. The balance sheet is strong. Brasil Foods (BRFS, OTC) is the dominant food processor in Brazil and Latin America, including poultry, which it raises; it also processes soybeans and producers frozen food for the domestic and export market.

Monsanto (MON, NY) is a controversial company, the manufacturer of "franken-food," especially genetically modified seeds that aim to resist disease and boost food production. CEO Hugh Grant claims the world has no chance of doubling agricultural output by 2050, as is required to meet growing food demand, without using genetically modified seeds. Most of Monsanto's sales come from seeds, which, along with pesticides and fertilizers, can raise yields in the rest of the world to U.S. levels. The American farmer raises about 160 bushels of corn per acre, versus 60 in Brazil and just 27 in sub-Saharan Africa. There is potential to boost food output just by increased efficiency. Another strong seed company is Switzerland's Syngenta (SYNN, Switzerland), which also generates most of its revenues from insecticides and herbicides. Like many Swiss companies, it has a very strong balance sheet and high margins.

Nestlé might be thought of as a long way from a resource invest-ment; indeed, if the price of agricultural commodities rises, other things being equal, this hurts a food processor like Nestlé. But Nestlé has attempted to improve food output by investing in new technolo-gies, such as genetically modified food. Chairman Peter Brabeck-Letmathe has loudly criticized "well-fed activists" whose decisions on new food technologies "are at the expense of those who are starving." Despite the challenges rising commodity prices pose for Nestlé, it is a great company that will do well in years to come and it is likely to be part of the solution to the world food crisis.

I mentioned before that China imports some of its grain and beef all the way from Argentina, and the key player there is Cresud (CRESY, Nasdaq). Cresud owns and leases farms in Argentina's rich Pampas region, and it raises grains of all types and both beef and dairy cattle. It has an asset-rich company, with a huge land bank. The stock can be volatile based on Argentina's politics and currency.

One of my top resource investments with a strong and growing interest in agriculture is Canada's Sprott Resources (SCP, Toronto). Founded by one of the most astute of Canada's resource investors, Eric Sprott, the company makes both direct and indirect investments in resources. The investments are focused now on three areas: oil and gas, gold and precious metals, and agriculture. The agriculture in-cludes both fertilizer ventures and farming. It has joint ventures in Peru on phosphate and in Newfoundland on potash. More impor-tant, however, is a massive partnership it organized with Canada's First Nations (aboriginal peoples), which plans to develop 1 mil-lion acres of farmland across Canada. Its goal is to become one of the largest corporate farms in the world. Well managed and well fi-nanced, Sprott has an attractive long-term potential with exposure to some key resource areas.

Finally, support industries include the companies that trade com-modities. Singapore's Noble Group (NOBL, Singapore) is another well-financed and conservatively managed company, a broad trading group deriving most of its revenues from the supply of bulk agricul-tural commodities, including sugar and soybeans. It also trades oil and gas and is involved heavily in the coal industry, as a financer and shipper. Itochu Corp. (8001, Tokyo) is another top trading firms spe-cializing in foodstuffs, as well as metals, minerals, wood, and other products.

Water Investments to Avoid

The water industry globally is enormous, the third-largest in terms of embedded capital (behind oil and electrical power). It is very diverse, with many component parts, and it is also very diffused, with numerous small players. This is one of the difficulties of investing in this sector. The other major risk is that of actual or potential political control. Many water utilities have their rates of return, as well as the fees they can charge, strictly controlled. This makes it difficult for the small utilities to justify spending the large amounts of capital necessary to improve infrastructure. But water everywhere is a political issue, and as shortages become more frequent and more extreme, that is only likely to increase. An owner of water or a utility delivering it to consumers is unlikely to be the master of his fate. This makes investments in this area potentially problematic.

There are four main stages in the water business: ownership of water, collection and treatment, distribution to consumers, and wastewater treatment. The first and third of these are the areas most subject to the political interference referred to before. The third also has the oldest infrastructure and companies involved are often more dependent on housing. The second and fourth—treatment and wastewater—involve much industrial technology—pumps, valves, filtration, and so on. Certainly, with the enormous infrastructure spend required over the next 30 years—both repairing and replacing existing pipes and plants and building new ones—makes some supplies to these companies attractive. Some of these companies specialize in the water industry while others are much more diversified. Good, profitable, politically independent pure water plays are not so common.

One of my top picks in the water industry is Singapore's Hyflux Water Trust (HYFT, Singapore), a company that invests in water infrastructure assets, including treatment plants, recycling, and desalination. Most of its investments are in China, India, and other developing markets. Its businesses include both building plants and operating them, the former providing huge potential, the latter more stable, long-term cash flow. Currently, it is building the largest desalination plant in the world, in Algeria. It avoids the problems in many water investments—the low-growth utility-like returns of water distribution and the potential for government control or interference in ownership of water. Instead, it focuses on the infrastructure area where governments will be willing to spend large amounts of money in coming years.

Without a doubt, agriculture, including water, is going to be a critical issue in the years to come, and prices of many commodities and the companies that produce, trade, and service the sectors will do very well. A combination of ETFs in the agricultural commodities themselves, and various producing and service companies, should see the investor well exposed in the years ahead.

Conclusion: Building a Portfolio

I have presented the facts and analysis that form a convincing argument why all resources are set to boom over the next three to five years and beyond. This is based primarily on twin factors: a huge step up in demand from China primarily and other emerging economies, and significant constraints on increasing supply.

These factors are more pronounced for some commodities, less for others. China *will* be buying more coal and copper and iron ore—of that there is little doubt. China's increased demand for silver, for example, is perhaps less certain, though the *potential* is enormous. The time frame for each will be different. Then there are some resources with their own fundamental story: geothermal is clean and cheap with or without China.

As an investor, you need to be exposed to this long-term story and avoid the temptation to sell too soon, either because you made some money or because of a temporary setback. Commodities will continue to be volatile, and if you are exposed to this sector, you must be prepared for that. Focus on the long-term fundamentals; trade around your core holdings by all means, but avoid panicking and selling when stocks decline. (Generally, I eschew the use of stops in this volatile sector.) Use volatility to your advantage, buying more when stocks or sectors decline temporarily.

Personal Decisions

The composition of your portfolio depends on your circumstances, risk tolerance, and other personal factors. Some investors should remain with mutual funds and managed accounts, others with individual equities or a combination. You cannot buy everything; obviously, the size of your allocation to the resource sector is important. If, for example, you have a $1 million portfolio and allocate about

20 percent to resources, you might hold 125 positions of $17,000 each. You do not want to hold many more positions than that unless it is a full-time job. Perhaps you need fewer positions or should use funds for some of the sectors. And do not forget to leave a cash cushion, both for taking advantage of particular bargains and also to have some liquidity if you might need the funds for unexpected expenses. You never want to be in a position of *having* to sell, because it will never be at the right time.

At this time, I would emphasize gold (for its defensive qualities), copper, agriculture, alternative energy, oil, platinum, and silver. Uranium and gas may be top buys a little later. If the global economy recovers strongly, then platinum and silver would move up the list.

Start with gold, either physical or an exchange-traded fund (ETF). Add some strong seniors (Franco-Nevada for example) and then some juniors, emphasizing first producers (such as Allied Nevada) or prospect generators (such as Virginia). Then buy some diversified base metal mines (such as BHP) as well as individual companies (Freeport, perhaps). Don't forget one of my favorite diversified companies, Altius.

Then buy some energy, starting with large solid independent exploration and development companies (commonly called E&P companies) like Devon and EOG, before moving on to the more specialized ones. In agriculture, you might start with an ETF (such as the Rogers Agriculture Fund), and then add individual companies, either Bunge or another agribusiness company and a fertilizer company.

Finally, you could add some uranium, platinum, silver (perhaps the silver ETF and some major and junior stocks), and the geothermal companies discussed.

Some Favorite Companies

SPDR Gold Trust	GLD New York
iShares Silver Trust	SLV New York
ETFS Platinum	PPLP Nasdaq
Central Fund	CEF New York
Franco–Nevada Corp.	FNV Toronto
Royal Gold	RGLD Nasdaq
Goldcorp	GG New York
Yamana Gold	AUY New York

Allied Nevada Gold	ANV New York
Almaden Minerals	AAU New York
Cartier Resource	ECR Toronto
Eurasian Minerals	EMX Toronto
Kiska Metals	KSK Toronto
Midland Exploration	MD Toronto
Miranda Gold	MAD Toronto
Virginia Mines	VGQ Toronto
Vista Gold	VGZ New York
Pan American Silver	PAAS Nasdaq
Silver Wheaton	SLW New York
Esperanza	EPZ Toronto
Fortuna Silver	FVI Toronto
BHP Billiton	BHP New York
Xstrata	XTA New York
Vale	VALE Nasdaq
Rio Tinto	RTP New York
Anglo American	AAL London
Freeport McMoRan Copper	FCX New York
Altius Minerals	ALS Toronto
Devon Energy	DVN New York
EOG Resources	EOG New York
Encana Corp.	ECA New York
Canadian Oil Sands	COS-U Toronto
Arc Energy	AET-U Toronto
Cameco Corp.	CCJ New York
Areva	CEI France
Uranium Participation	U Toronto
Magma Energy	MXY Toronto
Plutonic Power	PCC Toronto
Ram Power	RPG Toronto
Reservoir Capital	REO Toronto
Enel	ENEL Italy
Bunge Ltd.	BG New York
K+S Ag.	SDF Germany
Potash Corp	POT New York

Mosaic Co.	MOS New York
Monsanto Co.	MON New York
Sprott Resources	SCP Toronto
Hyflux Water Trust	HYFT Singapore
Cresud	CRESY Nasdaq
Noble Group	NOBL Singapore
Itochu Corp.	8001 Japan
Collectors Universe	CLCT Nasdaq
International Commodity Index	RJI New York
Agriculture Index	RJA New York
Energy Index	RJN New York
Metals Index	RJZ New York

Make sure you have at least some exposure to resources, such as in gold, or the broad agriculture ETF, and then as you build a portfolio and start buying individual equities, you can be more price conscious. However much it ever feels like it, you never have to chase stocks; there is always another opportunity, if not for the same stock, then for another. Try to keep emotions out of it, and remain disciplined in buying, patient in holding, and ruthless in selling.

In conclusion, you must be exposed to this sector and be prepared for volatility. But hold for the major long-term gains. Trade around your core holdings, by all means, but always remain focused on the big picture. At some point in the future, we will be selling, but not before we have made enormous profits on our resource investments, betting on the right side of history. Good luck!

Resource Directory

Rapidly changing events—political, military, economic, technological—can alter your investment perspective and decisions. I have laid out a fundamental, long-term case for buying and holding resources and stocks of miners and affiliated companies. It is crucial, however, that you the reader, if you are to make intelligent investment decisions, keep up-to-date with what is happening in the world. The newsletters and other publications I have listed in this directory will help you do that. Or you may prefer to use the services of a fund, broker, or manager who spends his professional life doing just that.

Free Follow-Up Report

I will also be writing a special update report, which I will make available free of charge to all buyers of this book. The report, which will be written at a suitable time in the next year or so, will update recommendations and describe new products and services of interest.

The report will be sent free of charge when available. Just send me your name and address on a postcard or letter, together with the words "Free Resource Report," and mail to Adrian Day, P.O. Box 6644, Annapolis, MD 21401, or email info@AdrianDay.com.

I also invite any readers who notices any errors or omissions, or have insights that they believe could be useful, to write to me so that I can include them in this report.

Books

- Bernstein, Peter, L. (2000). *The Power of Gold: The History of an Obsession.* New York: John Wiley & Sons Inc.

- Faber, Mark. (2002). *Tomorrow's Gold: Asia's Age of Discovery.* Hong Kong, CLSA.
- Jastram, Roy. (1977). *The Golden Constant: The English and American Experience 1560–1976.* New York: John Wiley & Sons Inc.
- Simmons, Matthew R. (2006). *Twilight in the Desert: The Coming Saudi Oil Shock and the World Economy.* New York: John Wiley & Sons Inc.
- Katz, John/Holmes, Frank. (2008). *The Goldwatcher; Demystifying Gold Investing.* New York: John Wiley & Sons Inc.
- Rogers, Jim. (2003). *Adventure Capitalist.* New York: Random House.
- Gibbon, Jim, ed. (2010). *The Golden Rule*; includes contributions from Peter Schiff, Ron Paul, myself, and many others. New York: John Wiley & Sons Inc.
- Skousen, Mark. (2007). *The Structure of Production.* New York: New York University Press.
- Truax, Martin, ed. (2010). *The Evergreen Portfolio;* includes contributions from Robert Prechter, Dr. Mark Skousen, myself, and others. New York: John Wiley & Sons Inc.

Periodicals

- *The Economist* (2007): www.economist.com
- Dr. Marc Faber, *The Gloom, Boom & Doom Report:* www.gloomboomdoom.com
- John Doody, *Gold Stock Analyst:* www.goldstockanalyst.com
- Brent Cook, *Exploration Insights:* www.explorationinsights.com
- David and Eric Coffin, *Hard Rock Analyst:* www.hraadvisory.com
- Douglas Casey and others, various publications: www.caseyresearch.com
- John Pugsley, *The Stealth Investor:* www.stealthinvestor.com
- Chris Mayer, *Capital & Crisis:* www.capitalandcrisis.agorafinancial.com

Web Sites

- The Gold Report: www.theaureport.com
- Kitco: www.kitco.com
- Mineweb: www.mineweb.com
- Resource Investor: www.resourceinvestor.com

- World Gold Council: www.gold.org
- US Global Investors: www.usfunds.com

Brokers

- Rick Rule, Global Resource Investments, Carlsbad, CA (800) 477-7853
- Martin Truax, Morgan Keegan & Company, Atlanta, GA (800) 742-4926
- Ed Johnson, Morgan Keegan & Company, Alpharetta, GA (800) 564-3589
- Ben Johnson, First Securities Northwest, Portland, OR (800) 547-4898
- Ed Caputo, International Assets, Orlando, FL (800) 432-0000

Mutual Funds

- US Global Investors: www.usfunds.com
- Tocqueville Asset Management: www.tocqueville.com
- First Eagle Funds (SoGen): www.firsteaglefunds.com

Coins

- Van Simmons, David Hall Rare Coins, Newport Beach, CA (800) 759-7575
- Michael Checkan, Asset Strategies International, Rockville, MD (800) 831-0007
- Pat Heller, Liberty Coin Service, Lansing, MI (800) 527-2375

Seminars

- New Orleans Conference: www.neworleansconference.com
- Prospectors and Developers Association of Canada (PDAC), Toronto: www.pdac.ca/pdac/conv
- Hard Assets Show, New York, San Francisco: www.the goldshow.com
- Las Vegas Freedom Fest: www.freedomfest.com

Adrian Day's Services

Adrian Day offers separate and distinct services through each of his two investment companies. He also speaks at numerous seminars around the world; details on upcoming appearances can be found on his Web site.

He is president of Adrian Day Asset Management, which offers separately managed accounts for individuals and businesses, in gold and resources, as well as in global markets. You can reach him at:

- 410-224-2037, AssetManagement@AdrianDay.com.
- www.AdrianDayAssetManagement.com

He also writes an e-mail advisory newsletter, *Global Analyst*, with specific recommendations on resource and global stocks: 410-224-8885, globalanalyst@AdrianDay.com and www.AdrianDay GlobalAnalyst.com.

About the Author

Adrian Day was born in London, England, and graduated from the London School of Economics. He is founder and President of Adrian Day Asset Management, which manages money for clients in global and resource markets, as well as the editor of *Adrian Day's Global Analyst* newsletter. He was a pioneer in global investing for Americans, with two books on the subject, *International Investment Opportunities: How and Where to Invest Overseas Successfully* and *Investing without Borders*. He also wrote *Thirty Minutes to Financial Freedom*, a money manual for beginners, and has contributed to several books, including *The Golden Rule* and *The Evergreen Portfolio* (both published by John Wiley & Sons in 2010). He was also early in investing in gold and other resources and has written widely on the subject. He is frequently interviewed by both domestic and international television, radio, and press, and is a popular speaker at financial conferences and seminars around the world. He travels widely and currently lives in Annapolis, Maryland. He loves the opera and fine food and wine, as well as reading history.

Index